DATE DUE

HIGHSMITH 45-102   PRINTED IN U.S.A.

An Authority Speaks
on Love

In this straightforward volume, Havelock Ellis, one of the world's great authorities on sex, presents a strong and knowing plea for the proper use and understanding of one of the most important forces in human behavior.

In lucid language, he covers every conceivable aspect of his subject: the relationships between husbands and wives, parents and children, the purposes of marriage, the functions of sex.

A great pioneer thinker whose works are now regarded as classics, Ellis has been called "the Darwin of Sex."

". . . It would be difficult to name anyone with a mind that has achieved a finer balance and harmony, a mind at once so rich, so widely curious and receptive. . . ."—*Nation*

SIGNET and MENTOR Books
of Related Interest

On Life and Sex

TWO VOLUMES IN ONE

1. Little Essays of Love and Virtue
2. More Essays of Love and Virtue

HAVELOCK ELLIS

A SIGNET BOOK

Published by THE NEW AMERICAN LIBRARY

Published as a SIGNET BOOK
By Arrangement with Doubleday & Company, Inc.
(New York) and William Heinemann, Ltd. (London)

FIFTH PRINTING

On Life and Sex is published in England
by William Heinemann, Ltd.

SIGNET BOOKS are published by
The New American Library, Inc.,
1301 Avenue of the Americas, New York, New York 10019

FIRST PRINTING, FEBRUARY, 1957

PRINTED IN THE UNITED STATES OF AMERICA
21923

CONTENTS

PART ONE:

Little Essays of Love and Virtue

PREFACE

IN THESE ESSAYS—little, indeed, as I know them to be, compared to the magnitude of their subjects—I have tried to set forth, as clearly as I can, certain fundamental principles, together with their practical application to the life of our time. Some of these principles were stated more briefly and technically, in my large *Studies* of sex; others were therein implied but only to be read between the lines. Here I have expressed them in simple language and with some detail. It is my hope that in this way they may more surely come into the hands of young people, youths and girls at the period of adolescence, who have been present to my thoughts in all the studies I have written of sex because I was myself of that age when I first vaguely planned them. I would prefer to leave to their judgment the question as to whether this book is suitable to be placed in the hands of older people. It might only give them pain. It is in youth that the questions of mature age can alone be settled, if they ever are to be settled, and unless we begin to think about adult problems when we are young all our thinking is likely to be in vain. There are but few people who are able when youth is over either on the one hand to re-mould themselves nearer to those facts of Nature and of Society they failed to perceive, or had not the courage to accept, when they were young, or, on the other hand, to mould the facts of the exterior world nearer to those of their own true interior world. One hesitates to bring home to them too keenly what they have missed in life. Yet, let us remember, even for those who have missed most, there always remains the fortifying and consoling thought that they may at least help to make the world better for those who come after them, and the possibilities of human adjustment easier for others than it has been for themselves. They must still remain true to their own traditions. We could not wish it to be otherwise.

The art of making love and the art of being virtuous—two aspects of the great art of living that are, rightly regarded, harmonious and not at variance—remain, indeed, when we cease to misunderstand them, essentially the same in all ages and among all peoples. Yet, always and everywhere, little modifications become necessary, little, yet, like so many little things, immense in their significance and results. In this way, if we are really alive, we flexibly adjust ourselves to the world in which we find ourselves, and in so doing simultaneously adjust to ourselves that ever-changing world, ever-changing, though its changes are within such narrow limits that it yet remains substantially the same. It is with such modification that we are concerned in these Little Essays.

H. E.

Chapter 1

CHILDREN AND PARENTS

THE TWENTIETH CENTURY, as we know, has frequently been called "the century of the child." When, however, we turn to the books of Ellen Key, who has most largely and sympathetically taken this point of view, one asks oneself whether, after all, the child's century has brought much to the child. Ellen Key points out, with truth, that, even in our century, parents may for the most part be divided into two classes: those who act as if their children existed only for their benefit, and those who act as if they existed only for their children's benefit, the results, she adds, being alike deplorable. For the first group of parents tyrannise over the child, seek to destroy its individuality, exercise an arbitrary discipline too spasmodic to have any of the good effects of discipline and would model him into a copy of themselves, though really, she adds, it ought to pain them very much to see themselves exactly copied. The second group of parents may wish to model their children not after themselves but after their ideals, yet they differ chiefly from the first class by their over-indulgence, by their anxiety to pamper the child by yielding to all his caprices and artificially protecting him from the natural results of those caprices, so that instead of learning freedom he has merely acquired self-will. These parents do not indeed tyrannise over their children but they do worse; they train their children to be tyrants. Against these two tendencies of our century Ellen Key declares her own Alpha and Omega of the art of education. Try to leave the child in peace; live your own life beautifully, nobly, temperately, and in so living you will sufficiently teach your children to live.

It is not my purpose here to consider how far this conception of the duty of parents towards children is justified, and whether or not peace is the best preparation for a world in which struggle dominates. All these questions about education are rather idle. There are endless theories of education but no agreement concerning the value of any of them, and the whole question of education remains open. I am here concerned less

11

with the duty of parents in relation to their children than with the duty of children in relation to their parents, and that means that I am not concerned with young children, to whom that duty still presents no serious problems, since they have not yet developed a personality with self-conscious individual needs. Certainly the one attitude must condition the other attitude. The reaction of children against their parents is the necessary result of the parents' action. So that we have to pay some attention to the character of parental action.

We cannot expect to find any coherent or uniform action on the part of parents. But there have been at different historical periods different general tendencies in the attitude of parents towards their children. Thus if we go back four or five centuries in English social history we seem to find a general attitude which scarcely corresponds exactly to either of Ellen Key's two groups. It seems usually to have been compounded of severity and independence; children were first strictly compelled to go their parents' way and then thrust off to their own way. There seems a certain hardness in this method, yet it is doubtful whether it can fairly be regarded as more unreasonable than either of the two modern methods deplored by Ellen Key. On the contrary it had points for admiration. It was primarily a discipline, but it was regarded, as any fortifying discipline should be regarded, as a preparation for freedom, and it is precisely there that the more timid and clinging modern way seems to fail.

We clearly see the old method at work in the chief source of knowledge concerning old English domestic life, the *Paston Letters*. Here we find that at an early age the sons of knights and gentlemen were sent to serve in the houses of other gentlemen: it was here that their education really took place, an education not in book knowledge, but in knowledge of life. Such education was considered so necessary for a youth that a father who kept his sons at home was regarded as negligent of his duty to his family. A knowledge of the world was a necessary part, indeed the chief part, of a youth's training for life. The remarkable thing is that this applied also to a large extent to the daughters. They realised in those days, what is only beginning to be realised in ours,[1] that, after all,

[1] This was illustrated in England when women first began to serve on juries. The pretext was frequently brought forward that there are certain kinds of cases and of evidence that do not concern women or that women ought not to hear. The pretext would have been more plausible if it had also been argued that there are certain kinds of cases and of evidence that men ought not to hear. As a matter of fact, whatever frontier there may be in these matters is not of a sexual kind. Everything that concerns men ultimately concerns women, and everything that concerns women ultimately concerns men. Neither women nor men are entitled to claim dispensation.

women live in the world just as much, though differently, as men live in the world, and that it is quite as necessary for the girl as for the boy to be trained to the meaning of life. Margaret Paston, towards the end of the fifteenth century, sent her daughter Ann to live in the house of a gentleman who, a little later, found that he could not keep her as he was purposing to decrease the size of his household. The mother writes to her son: "I shall be fain to send for her and with me she shall but lose her time, and without she be the better occupied she shall oftentimes move me and put me to great unquietness. Remember what labour I had with your sister, therefore do your best to help her forth"; as a result it was planned to send her to a relative's house in London.

It is evident that in the fifteenth century in England there was a wide prevalence of this method of education, which in France, a century later, was still regarded as desirable by Montaigne. His reason for it is worth noting; children should be educated away from home, he remarks, in order to acquire hardness, for the parents will be too tender to them. "It is an opinion accepted by all that it is not right to bring up children in their parents' laps, for natural love softens and relaxes even the wisest."[2]

In old France indeed the conditions seem similar to those in England. The great serio-comic novel of Antoine de la Salle, *Petit Jean de Saintré,* shows us in detail the education and the adventures, which certainly involved a very early introduction to life, of a page in a great house in the fifteenth century. We must not take everything in this fine comedy too solemnly, but in the fourteenth century *Book of the Knight of the Tour-Landry* we may be sure that we have at its best the then prevailing view of the relation of a father to his tenderly loved daughters. Of harshness and rigour in the relationship it is not easy to find traces in this lengthy and elaborate book of paternal counsels. But it is clear that the father takes seriously the right of a daughter to govern herself and to decide for herself between right and wrong. It is his object, he tells his girls, "to enable them to govern themselves." In this task he assumes that they are entitled to full knowledge, and we feel that he is not instructing them in the mysteries of that knowledge; he is taking for granted, in the advice he gives and the stories he tells them, that his "young and small daughters, not, poor things, overburdened with experience," already possess the most precise knowledge of the intimate facts of life, and that he may tell them, without turning a hair, the most outrageous incidents of de-

---

[2] Montaigne, *Essais,* Bk. I, ch. 25.

bauchery. Life already lies naked before them: that he
assumes; he is not imparting knowledge, he is giving good
counsel.[8]

It is clear that this kind of education and this attitude
towards children must be regarded as the outcome of the
whole mediæval method of life. In a state of society where
roughness and violence, though not, as we sometimes assume,
chronic, were yet always liable to be manifested, it was
necessary for every man and woman to be able to face the
crudest facts of the world and to be able to maintain his or
her own rights against them. The education that best secured
that strength and independence was the best education and it
necessarily involved an element of hardness. We must go back
earlier than Montaigne's day, when the conditions were becoming mitigated, to see the system working in all its vigour.

The lady of the day of the early thirteenth century has been
well described by Luchaire in his scholarly study of French
Society in the time of Philip Augustus. She was, he tells us,
as indeed she had been in the preceding feudal centuries, often
what we should nowadays call a virago, of violent temperament, with vivid passions, broken in from childhood to all
physical exercises, sharing the pleasures and dangers of the
knights around her. Feudal life, fertile in surprises and in risks,
demanded even in women a vigorous temper of soul and body,
a masculine air, and habits also that were almost virile. She
accompanied her father or her husband to the chase, while in
war-time, if she became a widow or if her husband was away
at the Crusades, she was ready, if necessary, to direct the de-
fences of the lordship, and in peace time she was not afraid
of the longest and most dangerous pilgrimages. She might even
go to the Crusades on her own account, and, if circumstances
required, conduct a war to come out victoriously.

We may imagine the robust kind of education required to
produce people of this quality. But as regards the precise
way in which parents conducted that education, we have, as

[8] If the Knight went to an extreme in his assumption of his daughters'
knowledge, modern fathers often go to the opposite and more foolish extreme of assuming in their daughters an ignorance that would be dangerous
even if it really existed. In *A Young Girl's Diary* (translated from the
German by Eden and Cedar Paul), a work that is highly instructive for
parents, and ought to be painful for many, we find the diarist noting at
the age of thirteen that she and a girl friend of about the same age overheard the father of one of them—both well brought up and carefully protected, one Catholic and the other Protestant—referring to "those innocent children." "We did laugh so, WE and *innocent children ! ! !* What
our fathers really think of us; we innocent ! ! ! At dinner we did not dare
look at one another or we should have exploded." It need scarcely be
added that, at the same time, they were more innocent than they knew.

Luchaire admits, little precise knowledge. It is for the most part only indirectly, by reading between the lines, that we glean something as to what it was considered befitting to inculcate in a good household, and as what we thus learn is mostly from the writings of Churchmen it is doubtless a little one-sided. Thus Adam de Perseigne, an ecclesiastic, writes to the Countess du Perche to advise her how to live in a Christian manner; he counsels her to abstain from playing games of chance and chess, not to take pleasure in the indecent farces of actors, and to be moderate in dress. Then, as ever, preachers expressed their horror of the ruinous extravagance of women, their false hair, their rouge, and their dresses that were too long or too short. They also reprobated their love of flirtation. It was, however, in those days a young girl's recognised duty, when a knight arrived in the household, to exercise the rites of hospitality, to disarm him, give him his bath, and if necessary massage him to help him to go to sleep. It is not surprising that the young girl sometimes made love to the knight under these circumstances, nor is it surprising that he, engaged in an arduous life and trained to disdain feminine attractions, often failed to respond.

It is easy to understand how this state of things gradually became transformed into the considerably different position of parents and child we have known, which doubtless attained its climax nearly a century ago. Feudal conditions, with the large household so well adapted to act as seminaries for youth, began to decay, and as education in such seminaries must have led to frequent mischances both for youths and maidens who enjoyed the opportunities of education there, the regret for their disappearance may often have been tempered for parents. Schools, colleges, and universities began to spring up and develop for one sex, while for the other home life grew more intimate, and domestic ties closer. Montaigne's warning against the undue tenderness of a narrow family life no longer seemed reasonable, and the family became more self-centred and more enclosed. Beneath this, and more profoundly influential, there was a general softening in social respects, and a greater expansiveness of affectional relationships, in reality or in seeming, within the home, compensating, it may be, the more diffused social feeling within a group which characterised the previous period.

So was cultivated that undue tenderness, deplored by Montaigne, which we now regard as almost normal in family life, and solemnly label, if we happen to be psychoanalysts, the Œdipus-complex or the Electra-complex. Sexual love is closely related to parental love; the tender emotion, which is an in-

timate part of parental love, is also an intimate part of sexual
love, and two emotions which are each closely related to a
third emotion cannot fail to become often closely associated
to each other. With a little thought we might guess beforehand, even while still in complete ignorance of the matter,
that there could not fail to be frequently a sexual tinge in
the affection of a father for his daughter, of a mother for
her son, of a son for his mother, or a daughter for her father.
Needless to say, that does not mean that there is present any
physical desire of sex in the narrow sense; that would be a
perversity, and a rare perversity. We are here on another plane
than that of crude physical desire, and are moving within the
sphere of the emotions. But such emotions are often strong,
and all the stronger because conscious of their own absolute
rectitude and often masked under the shape of Duty. Yet
when prolonged beyond the age of childhood they tend to
become a clog on development, and a hindrance to a wholesome life. The child who cherishes such emotions is likely to
suffer infantile arrest of development, and the parent who is
so selfish as to continue to expend such tenderness on a child
who has passed the age of childhood, or to demand it, is guilty
of a serious offence against the child.

That the intimate family life which sometimes resulted—
especially when, as frequently happened, the seeming mutual
devotion was also real—might often be regarded as beautiful
and almost ideal, it has been customary to repeat with an
emphasis that in the end has even become nauseous. For it
was usually overlooked that the self-centred and enclosed
family, even when the mutual affection of its members was
real enough to bear all examination, could scarcely be more
than partially beautiful, and could never be ideal. For the
family only represents one aspect, however important an
aspect, of a human being's functions and activities. He cannot,
she cannot, be divorced from the life of the social group, and
a life is beautiful and ideal, or the reverse, only when we have
taken into our consideration the social as well as the family
relationship. When the family claims to prevent the free association of an adult member of it with the larger social organisation, it is claiming that the part is greater than the whole, and
such a claim cannot fail to be morbid and mischievous.

The old-world method of treating children, we know, has
long ago been displaced as containing an element of harsh
tyranny. But it was not perceived, and it seems indeed not
even yet to be generally recognised, that the system which replaced it, and is only now beginning to pass away, involved
another and more subtle tyranny, the more potent because not

seemingly harsh. Parents no longer whipped their children even when grown up, or put them in seclusion, or exercised physical force upon them after they had passed childhood. They felt that that would not be in harmony with the social customs of a world in which ancient feudal notions were dead. But they merely replaced the external compulsion by an internal compulsion which was much more effective. It was based on the moral assumption of claims and duties which were rarely formulated because parents found it quite easy and pleasant to avoid formulating them, and children, on the rare occasions when they formulated them, usually felt a sense of guilt in challenging their validity. It was in the nineteenth century that this state of things reached its full development. The sons of the family were usually able, as they grew up, to escape and elude it, although they thereby often created an undesirable divorce from the home, and often suffered, as well as inflicted, much pain in tearing themselves loose from the spiritual bonds —especially perhaps in matters of religion—woven by long tradition to bind them to their parents. It was on the daughters that the chief stress fell. For the working class, indeed, there was often the possibility of escape into hard labour, if only that of marriage. But such escape was not possible, immediately or at all, for a large number. During the nineteenth century many had been so carefully enclosed in invisible cages, they had been so well drilled in the reticences and the duties and the subserviences that their parents silently demanded of them, that we can never know all the tragedies that took place. In exceptional cases, indeed, they gave a sign. When they possessed unusual power of intellect, or unusual power of character and will, they succeeded in breaking loose from their cages, or at least in giving expression to themselves. This is seen in the stories of nearly all the women eminent in life and literature during the nineteenth century, from the days of Mary Wollstonecraft onwards. The Brontës, almost, yet not quite, strangled by the fetters placed upon them by their stern and narrow-minded father, and enabled to attain the full stature of their genius only by that brief sojourn in Brussels, are representative. Elizabeth Barrett, chained to a couch of invalidism under the eyes of an imperiously affectionate father until with Robert Browning's aid she secretly eloped into the open air of freedom and health, and so attained complete literary expression, is a typical figure. It is only because we recognise that she is a typical figure among the women who attained distinction that we are able to guess at the vast number of mute inglorious Elizabeth Barretts who were never able to escape

by their own efforts and never found a Browning to aid them
to escape.

It is sometimes said that those days are long past and that
young women, in all the countries which we are pleased to
call civilised, are now emancipated, indeed, rather too much
emancipated. Critics come forward to complain of their undue
freedom, of their irreverent familiarity to their parents, of their
language, of their habits. But there were critics who said the
very same things, in almost the same words, of the grandmothers of these girls! These incompetent critics are as ignorant of
the social history of the past as they are of the social significance of the history of the present. We read in *Once a Week* of
sixty years ago (10th August, 1861), the very period when the
domestic conditions of girls were the most oppressive in the
sense here understood, that these same critics were about at that
time, and as shocked as they are now at "the young ladies who
talk of 'awful swells' and 'deuced bores,' who smoke and
venture upon free discourse, and try to be like men." The writer
of this anonymous article, who was really (I judge from internal
evidence) so distinguished and so serious a woman as Harriet
Martineau, duly snubs these critics, pointing out that such
accusations are at least as old as Addison and Horace Walpole;
she remarks that there have no doubt been so-called "fast
young ladies" in every age, "varying their doings and sayings
according to the fopperies of the time." The question, as she
pertinently concludes is, as indeed it still remains to-day: "Have
we more than the average proportion? I do not know." Nor
to-day do we know.

But while to-day, as ever before, we have a certain proportion of these emancipated girls, and while to-day, as perhaps
never before, we are able to understand that they have an
element of reason on their side, it would be a mistake to suppose that they are more than exceptions. The majority are
unable, and not even anxious, to attain this light-hearted social
emancipation. For the majority, even though they are workers,
the anciently subtle ties of the home are still, as they should be,
an element of natural piety, and, also, as they should not be,
clinging fetters which impede individuality and destroy personal initiative.

We all know so many happy homes beneath whose calm
surface this process is working out. The parents are deeply
attached to their children, who still remain children to them
even when they are grown up. They wish to guide them and
mould them and cherish them, to protect them from the world,
to enjoy their society and their aid, and they expect that their
children shall continue indefinitely to remain children. The

children, on their side, remain and always will remain tenderly attached to their parents, and it would really pain them to feel that they are harbouring any unwillingness to stay in the home even after they have grown up, so long as their parents need their attention. It is, of course, the daughters who are thus expected to remain in the home and who feel this compunction about leaving it. It seems to us—although, as we have seen, so unlike the attitude of former days—a natural, beautiful, and rightful feeling on both sides.

Yet, in the result, all sorts of evils tend to ensue. The parents often take as their moral right the services which should only be accepted, if accepted at all, as the offering of love and gratitude, and even reach a degree of domineering selfishness in which they refuse to believe that their children have any adult rights of their own, absorbing and drying up that physical and spiritual life-blood of their offspring which it is the parents' part in Nature to feed. If the children are willing there is nothing to mitigate this process; if they are unwilling the result is often a disastrous conflict. Their time and energy are not their own; their tastes are criticised and so far as possible crushed; their political ideas, if they have any, are treated as pernicious; and—which is often on both sides the most painful of all—differences in religious belief lead to bitter controversy and humiliating recrimination. Such differences in outlook between youth and age are natural and inevitable and right. The parents themselves, though they may have forgotten it, often in youth similarly revolted against the cherished doctrines of their own parents; it has ever been so, the only difference being that to-day, probably, the opportunities for variation are greater. So it comes about that what James Hinton said half a century ago is often true to-day: "Our happy Christian homes are the real dark places of the earth."

It is evident that the problem of the relation of the child to the parent is still incompletely solved even in what we consider our highest civilisation. There is here needed an art in which those who have to exercise it can scarcely possess all the necessary skill and experience. Among trees and birds and beasts the art is surer because it is exercised unconsciously, on the foundation of a large tradition in which failure meant death. In the common procreative profusion of those forms of life the frequent death of the young was a matter of little concern, but biologically there was never any sacrifice of the offspring to the well-being of the parents. Whenever sacrifice is called for it is the parents who are sacrificed to their offspring. In our superior human civilisation, in which quantity ever tends to give place to quality, the higher value of the individual involves an effort to avoid sacrifice which sometimes proves worse than abortive. An avian philosopher would be unlikely to feel called upon to denounce nests as the dark places of the earth, and in laying down our human moral laws we have always to be aware of forgetting the fundamental biological relationship of parent and child to which all such moral laws must conform. To some would-be parents that necessity may seem hard. In such a case it is well for them to remember that there is no need to become parents and that we live in an age when it is not difficult to avoid becoming a parent. The world is not dying for lack of parents. On the contrary we have far too many of them—ignorant parents, silly parents, unwilling parents, undesirable parents—and those who aspire to the high dignity of creating the future race, let them be as few as they will—and perhaps at the present time the fewer the better— must not refuse the responsibilities of that position, its pains as well as its joys.

In our human world, as we know, the moral duties laid upon us—the duties in which, if we fail, we become outcasts in our own eyes or in those of others or in both—are of three kinds: the duties to oneself, the duties to the small circle of those we love, and the duties to the larger circle of mankind to which ultimately we belong, since out of it we proceed, and to it we owe all that we are. There are no maxims, there is only an art and a difficult art, to harmonise duties which must often conflict. We have to be true to all the motives that sanctify our lives. To that extent George Eliot's Maggie Tulliver was undoubtedly right. But the renunciation of the self is not the routine solution of every conflict, any more than is the absolute failure to renounce. In a certain sense the duty towards the self comes before all others, because it is the condition on which duties towards others possess any significance and worth. In that sense, it is true according to the familiar saying of Shakespeare—though it was only Polonius, the man of maxims, who voiced it—that one cannot be true to others unless one is first true to oneself, and that one can know nothing of giving aught that is worthy to give unless one also knows how to take.

We see that the problem of the place of parents in life, after their function of parenthood has been adequately fulfilled, a problem which offers no difficulties among most forms of life, has been found hard to solve by Man. At some places and periods it has been considered most merciful to put them to death; at others they have been almost or quite deified and allowed to regulate the whole lives of their descendants. Thus in New Caledonia aged parents, it is said by Mrs. Hadfield, were formerly taken up to a high mountain and left with enough food to last a few days; there was at the same time great regard for the aged, as also among the Hottentots who asked: "Can you see a parent or a relative shaking and freezing under a cold, dreary, heavy, useless old age, and not think, in pity of them, of putting an end to their misery?" It was generally the opinion of the parents themselves, but in some countries the parents have dominated and overawed their children to the time of their natural death and even beyond, up to the point of ancestor worship, as in China, where no man of any age can act for himself in the chief matters of life during his parents' life-time, and to some extent in ancient Rome, whence an influence in this direction which still exists in the laws and customs of France.[4] Both extremes have proved compatible with a beautifully human life. To steer midway between them seems to-day, however, the wisest course. There ought to be no reason, and under happy conditions there is no reason, why the relationship between parent and child, as one of mutual affection and care, should ever cease to exist. But that the relationship should continue to exist as a tie is unnatural and tends to be harmful. At a certain stage in the development of the child the physical tie with the parent is severed, and the umbilical cord cut. At a later stage in development, when puberty is attained and adolescence is feeling its way towards a complete adult maturity, the spiritual tie must be severed. It is absolutely essential that the young spirit should begin to essay its own wings. If its energy is not equal to this adventure, then it is the part of a truly loving parent to push it over the edge of the nest. Of course there are dangers and risks. But the worst dangers and risks come of the failure to adventure, of the refusal to face the tasks of the world and to assume the full function of life. All that Freud has told of the paralysing and maiming influence of infantile arrest or regression is here profitable to consider. In order, moreover, that the relationship between parents and children may retain its early beauty and love, it is essential that it shall adapt itself to adult conditions and the absence of ties so rendered necessary. Otherwise there is little likelihood of anything but friction and pain on one side or the other, and perhaps on both sides.

The parents have not only to train their children: it is of at least equal importance that they should train themselves. It is desirable that children, as they grow up, should be alive to this necessity, and consciously assist in the process, since they are

[4] The varying customs of different peoples in this matter are set forth by Westermarck, *The Origin and Development of the Moral Ideas*, Ch. XXV.

in closer touch with a new world of activities to which their more lethargic parents are often blind and deaf. For every fresh stage in our lives we need a fresh education, and there is no stage for which so little educational preparation is made as that which follows the reproductive period. Yet at no time—especially in women, who present all the various stages of the sexual life in so emphatic a form—would education be more valuable. The great burden of reproduction, with all its absorbing responsibilities, has suddenly been lifted; at the same time the perpetually recurring rhythm of physical sex manifestations, so often disturbing in its effect, finally ceases; with that cessation, very often, after a brief period of perturbation, there is an increase both in physical and mental energy. Yet, too often, all that one can see is that a vacuum has been created, and that there is nothing to fill it. The result is that the mother—for it is most often of the mother that complaint is made—devotes her own new found energies to the never-ending task of hampering and crushing her children's developing energies. How many mothers there are who bring to our minds that ancient and almost inspired statement concerning those for whom "Satan finds some mischief still"! They are wasting, worse than wasting, energies that might be profitably applied to all sorts of social service in the world. There is nothing that is so much needed as the "maternal in politics," or in all sorts of non-political channels of social service, and none can be better fitted for such service than those who have had an actual experience of motherhood and acquired the varied knowledge that such experience should give. There are numberless other ways, besides social service, in which mothers who have passed the age of forty, providing they possess the necessary aptitudes, can more profitably apply themselves than in hampering, or pampering, their adult children. It is by wisely cultivating their activities in a larger sphere that women whose chief duties in the narrower domestic sphere are over may better ensure their own happiness and the welfare of others than either by fretting and obstructing, or by worrying over, their own children who are no longer children. It is quite true that the children may go astray even when they have ceased to be children. But the time to implant the seeds of virtue, the time to convey a knowledge of life, was when they were small. If it was done well, it only remains to exercise faith and trust. If it was done ill, nothing done later will compensate, for it is merely foolish for a mother who could not educate her children when they were small to imagine that she is able to educate them when they are big.

So it is that the problem of the attitude of the child to its parents circles round again to that of the parents to the child. The wise parent realises that childhood is simply a preparation for the free activities of later life, that the parents exist in order to equip children for life and not to shelter and protect them from the world into which they must be cast. Education, whatever else it should or should not be, must be an inoculation against the poisons of life and an adequate equipment in knowledge and skill for meeting the chances of life. Beyond that, and no doubt in the largest part, it is a natural growth and takes place of itself.

Chapter 2

THE PLACE
OF THE GRANDPARENTS

THE PLACE IN FAMILY LIFE OF THE GRANDPARENT seems to be but little discussed. It has of late come before me as a problem. But I do not know where to find it dealt with. Yet it is surely a subject of growing importance. We are always hearing about the increased expectation of life, and more especially for women, in our modern world. Alarmed statisticians tell us of a population more and more tending to consist largely of old people, and especially of old women. We may not agree to view the situation with alarm, but we seem to have to accept the fact that never before has there been in the population so large a proportion of grandparents and especially of grand-mothers.

I emphasise the prominence of grandmothers, not only because they are more numerous but because, for quite natural reasons, the grandmother is generally a more active element in family life, for evil sometimes as well as for good, than the grandfather.

So that the significant elements of the situation we are here concerned with are most likely to be: Child, mother, grand-mother. In all such triangular situations, as we may well know by experience or observation, difficulties are apt to arise. But as we are here in presence of a natural and not an artificial relationship, it should be quite possible to avoid or to overcome the difficulties. We may take each member of the trio in turn.

The prospect of a grandchild is often delightful to a woman. Her own reproductive life is over; her own children no longer need maternal care and are perhaps widely scattered by the chances of life; at the same time, if she has acquired few active interests in society or the world, she may have more time on her hands than ever before. The maternal instinct never dies, and the possibility of being to some extent able to renew it with a child who, from the closeness of the relationship, will bring back the association with her own child, is a precious

24

privilege. It is, though at a further remove, a return to the reproductive life, and a renewal of youth.

Under fortunate circumstances the grandmother relationship is thus a singularly happy one. It is a partial restoration of motherhood with the pains and responsibilities of motherhood diminished, if not abolished. But to be thus enjoyed the grandmotherly relationship usually needs to be exercised with much skill and consideration, for it is often surrounded by risks.

There is, especially, the need for self-control. The grandmother, with all her early experiences of motherhood, is tempted to domineer in this sphere. She sees a much younger woman, still quite inexperienced and only feeling her way, and she is tempted to lay down peremptorily the rules she had herself learnt and practiced in days long past. The central facts of motherhood are indeed always the same, and unchangeable. But manners and customs are always changing; the approach to motherhood becomes different from age to age; indeed the whole treatment of the child, even the very conception of the child's place in the family. So that the young mother, however inexperienced, is struggling to grasp new methods of life, and to embody new conceptions, which her own mother or mother-in-law a quarter of a century earlier had never heard of. I am especially referring to what I have elsewhere described as the "New Mother," who, often warned by unhappy experiences of her own childhood, seeks to avoid both excessive indulgence and rigid discipline in bringing up her child. She realises the need of discipline but rejects any artificial discipline in order to rely on that of real life, in which mistakes bring their own punishment; she desires to leave the child as free as possible, to advise rather than command, and to become the trusted friend and confidante as well as the mother, even though this process may sometimes bring her trouble and inconvenience before it begins to work beneficially.

There is a temptation for the grandmother to regard the new-fangled ideas and practices as altogether dangerous and pernicious, and to set herself against them. She may need a high degree of intelligence, as well as a just sense for the primary responsibilities of parenthood, if she is to enjoy in peace that secondary position, to which alone, in spite of her experience, she is entitled.

That is where the mother becomes important in this trio. It is normally only by her acquiescence and aid that the grandmother's position is assured. All her skill may be needed to allow fair scope to the grandmother and to avail herself of her experience while maintaining her own primary rights.

A not uncommon risk is that of jealousy. When the mother's work takes her much away from the home, or when she is absorbed by a constant round of social duties and pleasures, the child is left with a succession of nannies and servants, and may find a haven of refuge in the grandmother's skirts. She may here bestow the love that normally belongs to the mother who, in the child's eyes, falls into the place of an outside stranger. The mother grows jealous, and the position becomes uncomfortable, if not painful, for all the members of this trio.

For such a state of things cure may sometimes be difficult, but prevention is easy. A very little foresight, in addition to genuine maternal love, should enable the mother to realise the importance of keeping the first place in her child's affections and the natural risks of failing to do so. In a wholesome family life such risks are small, and if the mother's jealousy of the grandmother tends to occur that is because the relationships of family life often fail to be wholesome. Under favourable conditions the grandmother may become for her daughter or daughter-in-law a most valuable coadjutor and counsellor, as well as a devoted assistant in those practical cares of motherhood which are unending.

We come to the grandchild. This is the really important member of the trio, for whom the relationship in question may be of most significance. After all, the grandmother's experience comes towards the end of her active life, and the mother's part in the trio is consequently but an episode. For the child the influence of this relationship is sometimes life-long.

It is now a familiar fact that the passing on of the elements that make up heredity is not confined to an inheritance from parents to child. Some elements are latent in the parents; some that appear in the child may come from far back. The child is more than the child of its parents. It is thus quite normal and natural for the child to reveal an affinity—supplementary and by no means necessarily hostile to that with the parents—to one or other grandparent. It is possible, for instance, for a grandson who is affectionately devoted to his parents to realise that in his father's father and his mother's mother there had been spiritual affinities—intellectual, artistic, or moral—which, had circumstances permitted, he would have found more akin than the corresponding traits in his parents. There may thus be said to be a solid basis for the possibility of a close relationship between grandparent and grandchild even when the difference of years or too early death has not enabled it to develop.

The relationship may become intimate without assuming any such foundation for it. The circumstances of the family life are themselves favourable for its development. Every reader of Marcel Proust will recall the deep and intimate affection which the hero experiences for his grandmother. As a matter of fact, it appears that Proust has transferred to the grandmother the deep love which in real life he experienced for his mother. But it is significant that so subtle and clairvoyant a psychologist should have found no incongruity in substituting the grandmother.

To many a child a grandmother has been a precious possession, a helpful support in an otherwise uncongenial home, and an endeared memory for life. It is not every child who owns a New Mother. The mother may be keen to carry on the educational doctrines, in which she was herself brought up, of harsh discipline, of suppression of demonstrative emotion, of restraint of all unconventional activities, and a long code of Don'ts. Neither the child's natural energies and impulses, nor any special individual tendencies, can thus find scope. But the grandmother—it may be the paternal grandmother—is outside the maternal plan. She is not called upon to exercise the disciplinarian restraint; she may be ready to understand and comfort and sympathise. The child, beginning to pass out of childhood, realises that here has been found something that was longed for and missed in the real mother. It may be an inestimable boon that has thus been conferred on the child.

We are concerned here, it will be realised, with a relationship which, since it involves three generations, is apt to be beset with difficulties. But since it also contains the promise of fine possibilities we may well study to surmount those difficulties.

Chapter 3

THE MEANING OF PURITY

WE LIVE IN A WORLD in which, as we nowadays begin to realise, we find two antagonistic streams of traditional platitude concerning the question of sexual purity, both flowing from the far past.

The people who embody one of these streams of tradition, basing themselves on old-fashioned physiology, assume, though they may not always assert, that the sexual products are excretions, to be dealt with summarily like other excretions. That is an ancient view and it was accepted by such wise philosophers of old times as Montaigne and Sir Thomas More. It had, moreover, the hearty support of so eminent a theological authority as Luther, who on this ground preached early marriage to men and women alike. It is still a popular view, sometimes expressed in the crudest terms, and often by people who, not following Luther's example, use it to defend prostitution, though they generally exclude women from its operation, as a sex to whom it fails to apply and by whom it is not required.

But on the other hand we have another stream of platitude. On this side there is usually little attempt either to deny or to affirm the theory of the opposing party, though they would contradict its conclusions. Their theory, if they have one, would usually seem to be that sexual activity is a response to stimulation from without or from within, so that if there is no stimulation there will be no sexual manifestation. They would preach, they tell us, a strenuous ideal; they would set up a wholesome dictate of hygiene. The formula put forward on this basis usually runs: Continence is not only harmless but beneficial. It is a formula which, in one form or another, has received apparently enthusiastic approval in many quarters, even from distinguished physicians. We need not be surprised. A proposition so large and general is not easy to deny, and is still more difficult to reverse; therefore it proves welcome to the people—especially the people occupying public and professional positions—who wish to find the path of least resistance, under pressure of a vigorous section of public opinion. Yet in its vagueness the proposition is a little disingenuous; it condescends to no definitions and no qualifications; it fails even to make clear how it is to be reconciled with any enthusiastic approval of marriage, for if continence is beautiful how can marriage make it cease to be so?

Both these streams of feeling, it may be noted, sprang from a common source far back in the primitive human world. All the emanations of the human body, all the spontaneous manifestations of its activities, were mysterious and ominous to early man, pregnant with terror unless met with immense precautions and surrounded by careful ritual. The manifestations of sex were the least intelligible and the most spontaneous. Therefore the things of sex were those that most lent themselves to feelings of horror and awe, of impurity and of purity. They seemed so highly charged with magic potency that there were no things that men more sought to avoid, yet none to which they were impelled to give more thought. The manifold echoes of that primitive conception of sex, and all the violent reactions that were thus evolved and eventually bound up with the original impulse, compose the streams of tradition that feed our modern world in this matter and determine the ideas of purity that surround us.

At the present day the crude theory of the sexual impulse held on one side, and the ignorant rejection of theory altogether on the other side, are beginning to be seen as both alike unjustified. We begin to find the grounds for a sounder theory. Not indeed that the problems of sex, which go so deeply into the whole personal and social life, can ever be settled exclusively upon physiological grounds. But we have done much to prepare even the loftiest Building of Love when we have attained a clear view of its biological basis.

The progress of chemico-physiological research during recent years has now brought us to new ground for our building. Indeed the image might well be changed altogether, and it might be said that science has entirely transferred the drama of reproduction to a new stage with new actors. Therewith the immense emphasis placed on excretion, and the inevitable reaction that emphasis aroused, both alike disappear. The sexual protagonists are no longer at the surface but within the most secret recesses of the organism, and they appear to science under the name of Hormones or Internal Secretions, always at work within and never themselves condescending to appear at all. Those products of the sexual glands which in both sexes are cast out of the body, and at an immature stage of knowledge appeared to be excretions, are of primary reproductive importance, but, as regards the sexual constitution of the individual, they are of far less importance than the internal secretions of these very same glands. It is, however, by no means only the specifically sexual glands which thus exert a sexual influence within the organism. Other glands in the brain, the throat, and the abdomen—such as the thyroid and the adrenals—are also elaborating fermentative secretions to throw into the system. Their mutual play is so elaborate that it is only beginning to be understood. Some internal secretions stimulate, others inhibit, and the same secretions may under different conditions do either. This fact is the source of many degrees and varieties of energy and formative power in the organism. Taken altogether, the internal secretions are the forces which build up the man's and woman's distinctively sexual constitution: the special disposition and growth of hair, the relative development of breasts and pelvis, the characteristic differences in motor activity, the varying emotional desires and needs. It is in the complex play of these secretions that we now seek the explanation of all the peculiarities of sexual constitution, imperfect or one-sided physical and psychic development, the various approximations of the male to female bodily and emotional disposition, of the female to the male, all the numerous gradations that occur, naturally as we now see, between the complete man and the complete woman.

When we turn the light of this new conception on to our old ideas of purity—to the virtue or the vice, accordingly as we may have been pleased to consider it, of sexual abstinence—we begin to see that those ideas need radical revision. They appear in a new light, their whole meaning is changed. No doubt it may be said they never had the validity they appeared to possess, even when we judge them by the crudest criterion, that of practice. Thus, while it is the rule for physicians to proclaim the advantages of sexual continence, there is no good reason to believe that they have themselves practised it in any eminent degree. A few years ago an inquiry among thirty-five distinguished physicians, chiefly German and Russian, showed that they were nearly all of opinion that continence is harmless, if not beneficial. But Meirowsky found by inquiry of eighty-six physicians, of much the same nationalities, that only one had himself been sexually abstinent before marriage. There seem to be no similar statistics for the English-speaking countries, where there exists a greater modesty—though not perhaps notably less need for it—in the making of such confessions. But if we turn to the allied profession which is strongly on the side of sexual abstinence, we find that among theological students, as has been shown in the United States, while prostitution may be infrequent, no temptation is so frequent or so potent, and in most cases so irresistible, as that to solitary sexual indulgence. Such is the actual attitude towards the two least ideal forms of sexual practice—as distinguished from mere theory—on the part of the two professions which most definitely pronounce in favour of continence.

It is necessary, however, as will now be clearer, to set our net more widely. We must take into consideration every form and degree of sexual manifestation, normal and abnormal, gross and ethereal. When we do this, even cautiously and without going far afield, sexual abstinence is found to be singularly elusive. Rohleder, a careful and conscientious investigator, has asserted that such abstinence, in the true and complete sense, is absolutely non-existent, the genuine cases in which sexual phenomena of some kind or other fail to manifest themselves being simply cases of inborn lack of sexual sensibility. He met, indeed, a few people who seemed exceptions to the general rule, but, on better knowledge, he found that he was mistaken, and that so far from being absent in these people the sexual instinct was present even in its crudest shapes. The activity of sex is an activity that on the physical side is generated by the complex mechanism of the ductless glands and displayed in the whole organism, physical and psychic, of the individual, who cannot abolish that activity, although to some extent able to regulate the forms in which it is manifested, so that purity cannot be the abolition or even the indefinite suspension of sexual manifestations; it must be the wise and beautiful control of them.

It is becoming clear that the old platitudes can no longer be maintained, and that if we wish to improve our morals we must first improve our knowledge.

II

We have seen that various popular beliefs and conventional assumptions concerning the sexual impulse can no longer be maintained. The sexual activities of the organism are not mere responses to stimulation, absent if we choose to apply no stimulus, never troubling us if we run away from them, harmless if we enclose them within a high wall. Nor do they constitute a mere excretion, or a mere appetite, which we can control by a crude system of hygiene and dietetics. We better understand the psycho-sexual constitution if we regard the motive power behind it as a dynamic energy, produced and maintained by a complex mechanism at certain inner foci of the body, and realise that whatever periodic explosive manifestations may take place at the surface, the primary motive source lies in the intimate recesses of the organism, while the outcome is the whole physical and spiritual energy of our being under those aspects which are most forcible and most aspiring and even most ethereal.

This conception, we find, is now receiving an admirable and beautifully adequate physical basis in the researches of distinguished physiologists in various lands concerning the parts played by the ductless glands of the body, in sensitive equilibrium with each other, pouring out into the system stimulating and inhibiting hormones, which not only confer on the man's or woman's body those specific sexual characters which we admire but at the same time impart the special tone and fibre and polarity of masculinity or femininity to the psychic disposition. Yet, even before Brown-Séquard's first epoch-making suggestion had set physiologists to search for internal secretions, the insight of certain physicians on the medico-psychological side was independently leading towards the same dynamic conception. In the middle of the last century Anstie, an acute London physician, more or less vaguely realised the transformations of sexual energy into nervous disease and into artistic energy. James Hinton, whose genius rendered him the precursor of many modern ideas, had definitely grasped the dynamic nature of sexual activity, and daringly proposed to utilise it, not only as a solution of the difficulties of the personal life but for the revolutionary transformation of morality.[1] It was the wish to group to-

[1] "The man who separated the thought of chastity from Service and made it revolve around Self," wrote Hinton half a century ago in his unpublished M.S.S., "betrayed the human race." "The rule of Self," he wrote again, "has two forms: Self-indulgence and Self-virtue; and Nature has two weapons against it; pain and pleasure. . . . A restraint must always be put away when another's need can be served by putting it away; for so is restored to us the force by which Life is made. . . . How curious it seems! the true evil things are our *good* things. Our thoughts of duty and goodness and chastity, those are the things that need to be altered and put aside; these are the barriers to true goodness. . . . I foresee the positive denial of *all* positive morals, the removal of *all* restrictions. I feel I do not know what 'license,' as we should term it, may not truly belong to the perfect state of Man. When there is no self surely there is no restriction; as we see there is none in Nature. . . . May we not say of marriage as St. Augustine said of God: 'Rather would I, not finding, find Thee, than finding, not find Thee?' . . . 'Because we like' is the sole legitimate and perfect motive of human action. . . . If this is what Nature affirms then it will be what I believe." This dynamic conception of the sexual impulse, as a force, that under natural conditions, may be trusted to build up a new morality, obviously belongs to an indefinitely remote future. It is a force whose blade is two-edged, for while it strikes at unselfishness it also strikes at selfishness, and at present we cannot easily conceive a time when "there is no self"; we should be more disposed to regard it as a time when "there is much humbug. Yet for the individual this conception of the constructive power of love retains much enlightenment and inspiration.

gether all the far-flung manifestations of the inner irresistible process of sexual activity that underlay my own conception of *auto-erotism*, or the spontaneous erotic impulse which arises from the organism apart from all definite external stimulation, to be manifested, or it may be transformed, in mere solitary physical sex activity, in dreams of the night, in day-dreams, in shapes of literature and art, in symptoms of nervous disorder such as some forms of hysteria, and even in the most exalted phases of mystical devotion. Since then, a more elaborate attempt to develop a similar dynamic conception of sexual activity has been made by Freud; and the psychoanalysts who have followed him, or sometimes diverged, have with endless subtlety, and courageous thoroughness, traced the long and sinuous paths of sexual energy in personality and in life, indeed in all the main manifestations of human activity.

It is important for us to note about this dynamic sexual energy in the constitution that while it is very firmly and organically rooted, and quite indestructible, it assumes very various shapes. On the physical side all the characters of sexual distinction and all the beauties of sexual adornment are wrought by the power furnished by the co-operating furnaces of the glands, and so also, on the psychic side, are emotions and impulses which range from the simplest longings for sensual contact to the most exalted rapture of union with the Infinite. Moreover, there is a certain degree of correlation between the physical and the psychic manifestation of sexual energy, and, to some extent, transformation is possible in the embodiment of that energy.

A vague belief in the transformation of sexual energy has long been widespread. It is apparently shown in the idea that continence, as an economy in the expenditure of sexual force, may be practised to aid the physical and mental development, while folklore reveals various sayings in regard to the supposed influence of sexual abstinence in the causation of insanity. There is a certain underlying basis of reason in such beliefs, though in an unqualified form they cannot be accepted, for they take no account of the complexity of the factors involved, of the difficulty and often impossibility of effecting any complete transformation, either in a desirable or undesirable direction, and of the serious conflict which the process often involves. The psychoanalysts have helped us here. Whether or not we accept their elaborate and often shifting conceptions, they have emphasised and developed a psychological conception of sexual energy and its transformations, before only vaguely apprehended, which is now seen to harmonise with the modern physiological view.

The old notion that sexual activity is merely a matter of the voluntary exercise, or abstinence from exercise, of the reproductive functions of adult persons has too long obstructed any clear vision of the fact that sexuality, in the wide and deep sense, is independent of the developments of puberty. This has long been accepted as an occasional and therefore abnormal fact, but we have to recognise that it is true, almost or quite normally, even of early childhood. No doubt we must here extend the word "sexuality"[2]—in what may well be considered an illegitimate way—to cover manifestations which in the usual sense are not sexual or are at most called "sexual perversions." But this extension has a certain justification in view of the fact that these manifestations can be seen to be definitely related to the ordinary adult forms of sexuality. However we define it, we have to recognise that the child takes the same kind of pleasure in those functions which are natural to his age as the adult is capable of taking in localised sexual functions, that he may weave ideas around such functions, sometimes cultivate their exercise from love of luxury, make them the basis of day-dreams which at puberty, when the ideals of adult life are ready to capture his sexual energy, he begins to grow ashamed of.

At this stage, indeed, we reach a crucial point, though it has usually been overlooked, in the lives of boys and girls, more especially those whose heredity may have been a little tainted or their upbringing a little twisted. For it is here that the transformation of energy and the resulting possibilities of conflict are wont to enter. In the harmoniously developing organism, one may say, there is at this period a gradual and easy transmutation of the childish pleasurable activities into adult activities, accompanied perhaps by a feeling of shame for the earlier feelings, though this quickly passes into a forgetfulness which often leads the adult far astray when he attempts to understand the psychic life of the child. The childish manifestations, it must be remarked, are not necessarily unwholesome; they probably perform a valuable function and develop budding sexual emotions, just as the petals of flowers are developed in pale and contorted shapes beneath the enveloping sheaths.

But in our human life the transmutation is often not so

[2] Perhaps, as applied to the period below puberty, it would be more exact to say "pseudo-sexuality." Matsumato has lately pointed out the significance of the fact that the interstitial testicular tissue, essential to the hormonic function of the testes, only becomes active at puberty.

easy as in flowers. Normally, indeed, the adolescent transformations of sex are so urgent and so manifold—now definite sensual desire, now muscular impulses of adventure, now emotional aspirations in the sphere of art or religion—that they easily overwhelm and absorb all its vaguer and more twisted manifestations in childhood. Yet it may happen that by some aberration of internal development or of external influence this conversion of energy may at one point or another fail to be completely effected. Then some fragment of infantile sexuality survives, in rare cases to turn all the adult faculties to its service and become reckless and triumphant, in minor and more frequent cases to be subordinated and more or less repressed into the subconscious sphere by voluntary or even involuntary and unconscious effort. Then we may have conflict, which, when it works happily, exerts a fortifying and ennobling influence on character, when more unhappily a disturbing influence which may even lead to conditions of definite nervous disorder.

The process by which this fundamental sexual energy is elevated from elementary and primitive forms into complex and developed forms is termed sublimation, a term originally used for the process of raising by heat a solid substance to the state of vapour, which was applied even by such early writers as Drayton and Davies in a metaphorical and spiritual sense.[8] In the sexual sphere sublimation is of vital importance because it comes into question throughout the whole of life, and our relation to it must intimately affect our conception of morality. The element of athletic asceticism which is a part of all virility, and is found even—indeed often in a high degree —among savages, has its main moral justification as one aid to sublimation. Throughout life sublimation acts by transforming some part at all events of the creative sexual energy from its elementary animal manifestations into more highly individual and social manifestations, or at all events into finer forms of sexual activity, forms that seem to us more beautiful and satisfy us more widely. Purity, we thus come to see, is in one aspect, the action of sublimation, not abolishing sexual activity,

---

[8] We may gather the history of the term from the *Oxford Dictionary*. "Bodies," said Davies, "are transformed to spirit 'by sublimation strange,'" and Ben Jonson in *Cynthia's Revels* spoke of a being "sublimated and refined"; Purchas and Jackson, early in the same seventeenth century, referred to religion as "sublimating" human nature, and Jeremy Taylor, a little later, to "subliming" marriage into a sacrament; Shaftesbury, early in the eighteenth century, spoke of human nature being "sublimated by a sort of spiritual chemists" and Welton, a little later, of "a love sublimate and refined" while, finally, and altogether in our modern sense, Peacock in 1816, in his *Headlong Hall* referred to "that enthusiastic sublimation which is the source of greatness and energy."

but lifting it into forms of which our best judgment may approve.

We must not suppose—as is too often assumed—that sublimation can be carried out easily, completely, or even with unmixed advantage. If it were so, certainly the old-fashioned moralist would be confronted by few difficulties, but we have ample reason to believe that it is not so. It is with sexual energy, well observes Freud, who yet attaches great importance to sublimation, as it is with heat in our machines: only a certain proportion can be transformed into work. Or, as it is put by Löwenfeld, who is not a constructive philosopher but a careful and cautious medical investigator, the advantages of sublimation are not received in specially high degree by those who permanently deny to their sexual impulse every natural direct relief. The celibate Catholic clergy, notwithstanding their heroic achievements in individual cases, can scarcely be said to display a conspicuous excess of intellectual energy, on the whole, over the non-celibate Protestant clergy; or, if we compare the English clergy before and after the Protestant Reformation, though the earlier period may reveal more daring and brilliant personages, the whole intellectual output of the later Church may claim comparison with that of the earlier Church. There are clearly other factors at work besides sublimation, and even sublimation may act most potently, not when the sexual activities sink or are driven into a tame and monotonous subordination, but rather when they assume a splendid energy which surges into many channels. Yet sublimation is a very real influence, not only in its more unconscious and profound operations, but in its more immediate and temporary applications, as part of an athletic discipline, acting best perhaps when it acts most automatically, to utilise the motor energy of the organism in the attainment of any high physical or psychic achievement.

We have to realise, however, that these transmutations do not only take place by way of a sublimation of sexual energy, but also by way of a degradation of that energy. The new form of energy produced, that is to say, may not be of a beneficial kind; it may be of a mischievous kind, a form of perversion or disease. Sexual self-denial, instead of leading to sublimation, may lead to nervous disorder when the erotic tension, failing to find a natural outlet and not sublimated to higher erotic or non-erotic ends in the real world, is transmuted into an unreal dreamland, thus undergoing what Jung terms introversion; while there are also the people already referred to, in whom immature childish sexuality persists into an adult stage of development it is no longer altogether in accord with, so that conflict, with various possible trains of nervous symptoms, may result. Disturbances and conflicts in the emotional sexual field may, we know, in these and similar ways become transformed into physical symptoms of disorder which can be seen to have a precise symbolic relationship to definite events in the patient's emotional history, while fits of nervous terror, or anxiety-neurosis, may frequently be regarded as a degradation of thwarted or disturbed sexual energy, manifesting its origin by presenting a picture of sexual excitation transposed into a non-sexual shape of an entirely useless or mischievous character.

Thus, to sum up, we may say that the sexual energy of the organism is a mighty force, automatically generated throughout life. Under healthy conditions that force is transmuted in more or less degree, but never entirely, into forms that further the development of the individual and the general ends of life. These transformations are to some extent automatic, to some extent within the control of personal guidance. But there are limits to such guidance, for the primitive human personality can never be altogether rendered an artificial creature of civilisation. When these limits are reached the transmutation of sexual energy may become useless or even dangerous, and we fail to attain the exquisite flower of Purity.

III

It may seem that in setting forth the nature of the sexual impulse in the light of modern biology and psychology, I have said but little of purity and less of morality. Yet that is as it should be. We must first be content to see how the machine works and watch the wheels go round. We must understand before we can pretend to control; in the natural world, as Bacon long ago said, we can only command by obeying. Moreover, in this field Nature's order is far older and more firmly established than our civilised human morality. In our arrogance we often assume that Morality is the master of Nature. Yet except when it is so elementary or fundamental as to be part of Nature, it is but a guide, and a guide that is only a child, so young, so capricious, that in every age its wayward hand has sought to pull Nature in a different direction. Even only in order to guide we must first see and know.

We realise that never more than when we observe the distinction which conventional sex-morals so often makes between men and women. Failing to find in women exactly the same kind of sexual emotions as they find in themselves, men have concluded that there are none there at all. So man has regarded himself as the sexual animal, and woman as either the passive object of his adoring love or the helpless victim of his degrading lust, in either case as a being who, unlike man, possessed an innocent "purity" by nature, without any need for the trouble of acquiring it. Of woman as a real human being, with sexual needs and sexual responsibilities, morality has often known nothing. It has been content to preach restraint to man, an abstract and meaningless restraint even if it were possible. But when we have regard to the actual facts of life, we can no longer place virtue in a vacuum. Women are just as apt as men to be afflicted by the petty jealousies and narrownesses of the crude sexual impulse; women just as much as men need the perpetual sublimation of erotic desire into forms of more sincere purity, of larger harmony, in gaining which ends all the essential ends of morality are alone gained. The delicate adjustment of the needs of each sex to the needs of the other sex to the end of what Chaucer called fine loving, the adjustment of the needs of both sexes to the larger ends of fine living, may well furnish a perpetual moral discipline which extends its fortifying influence to men and women alike.

It is this universality of sexual emotion, blending in its own mighty stream, as is now realised, many other currents of emotion, even the parental and the filial, and traceable even in childhood—the wide efflorescence of an energy constantly generated by a vital internal mechanism—which renders vain all attempts either to suppress or to ignore the problem of sex, however immensely urgent we might foolishly imagine such attempts to be. Even the history of the early Christian ascetics in Egypt, as recorded in the contemporary *Paradise* of Palladius, illustrates the futility of seeking to quench the unquenchable, the flame of fire which is life itself. These "athletes of the Lord" were under the best possible conditions for the conquest of lust; they had been driven into the solitude of the desert by a genuine deeply-felt impulse, they could regulate their lives as they would, and they possessed an almost inconceivable energy of resolution. They were prepared to live on herbs, even to eat grass, and to undertake any labour of self-denial. They were so scrupulous that we hear of a holy man who would even efface a woman's footprints in the sand lest a brother might thereby be led into thoughts of evil. Yet they were perpetually tempted to seductive visions and desires, even after a monastic life of forty years, and the women seem to have been not less liable to yield to temptation than the men.

It may be noted that in the most perfect saints there has not always been a complete suppression of the sexual impulse even on the normal plane, nor even, in some cases, the attempt at such complete suppression. In the early days of Christianity the exercise of chastity was frequently combined with a close and romantic intimacy of affection between the sexes which shocked austere moralists. Even in the eleventh century we find that the charming and saintly Robert of Arbrissel, founder of the order of Fontevrault, would often sleep with his nuns, notwithstanding the remonstrances of pious friends who thought he was displaying too heroic a manifestation of continence, failing to understand that he was effecting a sweet compromise with continence. If, moreover, we consider the rarest and finest of the saints we usually find that in their early lives there was a period of full expansion of the organic activities in which all the natural impulses had full play. This was the case with the two greatest and most influential saints of the Christian Church, St. Augustine and St. Francis of Assisi, absolutely unlike as they were in most other respects. Sublimation, we see again and again, is limited, and the best developments of the spiritual life are not likely to come about by the rigid attempt to obtain a complete transmutation of sexual energy.

The old notion that any strict attempt to adhere to sexual abstinence is beset by terrible risks, insanity and so forth, has no foundation, at all events where we are concerned with reasonably sound and healthy people. But it is a very serious error to suppose that the effort to achieve complete and prolonged sexual abstinence is without any bad results at all, physical or psychic, either in men or women who are normal and healthy. This is now generally recognised everywhere, except in the English-speaking countries, where the supposed interests of a prudish morality often lead to a refusal to look facts in the face. As Professor Näcke, a careful and cautious physician, stated shortly before his death, a few years ago, the opinion that sexual abstinence has no bad effects is not to-day held by a single authority on questions of sex; the fight is only concerned with the nature and degree of the bad effects which, in Näcke's belief—and he was doubtless right—are never of a gravely serious character.

Yet we have also to remember that not only, as we have seen, is the effort to achieve complete abstinence—which we ignorantly term "purity"—futile, since we are concerned with a force which is being constantly generated within the organism, but in the effort to achieve it we are abusing a great source of beneficent energy. We lose more than half of what we might gain when we cover it up, and try to push it back, to produce, it may be, not harmonious activity in the world, but merely internal confusion and distortion, and perhaps the paralysis of half the soul's energy. The sexual activities of the organism, we cannot too often repeat, constitute a mighty source of energy which we can never altogether repress though by wise guidance we may render it an aid not only to personal development and well-being but to the moral betterment of the world. The attraction of sex, according to a superstition which reaches far back into antiquity, is a baleful comet pointing to destruction, rather than a mighty star to which we may harness our chariot. It may certainly be either, and which it is likely to become depends largely on our knowledge and our power of self-guidance.

In old days, when, as we have seen, tradition, aided by the most fantastic superstitions, insisted on the baleful aspects of sex, the whole emphasis was placed against passion. Since knowledge and self-guidance, without which passion is likely to be in fact pernicious, were then usually absent, the emphasis was needed, and when Böhme, the old mystic, declared that the art of living is to "harness our fiery energies to the service of the light," it has recently been even maintained that he was the solitary pioneer of our modern doctrines. But the ages in which ill-regulated passion exceeded—ages at least full of vitality and energy—gave place to a more anæmic society. To-day the conditions are changed, even reversed. Moral maxims that were wholesome in feudal days are deadly now. We are in no danger of suffering from too much vitality, from too much energy in the explosive splendour of our social life. We possess, moreover, knowledge in plenty and self-restraint in plenty, even in excess, however wrongly they may sometimes be applied. It is passion, more passion and fuller, that we need. The moralist who bans passion is not of our time; his place these many years is with the dead. For we know what happens in a world when those who ban passion have triumphed. When Love is suppressed Hate takes its place. The least regulated orgies of Love grow innocent beside the orgies of Hate. When nations that might well worship one another cut one another's throats, when Cruelty and Self-righteousness and Lying and Injustice and all the Powers of Destruction rule the human heart, the world is devastated, the fibre of the whole organism of society grows flaccid, and all the ideals of civilisation are debased. If the world is not now sick of Hate we may be sure it never will be; so whatever may happen to the world let us remember that the individual is still left, to carry on the tasks of Love, to do good even in an evil world.

It is more passion and ever more that we need if we are to undo the work of Hate, if we are to add to the gaiety and splendour of life, to the sum of human achievement, to the aspiration of human ecstasy. The things that fill men and women with beauty and exhilaration, and spur them to actions beyond themselves, are the things that are now needed. The entire intrinsic purification of the soul, it was held by the great Spanish Jesuit theologian, Suarez, takes place at the moment when, provided the soul is of good disposition, it sees God; he meant after death, but for us the saying is symbolic of the living truth. It is only in the passion of facing the naked beauty of the world and its naked truth that we can win intrinsic purity. Not all, indeed, who look upon the face of God can live. It is not well that they should live. It is only the metals that can be welded in the fire of passion to finer services that the world needs. It would be well that the rest should be lost in those flames. That indeed were a world fit to perish, wherein the moralist had set up the ignoble maxim: Safety first.

Chapter 4

MARRIAGES NOT MADE
IN HEAVEN

MARRIAGE, IT USED TO BE SAID, WAS MADE IN HEAVEN. Nowadays we usually expect to see the heavenly bloom rubbed off in a year or two, to reveal a commonplace friendly partnership. One marriage in four, it is sometimes estimated, is about the proportion of really happy marriages. In ancient days, it is argued, happy marriages were surely more frequent.

I doubt it. The marriage of romance was outside real life. One may even doubt if the happiness to-day demanded in marriage—whether or not often found—had any existence in ancient days. Marriage then was a duty for the partners, who were bound together in wedlock, and a convenience socially and financially, for the families who usually had the chief part in so binding them. Many love letters have come down to us from days of old—beautiful and romantic many of them—but they were written by unmarried lovers. I know that I might search long to find among the old letters of married women what I see in a letter I chanced to receive this morning from a woman, married and a mother: "We are happy, our love is beautiful; our lives, our interests, grow ever closer and dearer."

The established permanence of marriage in old days offered no practicable alternative to acceptance. If the germs of discontent were generated, they led to a slow spiritual death below the surface, but to no open conflict between the forces of happiness and unhappiness. If marriages appear less happy to-day it is because we are less willing to submit to unhappiness and make-believes. When the burdens seem intolerable new ways of meeting the difficulties are now at hand, and they can be met in the open, no longer concealed to gnaw slowly at the vitals. A degree of sexual equality, also, even though not always legally and economically achieved by women, has tended to become marked in social and spiritual respects. Business and religion alike no longer offer so many barriers to the independently-minded woman.

So that to-day the difficulties of marriage may be openly and fairly met. What are we doing to meet them? It is obvious that in this matter, as is recognised in the science of warfare, defence must be concurrently developed with offence. The increased attacks on marriage happiness must be met by increased methods of protection.

There is one method of protection to which attention is often called. I refer to the fitting choice of a mate. All attempts at adjustment after marriage may be in vain if the two parties—by traditions, or temperaments, or mental and emotional outlooks—are not fitted for adjustment. "I broke it off," said a girl, "because our opinions on religion and art were too far apart," and I am not sure that she was wrong. A difference in religious faith may easily be fatal to the deepest kind of union, though we may not be accustomed to think so of art. Yet differences about art may lead to fierce quarrels, and certainly a man who is a sedentary worker and hates all forms of noise becomes be tempted to cherish thoughts of divorce when his wife becomes an enthusiastic musician. We may, again, democratically despise the distinctions of "class." But when one's partner is constantly shocking one's life-long habits of living, marriage becomes difficult; if a cultured girl desires to marry some splendid "man of the people" she seldom fails soon to outgrow her infatuation. In our days of education for all, social equality becomes ever more easy, but even American experience has shown that the happiest marriages tend to be those in which the two partners spring from a similar social background. Differences in race and nationality are also of a kind which can only be considered before marriage; if slight they often constitute an attraction (and remarkably often have an advantageous influence on the offspring) but if extreme they may prove a growing source of alienation.

A marriage may be wrecked on its intimate side, or burdened with a perpetual handicap, because of ignorance or misinformation, or falsely puritanic superstitions in early life. Or an unfortunate early experience, a virtual rape, may cause a nervous shock which long after, if not for ever, impairs a woman's satisfaction with even the most fitting mate. Dr. Katharine Davis in her instructive *Factors in the Sex Life of Twenty-Two Hundred Women*, made a point of asking the women what was their first reaction to marriage. Too often we find such answers as "stunned," "frightened," "disgusted," "bewildered," "indignant," "astonished," "shocked." It is scarcely more satisfactory to find that some were "resigned" or "amused," and that a large number merely "took it as a matter of fact." Such failures of adequate response to the marriage relationship do not proceed from natural sex differences. But they bear witness to defective preparation for marriage. Education for marriage is needed by all normal young persons. The preparation needs to begin before any final choice is made, since the haphazard attack of romance is apt to cloud for a time the real qualities of its object when no definite standard has been set up.

It is foolish to overlook the importance of selection in sexual union for the production of offspring; even animals recognise it, whether or not we accept the full Darwinian doctrine of sexual selection. There should be nothing but praise for such an initiative as that now being taken by the Eugenics Society in preparing schedules for each of the couple proposing marriage, to fill in (with his or her physician's help) for the information of the other partner. These schedules, aided by the advice of practical experts, have been drawn up with much care and consideration; they do not merely cover heredity and health; they enter into such subjects as knowledge of what sexual relations mean and what the feeling is about such relations. These schedules may freely be obtained from the Secretary of the Eugenics Society. Every doctor should be in possession of them and bring the matter to the notice of patients who contemplate marriage. If this were generally done no one can measure the amount of marital unhappiness which might have been avoided.

II

It will be seen from the previous article that I do not underestimate the immense importance for married happiness of right selection of a partner and adequate preparation for the privileges and the duties of marriage. What I am, however, specially concerned to emphasise is that right sexual selection and right preparation—important as they both are and even essential—do not alone suffice to make a happy marriage. The child emerging from the womb may arrive with a perfect equipment for life, but that is only half its fate; the other half depends on the nature of its contact with the environment. A perfect equipment for marriage, similarly, will only account for half the fate in marriage; the rest will depend on what happens in the mutual reactions of the two partners. In other words marriage is an art.

That is a central fact about marriage. Only in recent years set forth, it already for some people seems so obvious that they are inclined to think it a truism. Far from it! Although in ancient days, as far back as the time of Ovid, an "art of love" was recognised, it was an illegitimate art, to be confined to illicit love, and held in disrepute. It had no place in marriage. In a virtuous marriage morality lay in confining "love" to its most animal functions, in the absence of which marriage is excluded. That viewpoint is still common.

It is so especially, I regret to say, among men. For this there are at least two reasons. In the first place the world of men remains more traditionalised in matters of sex than that of women. "Women live in a man-made world," one still often hears. But women are modifying their position in that world. In innumerable ways the status of women has been changed during the past century, alike legally, economically, politically, and socially. The process is still going on. We cannot be surprised that it should spread to the sexual sphere. A century ago, almost to a day, in a district close to that where I now write, two women, the mothers of illegitimate children, publicly testified their sorrow for their sins at a special ceremony at the parish church as ordered by the Ecclesiastical Court, in the presence of a large congregation. They were habited in white robes made for the occasion and stood one on each side of the church door with long white wands in their hands. They were then conducted into the church and placed before the desk of the minister who, we are told, delivered a very excellent and appropriate discourse, after which the ladies were dispossessed of their penitential habiliments and allowed to depart. We hear nothing of any penance inflicted on the men who were at least equally responsible for these misdeeds. We still do not usually regard such feminine adventurers with approval, but at all events we are prepared to be less brutal and more considerate. And it has been possible to insist, with wide approval, on the erotic rights of women.

There is another, and organic, reason for their sexual difference. That is women's wider possibilities of response. Women's special functions in reproduction furnish them with a greater range of sexual centres, and their readier reaction to affective stimuli co-operates in the same direction. The keyboard has more keys. And Balzac's ancient and often quoted simile of the man with a woman in his arms to an orang-utan with a violin cannot, unfortunately, yet be called out-of-date. So it is that women are readier than men for the art of love.

That is why I feel that we are to-day called upon to face a new situation. It is a period of transition. We are beginning to realise that, in matters of love, a "man-made world" is a bad world. Men themselves are realising this. It is becoming clear that even those supposedly feminine qualities which stand in the way of betterment are qualities which men themselves have imposed on women. Conventionality and prudery, incompatible with any art, are not really so native to women in matters of love as we have come to suppose; they are merely the fictitious masculine ideals which women have been forced to accept. If we now so often see an open dissatisfaction it is due to the revolt of those who of old meekly submitted to unnatural conditions. The existence of easier divorce is really an encouraging sign. It offers greater possibilities for real marriage and is only fatal to false marriage. The dissatisfied of to-day feel heartened to seek the art of love. It is an art which, like other arts, may be learnt though it cannot be taught, and until it is learnt the search of happiness in marriage is in vain.

In laying this emphasis on the art of love, I am not proposing that we run to the opposite extreme to those who insist on the importance of eugenic and temperamental selection. It is not true that, in our civilization, any marriage may be made happy. We must not forget—though it is often forgotten—that in every department of life good seed and good soil are both alike essential. The best husband like the best husbandman—as of old they wisely called the farmer—cannot expect by the fine quality of the seed he supplies to make up entirely for inferiority in his partner. It will nevertheless always help.

It is a sad spectacle for those who have an intimate knowledge of marriage to observe the frequent bad husbandry of husbands and its fatal effect on love. We see, for instance, a woman of the typical feminine type, with less self-will and independence of character than some of her sisters, but of admirable material to make a happy wife. She is in love with her husband and he is in love with her, indeed perhaps absurdly jealous. But he is also completely ignorant of the art of loving, and even neglectful of the elementary rights of personality. And far too often he imagines that marriage has brought courtship to an end. Love-making becomes for him a routine for which no preparation is necessary, unless, it may be, of a precautionary nature. He is not aware that for his wife to be brought into the right condition for love-making, alike physically and psychically, a preliminary courtship is necessary. Nothing can ever be taken for granted in love. That recognition is essential for happy marriage.

There are other rights which it is important the wife should possess if the union is to be happy. She should be able to cherish her own personality on those aspects of it which do not affect her husband. There is always a realm of personality to which other persons, however intimately near, can only enter as a privilege and not by right. Even children should be encouraged to cherish this source of personality. I do not know if there are many husbands who consider that they may demand to see all the letters their wives receive or write. But such husbands are still not unknown. It is a demand that should never be made and never admitted. (These words were only just written when I came on the letter of a correspondent who remarks: "My wife and I do not open or read each other's letters: this was enunciated by her and is an excellent rule; we have no secrets, but we don't express or feel curiosity about each other's affairs.") Love is always free to give but never free to demand, even within the proper love sphere. Marriage is still too much based on demands. The wife may merely demand maintenance, the husband merely a housekeeper. Maintenance and housekeeping may still both be essential. But they are matters of business arrangement and outside the art of love. As sources of marital happiness they must in time largely disappear in so far as we acquire a common-sense conception of the business of life. The discontent we find is largely of those who refuse to accept these as the primary demands of marriage.

Thus while we recognise the importance of due selection of partners before marriage we also accept the possibility of constructive selection after marriage. Each partner enters the union with a large number of possible qualities, many of them still latent, and among these selection may still be effected. It has been asserted that "the person one marries really has the possibility of being a dozen different people." On the intellectual side certainly that may sometimes be seen. An example I sometimes quote is that of Mrs. Mark Pattison, the wife of a man absorbed in scholarship, who became herself a brilliant and scholarly authority on eighteenth century French art, and when, later, she became the wife of Sir Charles Dilke, Radical statesman, became equally brilliant as a student of Labour questions, in both phases, we may be sure, as a voluntary giving. On a less intellectual plane of character in the domestic sphere, manifestations of changed personality occur, though often in response to demands and much less satisfactory. When we observe a husband who is domineering in the home, or, on the other hand, manifesting a quite reverse attitude, we may often need to observe his wife for an explanation of the personality he has developed. More often, no doubt, it is the wife who is apparently moulded by the influences with which her husband's temperament has surrounded her. She may grow wise and tolerant and generous; she may grow sour and petty and pessimistic. But it is only by a process of giving out, in an atmosphere rendered favourable by a like attitude on the man's part, that a woman's powers can develop, and that both

mates may grow wise and tolerant and generous in a life
of shared interests.

This brings us again to what must always be regarded a
central fact of the situation: marriage is an art. And a great
deal of the art is in giving, and not only in giving love but in
giving understanding. As in all arts, success can only be the
outcome of practice and experience.

Preliminary enlightenment is not enough. Many a girl has
found on marriage that the knowledge she was confident
she possessed has failed to carry her far. From the wedding-
night—and indeed specially then—onwards, throughout the
whole course of marriage, the maintenance of love is an art
and in that art a golden rule on both sides is always to give
and never to demand. Since no two human beings are alike,
the only guide to the art is experience.

III

Marriage is an art, I have sought to show, and the guide to
that art is experience. Yet difficult questions sometimes remain.
There is, for instance, that craving for variety which has been
brought forward as a source of disturbance in married life.
No doubt of its existence. In Dr. Hamilton's careful investigation 41 per cent. husbands and 29 per cent. wives admitted a
craving for variety of one sort or another, the feminine desire
for variety being thus less acute than the masculine. This
craving is admitted even by so wise and cautious an upholder
of monogamy as Dr. Westermarck in his recent book on *The
Future of Marriage in Western Civilisation*. It has indeed long
been recognised by breeders even among animals; they are
excited by novelty. It cannot therefore be said that this impulse
is unnatural. The important point is that civilised man need
not be animal-like.

It has often been said, and it is still well to repeat, that
married lovers who have passed beyond the cruder stages may
find ample variety in themselves. The secrets of love-making
are many and there is now no need to search for them in the
pedantic lore of ancient books. Two lovers who are interested
in each other will discover those new mysteries of love which
best suit themselves, and now that sane ideas on these matters
are more common they will not be tempted to fear that they are
becoming morbid or vicious. The lovers who can always find
variety in themselves will be less likely to seek it outside.

But even when variety outside marriage becomes attractive,
the civilised lover may find satisfaction without the risks which
beset the crude animal search for novelty. In the complex network of our lives human beings are so unlike, and the gamut

of emotions so extended, that all sorts of relationships may be formed in the outside world without disturbing the deep central relationship. Indeed, when rightly understood, and the equal freedom of both partners is recognised, that central relationship is thereby enriched. I can never forget Edward Carpenter's image of the life of a family of grubs as revealed when one lifts some heavy stone in the garden which shelters them from the world. The happiness of the pigsty, however genuine, is not of the kind which we need seek to emulate.

Then, however, we have to face the problem of jealousy. That is a common and often difficult problem.

Jealousy is certainly natural. We may not hope to abolish it, but the significant fact is that civilisation affords possibilities of its modification, of its control, of its conquest. The very circumstance that through our increased intellectual and emotional development the possible occasions for jealousy are multiplied renders the approaches far more accessible to control than when a consummated act of bodily intercourse seemed the only reason for jealousy. If the manifold relationships of modern life make for the enrichment of personality, then the enrichment cannot but be increased when it is shared between two people who feel that they are in a unique relationship to each other. The sincerity and frankness involved by this sharing of experiences remove any sting that the experiences themselves might possess. Where the adjustments are less easy to effect happily, there is one vital consideration which in civilisation is readier of comprehension than in savagery. That is that, under our social conditions, jealousy is not only futile, but worse. It tends to fortify what it attacks, while the obstinately jealous lover makes still more difficult the restoration of what he fears he is losing. The lover who succeeds in being tender and considerate in the face of what might well arouse jealousy wins a reward of gratitude and affection which must ever be out of reach of the jealous lover.

It is necessary to add that it is not enough to insist on the need for self-control and affectionate consideration in one only of the two partners. We are entitled to expect an equal self-control and consideration in the partner whose conduct is liable to excite jealousy. However close the bonds uniting the partners, neither has the right to assume that the other totally lacks any impulse to suffer, if not from the crude emotion of jealousy, at all events from what may be felt as an invasion of the hitherto unique relationship. The love that has attained any fine degree of development instinctively avoids, as far as possible, making the beloved person feel pain.

Such considerations may serve to indicate that as we push

more deeply the development of married life the conception of happiness undergoes constant modification. The crude romance of mutual absorption, with which the innocent young couple may approach the altar, cannot survive the shocks of real life, and would be unwholesome if it could. The modifications are inevitable. The main point is that they should be of enlargement rather than of restriction, of elevation rather than of debasement.

After twenty years of married life, or less, happiness, however genuine, is no longer conceived in the same terms as on the wedding day. The emotional accompaniments to the original urge to physical gratification tend to acquire a more or less independent existence of their own. The sentiments of affection and sympathy and admiration for the beloved mate may develop to such a point as themselves to constitute a kind of passion, and almost, if not quite, to replace physical desire. But even in ceasing to exist, its spiritual transformation remains in lasting ties of happily mutual love and tenderness, provided it was really friendship and affection which brought the pair together. So it comes about that at no stage in the longest married life, even leaving out the possibilities introduced by parenthood, are the possibilities of happiness outgrown.

If we sum up the considerations we encounter in exploring the possibilities of happiness in marriage they mainly come under two heads: the need of enlightenment and the need of what in a wide sense may be called art, together with the discipline that all good art demands. Many of the impediments to married happiness are in reality so slight that they might easily be removed at the outset by better knowledge. But there are others which may involve struggle and tension, though of this we should not be impatient, for, as it has been truly said in this connection, there is no music save on tightened strings. It remains true, as in the days of the ancient Greeks, that "the beautiful is difficult."

Chapter 5

THE OBJECTS OF MARRIAGE

WHAT ARE THE LEGITIMATE OBJECTS OF MARRIAGE? We know that many people seek to marry for ends that can scarcely be called legitimate, that men may marry to obtain a cheap domestic drudge or nurse, and that women may marry to be kept when they are tired of keeping themselves. These objects in marriage may or may not be moral, but in any case they are scarcely its legitimate ends. We are here concerned to ascertain those ends of marriage which are legitimate when we take the highest ground as moral and civilised men and women living in an advanced state of society and seeking, if we can, to advance that state of society still further.

The primary end of marriage is to beget and bear offspring, and to rear them until they are able to take care of themselves. On that basis Man is at one with all the mammals and most of the birds. If, indeed, we disregard the originally less essential part of this end—that is to say, the care and tending of the young—this end of marriage is not only the primary but usually the sole end of sexual intercourse in the whole mammal world. As a natural instinct, its achievement involves gratification and well-being, but this bait of gratification is merely a device of Nature and not in itself an end having any useful function at the periods when conception is not possible. This is clearly indicated by the fact that among animals the female only experiences sexual desire at the season of impregnation, and that desire ceases as soon as impregnation takes place, though this is only in a few species true of the male, obviously because, if his sexual desire and aptitude were confined to so brief a period, the chances of the female meeting the right male at the right moment would be too seriously diminished; so that the attentive and inquisitive attitude towards the female by the male animal—which we may often think we see still traceable in the human species—is not the outcome of lustfulness for personal gratification ("wantonly to satisfy

51

carnal lusts and appetites like brute beasts," as the Anglican Prayer Book incorrectly puts it) but implanted by Nature for the benefit of the female and the attainment of the primary object of procreation. This primary object we may term the animal end of marriage.

This object remains not only the primary but even the sole end of marriage among the lower races of mankind generally. The erotic idea, in its deeper sense, that is to say the element of love, arose very slowly in mankind. It is found, it is true, among some lower races, and it appears that some tribes possess a word for the joy of love in a purely psychic sense. But even among European races the evolution was late. The Greek poets, except the latest, showed little recognition of love as an element of marriage. Theognis compared marriage with cattle-breeding. The Romans of the Republic took much the same view. Greeks and Romans alike regarded breeding as the one recognisable object of marriage; any other object was mere wantonness and had better, they thought, be carried on outside marriage. Religion, which preserves so many ancient and primitive conceptions of life, has consecrated this conception also, and Christianity—though, as I will point out later, it has tended to enlarge the conception—at the outset only offered the choice between celibacy on the one hand and on the other marriage for the production of offspring.

Yet, from an early period in human history, a secondary function of sexual intercourse had been slowly growing up to become one of the great objects of marriage. Among animals, it may be said, and even sometimes in man, the sexual impulse, when once aroused, makes but a short and swift circuit through the brain to reach its consummation. But as the brain and its faculties develop, powerfully aided indeed by the very difficulties of the sexual life, the impulse for sexual union has to traverse ever longer, slower, more painful paths, before it reaches—and sometimes it never reaches—its ultimate object. This means that sex gradually becomes intertwined with all the highest and subtlest human emotions and activities, with the refinements of social intercourse, with high adventure in every sphere, with art, with religion. The primitive animal instinct, having the sole end of procreation, becomes on its way to that end the inspiring stimulus to all those psychic energies which in civilisation we count most precious. This function is thus, we see, a by-product. But, as we know, even in our human factories, the by-product is sometimes more valuable than the product. That is so as regards the functional products of human evolution. The hand was produced out of the animal forelimb with the primary end of grasping the things we materially need, but as a by-product the hand has developed the function of making and playing the piano and the violin and that secondary functional by-product of the hand we account, even as measured by the rough test of money, more precious, however less materially necessary, than its primary function. It is, however, only in rare and gifted natures that transformed sexual energy becomes of supreme value for its own sake without ever attaining the normal physical outlet. For the most part the by-product accompanies the product, throughout, thus adding a secondary, yet peculiarly sacred and specially human, object of marriage to its primary animal object. This may be termed the spiritual object of marriage.

By the term "spiritual" we are not to understand any mysterious and supernatural qualities. It is simply a convenient name, in distinction from animal, to cover all those higher mental and emotional processes which in human evolution are ever gaining greater power. It is needless to enumerate the constituents of this spiritual end of sexual intercourse, for everyone is entitled to enumerate them differently and in different order. They include not only all that makes love a gracious and beautiful erotic art, but the whole element of pleasure in so far as pleasure is more than a mere animal gratification. Our ancient ascetic traditions often make us blind to the meaning of pleasure. We see only its possibilities of evil and not its mightiness for good. We forget that, as Romain Rolland says, "Joy is as holy as Pain." No one has insisted so much on the supreme importance of the element of pleasure in the spiritual ends of sex as James Hinton. Rightly used, he declares, Pleasure is "the Child of God," to be recognised as a "mighty storehouse of force," and he pointed out the significant fact that in the course of human progress its importance increases rather than diminishes.[1] While it is perfectly true that sexual energy may be in large degree arrested, and transformed into intellectual and moral forms, yet it is also true that pleasure itself, and above all, sexual pleasure, wisely used and not abused, may prove the stimulus and liberator of our finest and most exalted activities. It is largely this remarkable function of sexual pleasure which is decisive in settling the argument of those who claim that continence is the only alternative to the animal end of marriage. That argument ignores the liberating and harmonising influences, giving wholesome balance and sanity to the whole organism, imparted by a sexual union which is the outcome of the psychic as well as physical needs. There is, further, in the attainment of the spiritual end of marriage, much more than the benefit of each individual separately.

[1] Mrs. Havelock Ellis, *James Hinton: A Sketch*, Ch. IV.

There is, that is to say, the effect on the union itself. For through harmonious sex relationships a deeper spiritual unity is reached than can possibly be derived from continence in or out of marriage, and the marriage association becomes an apter instrument in the service of the world. Apart from any sexual craving, the complete spiritual contact of two persons who love each other can only be attained through some act of rare intimacy. No act can be quite so intimate as the sexual embrace. In its accomplishment, for all who have reached a reasonably human degree of development, the communion of bodies becomes the communion of souls. The outward and visible sign has been the consummation of an inward and spiritual grace. "I would base all my sex teaching to children and young people on the beauty and sacredness of sex," wrote a distinguished woman; "sex intercourse is the great sacrament of life, he that eateth and drinketh unworthily eateth and drinketh his own damnation; but it may be the most beautiful sacrament between two souls who have no thought of children."[2] To many the idea of a sacrament seems merely ecclesiastical, but that is a misunderstanding. The word "sacrament" is the ancient Roman name of a soldier's oath of military allegiance, and the idea, in the deeper sense, existed long before Christianity, and has ever been regarded as the physical sign of the closest possible union with some great spiritual reality. From our modern standpoint we may say, with James Hinton, that the sexual embrace, worthily understood, can only be compared with music and with prayer. "Every true lover," it has been well said by a woman, "knows this, and the worth of any and every relationship can be judged by its success in reaching, or failing to reach, this standpoint."[3]

I have mentioned how the Church—in part influenced by that clinging to primitive conceptions which always marks religions and in part by its ancient traditions of asceticism—tended to insist mainly, if not exclusively, on the animal object of marriage. It sought to reduce sex to a minimum because the pagans magnified sex; it banned pleasure because the Christian's path on earth was the way of the Cross; and even if theologians accepted the idea of a "Sacrament of Nature" they could only allow it to operate when the active interference of the priest was impossible, though it must in justice be said that, before the Council of Trent, the Western Church recognised that the sacrament of marriage was effected entirely by the act of the two celebrants themselves and not by the priest. Gradually, however, a more reasonable and humane opinion crept into the Church. Intercourse outside the animal end of marriage

---

[2] Olive Schreiner in a personal letter.
[3] Mrs. Havelock Ellis, *James Hinton*, p. 180.

was indeed a sin, but it became merely a venial sin. The great influence of St. Augustine was on the side of allowing much freedom to intercourse outside the aim of procreation. At the Reformation, John à Lasco, a Catholic bishop who became a Protestant and settled in England, laid it down, following various earlier theologians, that the object of marriage, besides offspring, was to serve as a "sacrament of consolation" to the united couple, and that view was more of less accepted by the founders of the Protestant churches. It is the generally accepted Protestant view to-day.[4] The importance of the spiritual end of intercourse in marriage, alike for the higher development of each member of the couple and for the intimacy and stability of their union, is still more emphatically set forth by the more advanced thinkers of to-day.

There is something pathetic in the spectacle of those among us who are still only able to recognise the animal end of marriage, and who point to the example of the lower animals— among whom the biological conditions are entirely different— as worthy of our imitation. It has taken God—or Nature, if we will—unknown millions of years of painful struggle to evolve Man, and to raise the human species above that helpless bondage to reproduction which marks the lower animals. But on these people it has all been wasted. They are at the animal stage still. They have yet to learn the A. B. C. of love. A representative of these people in the person of an Anglican bishop, the Bishop of Southwark, appeared as a witness before the National Birth-Rate Commission which, a few years ago, met in London to investigate the decline of the birth-rate. He declared that procreation is the sole legitimate object of marriage and that intercourse for any other end was a degrading act of mere "self-gratification." This declaration had the interesting result of evoking the comments of many members of the Commission, formed of representative men and women with various standpoints—Protestant, Catholic, and other—and it is notable that while not one identified himself with the Bishop's opinion, several decisively opposed that opinion, as contrary to the best beliefs of both ancient and modern times, as representing a low and not a high moral standpoint, and as involving the notion that the whole sexual activity of an individual should be reduced to perhaps two or three effective acts of intercourse in a lifetime. Such a notion obviously cannot be carried into general practice, putting aside the question as to whether it would be desirable, and it may be added that it would have the further result of shutting

[4] It is well set forth by the Rev. H. Northcote in his excellent book, *Christianity and Sex Problems.*

out from the life of love altogether all those persons who, for whatever reason, feel that it is their duty to refrain from having children at all. It is the attitude of a handful of Pharisees seeking to thrust the bulk of mankind into Hell. All this confusion and evil come of the blindness which cannot know that, beyond the primary animal end of propagation in marriage, there is a secondary but more exalted spiritual end.

It is needless to insist how intimately that secondary end of marriage is bound up with the practice of birth control. Without birth control, indeed, it could frequently have no existence at all, and even at the best seldom be free from disconcerting possibilities fatal to its very essence. Against these disconcerting possibilities is often placed, on the other side, the unæsthetic nature of the contraceptives associated with birth control. Yet, it must be remembered, they are of a part with the whole of our civilised human life. We at no point enter the spiritual save through the material. Forel has in this connection compared the use of contraceptives to the use of eye-glasses. Eye-glasses are equally unæsthetic, yet they are devices, based on Nature, wherewith to supplement the deficiencies of Nature. However in themselves unæsthetic, for those who need them they make the æsthetic possible. Eye-glasses and contraceptives alike are a portal to the spiritual world for many who, without them, would find that world largely a closed book.

Birth control is effecting, and promising to effect, many functions in our social life. By furnishing the means to limit the size of families, which would otherwise be excessive, it confers the greatest benefit on the family and especially on the mother. By rendering easily possible a selection in parentage and the choice of the right time and circumstances for conception it is, again, the chief key to the eugenic improvement of the race. There are many other benefits, as is now generally becoming clear, which will be derived from the rightly applied practice of birth control. To many of us it is not the least of these that birth control effects finally the complete liberation of the spiritual object of marriage.

Chapter 6

HUSBANDS AND WIVES

IT HAS ALWAYS BEEN COMMON to discuss the psychology of women. The psychology of men has usually been passed over, whether because it is too simple or too complicated. But the marriage question to-day is much less the wife-problem than the husband-problem. Women in their personal and social activities have been slowly expanding along lines which are now generally accepted. But there has been no marked change of responsive character in the activities of men. Hence a defective adjustment of men and women, felt in all sorts of subtle as well as grosser ways, most felt when they are husband and wife, and sometimes becoming acute.

It is necessary to make clear that, as is here assumed at the outset, "man" and "husband" are not quite the same thing, even when they refer to the same person. No doubt that is also true of "woman" and "wife." A woman in her quality as woman may be a different kind of person from what she is in her function as wife. But in the case of a man the distinction is more marked. One may know a man well in the world as a man and not know him at all in his home as a husband; not necessarily that he is unfavorably revealed in the latter capacity. It is simply that he is different.

The explanation is not really far to seek. A man in the world is in vital response to the influences around him. But a husband in the home is playing a part which was created for him long centuries before he was born. He is falling into a convention, which, indeed, was moulded to fit many masculine human needs but has become rigidly traditionalised. Thus the part no longer corresponds accurately to the player's nature nor to the circumstances under which it has to be played.

In the marriage system which has prevailed in our world for several thousand years, a certain hierarchy, or sacred order in authority, has throughout been recognised. The family has been regarded as a small State of which the husband and father is head. Classic paganism and Christianity differed on many points, but they were completely at one on this. The Roman system was on a patriarchal basis and continued to be so theoretically even when in practice it came to allow great independence to the wife. Christianity, although it allowed complete spiritual freedom to the individual, introduced no fundamentally new theory of the family, and, indeed, reinforced the old theory by regarding the family as a little church of which the husband was the head. Just as Christ is the head of the Church, St. Paul repeatedly asserted, so the husband is the head of the wife; therefore, as it was constantly argued during the Middle Ages, a man is bound to rule his wife. St. Augustine, the most influential of Christian Fathers, even said that a wife should be proud to consider herself as the servant of her husband, his *ancilla,* a word that had in it the suggestion of slave. That was the underlying assumption throughout the Middle Ages, for the Northern Germanic peoples, having always been accustomed to wife-purchase before their conversion, had found it quite easy to assimilate the Christian view. Protestantism, even Puritanism, with its associations of spiritual revolt, so far from modifying the accepted attitude, strengthened it, for they found authority for all social organisation in the Bible, and the Bible revealed an emphatic predominance of the Jewish husband, who possessed essential rights to which the wife had no claim. Milton, who had the poet's sensitiveness to the loveliness of woman, and the lonely man's feeling for the solace of her society, was yet firmly assured of the husband's superiority over his wife. He has indeed furnished the classical picture of it in Adam and Eve,

"He for God only, she for God in him,"

and to that God she owed "subjection," even though she might qualify it by "sweet reluctant amorous delay." This was completely in harmony with the legal position of the wife. As a subject she was naturally in subjection; she owed her husband the same loyalty as a subject owes the sovereign; her disloyalty to him was termed a minor form of treason; if she murdered him the crime was legally worse than murder and she rendered herself liable to be burnt.

We see that all the influences on our civilisation, religious and secular, southern and northern, have combined to mould the underlying bony structure of our family system in such a way that, however it may appear softened and disguised on the surface, the husband is the head and the wife subject to him. We must not be supposed hereby to deny that the wife has had much authority, many privileges, considerable freedom, and in individual cases much opportunity to domineer, whatever superiority custom or brute strength may have given the husband. There are henpecked husbands, it has been remarked, even in aboriginal Australia. It is necessary to avoid the error of those enthusiasts for the emancipation of women who, out of their eager faith in the future of women, used to describe their past as one of scarcely mitigated servitude and hardship. If women had not constantly succeeded in overcoming or eluding the difficulties that beset them in the past, it would be foolish to cherish any faith in their future. It must, moreover, be remembered that the very constitution of that ecclesiastico-feudal hierarchy which made the husband supreme over the wife, also made the wife jointly with her husband supreme over their children and over their servants. The Middle Ages, alike in England and in France, as doubtless in Christendom generally, accepted the rule laid down in Gratian's *Decretum,* the great mediæval text-book of Canon Law, that "the husband may chastise his wife temperately, for she is of his household," but the wife might chastise her daughters and her servants, and she sometimes exercised that right in ways that we should now-adays think scarcely temperate.

If we seek to observe how the system worked some five hundred years ago when it had not yet become, as it is to-day, both weakened and disguised, we cannot do better than turn to the *Paston Letters,* the most instructive documents we possess concerning the domestic life of excellent yet fairly average people of the upper middle class in England in the fifteenth century. Marriage was still frankly and fundamentally (as it was in the following century and less frankly later) a commercial transaction. The wooer, when he had a wife in view, stated as a matter of course that he proposed to "deal" in the matter; it was quite recognised on both sides that love and courtship must depend on whether the "deal" came off satisfactorily. John Paston approached Sir Thomas Brews, through a third person, with a view to negotiate a marriage with his daughter Margery. She was willing, even eager, and while the matter was still uncertain she wrote him a letter on Valentine's Day, addressing him as "Right reverent and worshipful and my right well-beloved Valentine," to tell him that it was impossible for her father to offer a larger dowry than he had already promised. "If that you could be content with that good, and my poor person, I would be the merriest maiden on ground." In his first letter—boldly written, he says, without her knowledge or license—he addresses her simply as "Mistress," and assures her that "I am and will be yours and at your commandment in every wise during my life." A few weeks later, addressing him as "Right worshipful master," she calls him "mine own sweet-heart," and ends up, as she frequently does, "your servant and bedeswoman." Some months later, a few weeks after marriage, she addresses her husband in the correct manner of the time as "Right reverent and worshipful husband," asking him to buy her a gown as she is weary of wearing her present one, it is so cumbrous. Five years later she refers to "all" the babies, and writes in haste: "Right reverent and worshipful Sir, in my most humble wise I recommend me unto you as lowly as I can," etc., though she adds in a postscript: "Please you to send for me for I think long since I lay in your arms." If we turn to another wife of the Paston family; a little earlier in the century, Margaret Paston, whose husband's name also was John, we find the same attitude even more distinctly expressed. She always addressed him in her most familiar letters, showing affectionate concern for his welfare, as "Right reverent and worshipful husband" or "Right worshipful master." It is seldom that he writes to her at all, but when he writes the superscription is simply "To my mistress Paston," or "my cousin," with little greeting at either beginning or end. Once only, with unexampled effusion, he writes to her as "My own dear sovereign lady" and signs himself "Your true and trusting husband." [1]

If we turn to France the relation of the wife to her husband was the same, or even more definitely dependent, for he occupied the place of father to her as well as of husband and sovereign, in this respect carrying on a tradition of Roman Law. She was her husband's "wife and subject"; she signed herself "Vostre humble obéissante fille et amye." If also we turn to the *Book of the Chevalier de la Tour-Landry* in Anjou, written at the end of the fourteenth century, we find a picture of the relations of women to men in marriage comparable to that presented in the *Paston Letters*, though of a different order. This book was, as we know, written for the instruction of his daughters by a Knight who seems to have been a fairly average man of his time in his beliefs, and in character, as he has been described, probably above it, "a man of the world, a Christian, a parent, and a gentleman." His book is full of interesting light on the customs and manners of his day, though it is mainly a picture of what the writer thought ought to be rather than what always was. Herein the Knight is sagacious and moderate, much of his advice is admirably sound for every age. He is less concerned with affirming the authority of husbands than with assuring the happiness and well-being of his

[1] We see just the same formulas in the fifteenth century letters of the Stonor family (*Stonor Letters and Papers*, Camden Society), though in these letters we seem often to find a lighter and more playful touch than was common among the Pastons. I may refer here to Dr. Powell's learned and well-written book (with which I was not acquainted when I wrote this chapter), *English Domestic Relations 1487-1653* (Columbia University Press).

procession of husbands which began long ages before he was born. It thus comes about that a man, even after he is married, and a husband are two different persons, so that his wife who mainly knows him as a husband may be unable to form any just idea of what he is like as a man. As a husband he has stepped out of the path that belongs to him in the world, and taken on another part which has called out altogether different reactions, so he is sometimes a much more admirable person in one of these spheres—whichever it may be—than in the other.

We must not be surprised if the husband's position has sometimes developed those qualities which from the modern point of view are the less admirable. In this respect the sovereign husband resembles the Sovereign State. The Sovereign State, as it has survived from Renaissance days in our modern world, may be made up of admirable people, yet as a State they are forced into an attitude of helpless egoism which nowadays fails to commend itself to the outside world, and the tendency of scientific jurists to-day is to deal very critically with the old conception of the Sovereign State. It is so with the husband in the home. He was thrust by ancient tradition into a position of sovereignty which impelled him to play a part of helpless egoism. He was a celestial body in the home around which all the other inmates were revolving satellites. The hours of rising and retiring, the times of meals and their nature and substance, all the activities of the household—in which he himself takes little or no part—are still arranged primarily to suit his work, his play, and his tastes. This is an accepted matter of course, and not the result of any violent self-assertion on his part. It is equally an accepted matter of course that the wife should be constantly occupied in keeping this little solar system in easy harmonious movement, evolving from it, if she has the skill, the music of the spheres. She has no recognised independent personality of her own, nor even any right to go away by herself for a little change and recreation. Any work of her own, play of her own, tastes of her own, must be strictly subordinated, if not suppressed altogether.

In the old days, from which our domestic traditions proceed, little hardship was thus inflicted on the wife. Her rights and privileges were far less than those of the modern woman, but for that very reason the home offered her a larger field; beneath the shelter of her husband the irresponsible wife might exert a maximum of influential activity with a minimum of rights and privileges of her own. To many men, even to-day, that state of things seems the realisation of an ideal.

Yet to women it seems increasingly less so, and of necessity since the cleavage between the position of woman in society and law, and the position of the wife in the sacramental bonds of wedlock, is daily becoming greater. To-day a woman, who possibly for ten years has been leading her own life of independent work, earning her own living, choosing her own conditions in accordance with her own needs, and selecting her own periods of recreation in accordance with her own tastes, whether or not this may have included the society of a man-friend—such a woman suddenly finds on marriage, and without any assertion of authority on her husband's part, that all the outward circumstances of her life are reversed and all her inner spontaneous movements arrested. There may be no signs of this on the surface of her conduct. She loves her husband too much to wish to hurt his feelings by explaining the situation, and she values domestic peace too much to risk friction by making unexpected claims. But beneath the surface there is often a profound discontent, and even in women who thought they had gained an insight into life, a sense of disillusion. Everyone knows this who is privileged to catch a glimpse into the hearts of women— often women of most distinguished intelligence as well as women of quite ordinary nature—who leave a life of spontaneous activity in the world to enter the home.[2]

It is not to be supposed that in this presentation of the situation in the home, as it is to-day visible to those who are privileged to see beneath the surface, any accusation is brought against the husband. He is no more guilty of an unreasonable conservatism than the wife is guilty of an unreasonable radicalism. Each of them is the outcome of a tradition. The point is that the events of the past hundred years have produced a discrepancy in the two lines of tradition, with a resultant

[2] While this condition of things is sometimes to be found in the more distinguished minority and in well-to-do families, it is, of course, among the great labouring majority that it is most conspicuous. Mrs. Will Crooks, of Poplar, speaking to a newspaper reporter (*Daily Chronicle*, 17 Feb., 1919), truly remarked: "At present the average married woman's working day is a flagrant contradiction of all trade-union ideals. The poor thing is slaving all the time! What she needs—what she longs for—is just a little break or change now and again, an opportunity to get her mind off her work and its worries. If her husband's hours are reduced to eight, well that gives her a chance, doesn't it? The home and the children are, after all as much his as hers. With his enlarged leisure he will now be able to take a fair share in home duties. I suggest that they take it turn and turn about—one night he goes out and she looks after the house and the children: the next night she goes out and he takes charge of things at home. She can sometimes go to the cinema, sometimes call on friends. Then, say once a week, they can both go out together, taking the children with them. That will be a little change and treat for everybody."

lack of harmony, independent of the goodwill of either husband or wife.

Olive Schreiner, in her *Woman and Labour,* has eloquently
set forth the tendency to parasitism which civilisation produces
in women; they no longer exercise the arts and industries
which were theirs in former ages, and so they become economically dependent on men, losing their energies and aptitudes, and becoming like those dull parasitic animals which
live as blood-suckers of their host. That picture, which was
of course never true of all women, is now ceasing to be true
of any but a negligible minority; it presents, moreover, a
parasitism limited to the economic side of life. For if the
wife has often been a lazy gold-sucking parasite on her husband in the world, the husband has yet oftener been a helpless
service-absorbing parasite on his wife in the home. There is,
that is to say, not only an economic parasitism with no adequate return for financial support, but a still more prevalent
domestic parasitism, with an absorption of services for which
no return would be adequate. There are many helpful husbands in the home, but there are a larger number who are
helpless and have never been trained to be anything else
but helpless, even by their wives, who would often detest
a rival in household work and management. The average
husband enjoys the total effect of his home but is usually
unable to contribute any of the details of work and organisation that make it enjoyable. He cannot keep it in order and
cleanliness and regulated movement, he seldom knows how
to buy things that are needed for its upkeep, nor how to
prepare and cook and present a decent meal; he cannot even
attend to his own domestic needs. It is the wife's consolation
that most husbands are not always at home.

"In ministering to the wants of the family, the woman has
reduced man to a state of considerable dependency on her in
all domestic affairs, just as she is dependent on him for bodily
protection. In the course of ages this has gone so far as to
foster a peculiar helplessness on the part of the man, which
manifests itself in a somewhat childlike reliance of the husband
on the wife. In fact, it may be said that the husband is, to
all intents and purposes, incapable of maintaining himself
without the aid of a woman." This passage will probably seem
to many readers to apply fairly well to men as they exist
to-day in most of those lands which we consider at the summit
of our civilisation. Yet it was not written of civilisation, or of
white men, but of the Bantu tribes of East Africa,[3] complete

[3] Hon. C. Dundas, *Journal of the Anthropological Institute,* Vol. 45,
1915, p. 302.

Negroes who, while far from being among the lowest savages, belong to a culture which is only just emerging from cannibalism, witchcraft, and customary bloodshed. So close a resemblance between the European husband and the Negro husband significantly suggests how remarkable has been the arrest of development in the husband's customary status during a vast period of the world's history.

It is in the considerable group of couples where the husband's work separates him but little from the home that the pressure on the wife is most severe, and without the relief and variety secured by his frequent absence. She has perhaps led a life of her own before marriage, she knows how to be economically independent; now they occupy a small dwelling, they have, maybe, one or two small children, they can only afford one helper in the work or none at all, and in this busy little hive the husband and wife are constantly tumbling over each other. It is small wonder if the wife feels a deep discontent beneath her willing ministrations and misses the devotion of the lover in the perpetual claims of the husband.

But the difficulty is not settled if she persuades him to take a room outside. He is devoted to his wife and his home, with good reason, for the wife makes the home and he is incapable of making a home. His new domestic arrangements sink into careless and sordid disorder, and he is conscious of profound discomfort. His wife soon realises that it is a choice between his return to the home and complete separation. Most wives never get even as far as this attempt at solution of the difficulty and hide their secret discontent.

This is the situation which to-day is becoming intensified and extended on a vast scale. The habit and the taste for freedom, adventure, and economic independence are becoming generated among millions of women who once meekly trod the ancient beaten paths, and we must not be so foolish as to suppose that they can suddenly renounce those habits and tastes at the threshold of marriage. Moreover, it is becoming clear to men and to women alike, and for the first time, that the world can be remoulded, and that the claims for better conditions of work, for a higher standard of life, and for the attainment of leisure, which previously had only feebly been put forward, may now be asserted drastically. We see therefore to-day a great revolutionary movement, mainly on the part of men in the world of Labour, and we see a corresponding movement, however less ostentatious, mainly on the part of women, in the world of the Home.

It may seem to some that this new movement of upheaval in the sphere of the Home is merely destructive. Timid souls have felt the like in every period of transition, and with as little reason. Just as we realise that the movement now in progress in the world of Labour for a higher standard of life and for, as it has been termed, a larger "leisure-ration," represents a wholesome revolt against the crushing conditions of prolonged monotonous work—the most deadening of all work —and a real advance towards those ideals of democracy which are still so remote, so it is with the movement in the Home. That also is the claim for a new and fairer allotment of responsibility, of larger opportunities for freedom and leisure. If in the home the husband is still to be regarded as the capitalist and the wife as the labourer, then at all events it has to be recognised that he owes her not only the satisfaction of her physical needs of food and shelter and clothing, but the opportunity to satisfy the personal spontaneous claims of her own individual nature. Just as the readjustment of Labour is really only an approach to the long-recognised ideals of Democracy, so the readjustment of the Home, far from being subversive or revolutionary, is merely an approximation to the long-recognised ideals of marriage.

How in practice, one may finally ask, is this readjustment of the home likely to be carried out?

In the first place we are justified in believing that in the future home men will no longer be so helpless, so domestically parasitic, as in the past. This change is indeed already coming about. It is an inestimable benefit throughout life for a man to have been forcibly lifted out of the routine comforts and feminine services of the old-fashioned home and to be thrown into an alien and solitary environment, face to face with Nature and the essential domestic human needs (in my own case I owe an inestimable debt to the chance that thus flung me into the Australian bush in early life), and one may note that the Great War has had, directly and indirectly, a remarkable influence in this direction, for it not only compelled women to exercise many enlarging and fortifying functions commonly counted as pertaining to men, it also compelled men, deprived of accustomed feminine services, to develop a new independent ability for organising domesticity, and that ability, even though it is not permanently exercised in rendering domestic services, must yet always make clear the nature of domestic problems and tend to prevent the demand for unnecessary domestic services.

But there is another quite different and more general line along which we may expect this problem to be largely solved. That is by the simplification and organisation of domestic life. If that process were carried to the full extent that is now becoming possible a large part of the problem before us would be at once solved. A great promise for the future of domestic life is held out by the growing adoption of birth control, by which the wife and mother is relieved from that burden of unduly frequent and unwanted maternity which in the past so often crushed her vitality and destroyed her freshness. But many minor agencies are helpful. To supply heat, light, and motive power even to small households, to replace the wasteful, extravagant, and often inefficient home-cookery by meals cooked outside, as well as to facilitate the growing social habit of taking meals in spacious public restaurants, under more attractive, economical, and wholesome conditions than can usually be secured within the narrow confines of the home, to contract with specially trained workers from outside for all those routines of domestic drudgery which are often so inefficiently and laboriously carried on by the household-worker, whether mistress or servant, and to seek perpetually by new devices to simplify, which often means to beautify, all the everyday processes of life—to effect this in any comprehensive degree is to transform the home from the intolerable burden it is sometimes felt to be into a possible haven of peace and joy.[4] The trouble in the past, and even to-day, has been not in any difficulty in providing the facilities, but in prevailing people to adopt them. Thus in England, even under the stress of the Great War, there was among the working population a considerable disinclination—founded on stupid conservatism and a meaningless pride—to take advantage of National Kitchens and National Restaurants, notwithstanding the superiority of the meals in quality, cheapness, and convenience, to the workers' home meals, so that many of these establishments, even while still fostered by the Government, had speedily to close their doors. Ancient traditions, that have now become not only empty but mischievous, in these matters still fetter the wife even more than the husband. We cannot regulate even the material side of life without cultivating that intelligence in the development of which civilisation so largely consists.

Intelligence, and even something more than intelligence, is needed along the third line of progress towards the modernised home. Simplification and organisation can effect nothing in the desired transformation if they merely end in themselves. They are only helpful in so far as they economise energy, offer a more ample leisure, and extend the opportunities for that play of the intellect, that liberation of the emotions with ac-

[4] This aspect of the future of domesticity was often set forth by Mrs. Havelock Ellis, *The New Horizon in Love and Life*, 1921.

companying discipline of the primitive instincts, which are needed not only for the development of civilisation in general, but in particular of the home. Domineering egotism, the assertion of greedy possessive rights, are out of place in the modern home. They are just as mischievous when exhibited by the wife as by the husband. We have seen, as we look back, the futility in the end of the ancient structure of the home, however reasonable it was at the beginning, under our different modern social conditions, and for women to attempt nowadays to reintroduce the same structure, merely reversed, would be not only mischievous but silly. That spirit of narrow exclusiveness and self-centred egoism—even if it were sometimes an *égoïsme à deux*—evoked, half a century ago, the scathing sarcasm of James Hinton, who never wearied of denouncing the "virtuous and happy homes" which he saw as "floating blotches of verdure on a sea of filth." Such outbursts seem extravagant, but they were the extravagance of an idealist at the vision which, as a physician in touch with realities, he had seen beneath the surface of the home.

It is well to insist on the organisation of the mechanical and material side of life. Some leaders of women movements feel this so strongly that they insist on nothing else. In old days it was conventionally supposed that women's sphere was that of the feelings; the result has been that women now often take ostentatious pleasure in washing their hands of feelings and accusing men of "sentiment." But that wrongly debased word stands for the whole superstructure of life on the basis of material organisation, for all the finer and higher parts of our nature, for the greater part of civilisation.[5] The elaboration of the mechanical side of life by itself may merely serve to speed up the pace of life instead of expanding leisure, to pile up the weary burden of luxury, and still further to dissipate the energy of life in petty or frivolous channels.[6] To bring order into the region of soulless machinery running at random, to raise the super-structure of a genuinely human civilisation,

[5] "The growth of the sentiments," remarks an influential psychologist of our own time (W. McDougall, *Social Psychology*, p. 160), "is of the utmost importance for the character and conduct of individuals and of societies; it is the organisation of the affective and conative life. In the absence of sentiments our emotional life would be a mere chaos, without order, consistency, or continuity of any kind; and all our social relations and conduct, being based on the emotions and their impulses, would be correspondingly chaotic, unpredictable, and unstable. . . . Again, our judgments of value and of merit are rooted in our sentiments; and our moral principles have the same source, for they are formed by our judgments of moral value."

[6] The destructive effects of the mechanisation of modern life have lately been admirably set forth, and with much precise illustration, by Dr. Austin Freeman, *Social Decay and Regeneration*.

is not a task which either men or women can afford to fling contemptuously to the opposite sex. It concerns them both equally and can only be carried out by both equally, working side by side in the most intimate spirit of mutual comprehension, confiding trust, and the goodwill to conquer the demon of jealousy, that dragon which slays love under the pretence of keeping it alive.

This task, it may finally be added, is always an adventure. However well organised the foundations of life may be, life must always be full of risks. We may smile, therefore, when it is remarked that the future developments of the home are risky. Birds in the air and fishes in the sea, quite as much as our own ancestors on the earth, have always found life full of risks. It was the greatest risk of all when they insisted on continuing on the old outworn ways and so became extinct. If the home is an experiment and a risky experiment, one can only say that life is always like that. We have to see to it that in this central experiment, on which our happiness so largely depends, all our finest qualities are mobilised. Even the smallest homes under the new conditions cannot be built to last with small minds and small hearts. Indeed the discipline of the home demands not only the best intellectual qualities that are available, but often involves—and in men as well as in women —a spiritual training fit to make sweeter and more generous saints than any cloister. The greater the freedom, the more complete the equality of husband and wife, the greater the possibilities of discipline and development. In view of the rigidities and injustices of the law, many couples nowadays dispense with legal marriage, and form their own private contract; that method has sometimes proved more favourable to the fidelity and permanence of love than external compulsion; it assists the husband to remain the lover, and it is often the lover more than the husband that the modern woman needs; but it has always to be remembered that in the present condition of law and social opinion a slur is cast on the children of such unions. No doubt, however, marriage and the home will undergo modifications, which will tend to make these ancient institutions a little more flexible and to permit a greater degree of variation to meet special circumstances. We can occupy ourselves with no more essential task, whether as regards ourselves or the race, than to make more beautiful the House of Life for the dwelling of Love.

Chapter 7

THE LOVE-RIGHTS
OF WOMEN

WHAT IS THE PART OF WOMAN, one is sometimes asked, in the sex act? Must it be the wife's concern in the marital embrace to sacrifice her own wishes from a sense of love and duty towards her husband? Or is the wife entitled to an equal mutual interest and joy in this act with her husband? It seems a simple problem. In so fundamental a relationship, which goes back to the beginning of sex in the dawn of life, it might appear that we could leave Nature to decide. Yet it is not so. Throughout the history of civilisation, wherever we can trace the feelings and ideas which have prevailed on this matter and the resultant conduct, the problem has *arisen*, often to produce discord, conflict and misery. The *problem* still exists to-day and with as important results as in the past.

In Nature, before the arrival of Man, it can scarcely be said indeed that any difficulty existed. It was taken for granted at that time that the female had both the right to her own body, and the right to a certain amount of enjoyment in the use of it. It often cost the male a serious amount of trouble—though he never failed to find it worth while—to explain to her the point where he may be allowed to come in, and to persuade her that he can contribute to her enjoyment. So it generally is throughout Nature, before we reach Man, and, though it is not invariably obvious, we often find it even among the unlikeliest animals. As is well known, it is most pronounced among the birds, who have in some species carried the erotic art—and the faithful devotion which properly accompanied the erotic art as being an essential part of it—to the highest point. We have here the great natural fact of courtship. Throughout Nature, wherever we meet with animals of a high type, often indeed when they are of a lowly type—provided they have not been rendered unnatural by domestication—

71

every act of sexual union is preceded by a process of courtship. There is a sound physiological reason for this courtship, for in the act of wooing and being wooed the psychic excitement gradually generated in the brains of the two partners acts as a stimulant to arouse into full activity the mechanism which ensures sexual union and aids ultimate impregnation. Such courtship is thus a fundamental natural fact.

It is as a natural fact that we still find it in full development among a large number of peoples of the lower races whom we are accustomed to regard as more primitive than ourselves. New conditions, it is true, soon enter to complicate the picture presented by savage courtship. The economic element of bargaining, destined to prove so important, comes in at an early stage. And among peoples leading a violent life, and constantly fighting, it has sometimes happened, though not always, that courtship also has been violent. This is not so frequent as was once supposed. With better knowledge it was found that the seeming brutality once thought to take the place of courtship among various peoples in a low state of culture was really itself courtship, a rough kind of play agreeable to both parties and not depriving the feminine partner of her own freedom of choice. This was notably the case as regards so-called "marriage by capture." While this is sometimes a real capture, it is more often a mock capture; the lover perhaps pursues the beloved on horseback, but she is as fleet and as skilful as he is, cannot be captured unless she wishes to be captured, and in addition, as among the Kirghiz, she may be armed with a formidable whip; so that "marriage by capture," far from being a hardship imposed on women, is largely a concession to their modesty and a gratification of their erotic impulses. Even when the chief part of the decision rests with masculine force, courtship is still not necessarily or usually excluded, for the exhibition of force by a lover—and this is true for civilised as well as for savage women—is itself a source of pleasurable stimulation, and when that is so the essence of courtship may be attained even more successfully by the forceful than by the humble lover.

The evolution of society, however, tended to overlay and sometimes even to suppress those fundamental natural tendencies. The position of the man as the sole and uncontested head of the family, the insistence on paternity and male descent, the accompanying economic developments, and the tendency to view a woman less as a self-disposing individual than as an object of barter belonging to her father, the consequent rigidity of the marriage bond and the stern insistence on wifely fidelity—all these conditions of developing civilisation, while still leaving courtship possible, diminished its significance and even abolished its necessity. Moreover, on the basis of the social, economic, and legal developments thus established, new moral, spiritual, and religious forces were slowly generated, which worked on these rules of merely exterior order, and interiorised them, thus giving them power over the souls as well as over the bodies of women.

The result was that, directly and indirectly, the legal, economic, and erotic rights of women were all diminished. It is with the erotic rights only that we are here concerned.

No doubt in its erotic aspects, as well as in its legal and economic aspects, the social order thus established was described, and in good faith, as beneficial to women, and even as maintained in their interests. Monogamy and the home, it was claimed, alike existed for the benefit and protection of women. It was not so often explained that they greatly benefited and protected men, with, moreover, this additional advantage that while women were absolutely confined to the home, men were free to exercise their activities outside the home, even, with tacit general consent, on the erotic side.

Whatever the real benefits and there is no occasion for questioning them, of the sexual order thus established, it becomes clear that in certain important respects it had an unnatural and repressive influence on the erotic aspect of woman's sexual life. It fostered the reproductive side of woman's sexual life, but it rendered difficult for her the satisfaction of the instinct for that courtship which is the natural preliminary of reproductive activity, an instinct even more highly developed in the female than in the male, and the more insistent because in the order of Nature the burden of maternity is preceded by the reward of pleasure. But the marriage order which had become established led to the indirect result of banning pleasure in women, or at all events in wives. It was regarded as too dangerous, and even as degrading. The women who wanted pleasure were not considered fit for the home, but more suited to be devoted to an exclusive "life of pleasure," which soon turned out to be not their own pleasure but men's. A "life of pleasure," in that sense or in any other sense, was not what more than a small minority of women ever desired. The desire of women for courtship is not a thing by itself, and was not implanted for gratification by itself. It is naturally interwined—and to a much greater degree than the corresponding desire in men

—with her deepest personal, family, and social instincts, so
that if these are desecrated and lost its charm soon fades.

The practices and the ideals of this established morality
were both due to men, and both were so thoroughly fashioned
that they subjugated alike the action and the feelings of
women. There is no sphere which we regard as so peculiarly
women's sphere as that of love. Yet there is no sphere which
in civilisation women have so far had so small a part in
regulating. Their deepest impulses—their modesty, their
maternity, their devotion, their emotional receptivity—were
used, with no conscious and deliberate Machiavellism, against
themselves, to mould a moral world for their habitation which
they would not themselves have moulded. It is not of modern
creation, nor by any means due, as some have supposed, to
the asceticism of Christianity, however much Christianity may
have reinforced it. Indeed one may say that in course of time
Christianity had an influence in weakening it, for Christianity
discovered a new reservoir of tender emotion, and such emotion may be transferred, and, as a matter of fact, was transferred, from its first religious channel into erotic channels
which were thereby deepened and extended, and without
reference to any design of Christianity. For the ends we
achieve are often by no means those which we set out to
accomplish. In ancient classic days this moral order was even
more severely established than in the Middle Ages. Montaigne,
in the sixteenth century, declared that "marriage is a devout
and religious relationship, the pleasures derived from it
should be restrained and serious, mixed with some severity."
But in this matter he was not merely expressing the Christian
standpoint but even more that of paganism, and he thoroughly
agreed with the old Greek moralist that a man should approach his wife "prudently and severely" for fear of inciting
her to lasciviousness; he thought that marriage was best
arranged by a third party, and was inclined to think, with the
ancients, that women are not fitted to make friends of.
Montaigne has elsewhere spoken with insight of women's
instinctive knowledge of the art and discipline of love and
has pointed out how men have imposed their own ideals and
rules of action on women from whom they have demanded
opposite and contradictory virtues; yet, we see, he approves
of this state of things and never suggests that women have
any right to opinions of their own or feelings of their own
when the sacred institution of marriage is in question.

Montaigne represents the more exalted aspects of the
Pagan-Christian conception of morality in marriage which

still largely prevails. But that conception lent itself to deductions, frankly accepted even by Montaigne himself, which were by no means exalted. "I find," said Montaigne, "that Venus, after all, is nothing more than the pleasure of discharging our vessels, just as nature renders pleasurable the discharge from other parts." Sir Thomas More among Catholics, and Luther among Protestants, said exactly the same thing in other and even clearer words, while untold millions of husbands in Christendom down to to-day, whether or not they have had the wit to put their theory into a phrase, have regularly put it into practice, at all events within the consecrated pale of marriage, and treated their wives, "severely and prudently," as convenient utensils for the reception of a natural excretion.

Obviously, in this view of marriage, sexual activity was regarded as an exclusively masculine function, in the exercise of which women had merely a passive part to play. Any active participation on her side thus seemed unnecessary, and even unbefitting, finally, though only in comparatively modern times, disgusting and actually degrading. Thus Acton, who was regarded half a century ago as the chief English authority on sexual matters, declared that, "happily for society," the supposition that women possess sexual feelings could be put aside as "a vile aspersion," while another medical authority of the same period stated in regard to the most simple physical sign of healthy sexual emotion that it "only happens in lascivious women." This final triumph of the masculine ideals and rule of life was, however, only achieved slowly. It was the culmination of an elaborate process of training. At the outset men had found it impossible to speak too strongly of the "wantonness" of women. This attitude was pronounced among the ancient Greeks and prominent in their dramatists. Christianity again, which ended by making women into the chief pillars of the Church, began by regarding them as the "Gate to Hell." Again, later, when in the Middle Ages this masculine moral order approached the task of subjugating the barbarians of Northern Europe, men were horrified at the licentiousness of those northern women at whose coldness they are now shocked.

That, indeed, was, as Montaigne had seen, the central core of conflict in the rule of life imposed by men on women. Men were perpetually striving, by ways the most methodical, the most subtle, the most far-reaching, to achieve a result in women, which, when achieved, men themselves viewed with dismay. They may be said to be moved in this sphere by two passions, the passion for virtue and the passion for vice. But it so happens that both these streams of passion have to be directed at the same fascinating object: Woman. No doubt nothing is more admirable than the skill with which women have acquired the duplicity necessary to play the two contradictory parts thus imposed upon them. But in that requirement the play of their natural reactions tended to become paralysed, and the delicate mechanism of their instincts often disturbed. They were forbidden, except in a few carefully etiquetted forms, the free play of courtship, without which they could not perform their part in the erotic life with full satisfaction either to themselves or their partners. They were reduced to an artificial simulation of coldness or of warmth, according to the particular stage of the dominating masculine ideal of woman which their partner chanced to have reached. But that is an attitude equally unsatisfactory to themselves and to their lovers, even when the latter have not sufficient insight to see through its unreality. It is an attitude so unnatural and artificial that it inevitably tends to produce a real coldness which nothing can disguise. It is true that women whose instincts are not perverted at the roots do not desire to be cold. Far from it. But to dispel that coldness the right atmosphere is needed, and the insight and skill of the right man. In the erotic sphere a woman asks nothing better of a man than to be lifted above her coldness, to the higher plane where there is reciprocal interest and mutual joy in the act of love. Therein her silent demand is one with Nature's. For the biological order of the world involves those claims which, in the human range, are the erotic rights of women.

The social claims of women, their economic claims, their political claims, have long been before the world. Women themselves have actively asserted them, and they are all in process of realisation. The erotic claims of women, which are at least as fundamental, are not publicly voiced, and women themselves would be the last to assert them. It is easy to understand why that should be so. The natural and acquired qualities of women, even the qualities developed in the art of courtship, have all been utilised in building up the masculine ideal of sexual morality; it is on feminine characteristics that this masculine ideal has been based, so that women have been helpless to protest against it. Moreover, even if that were not so, to formulate such rights is to raise the question whether there so much as exists anything that can be called "erotic rights." The right to joy cannot be claimed in the same way as one claims the right to put a voting paper in a ballot box. A human being's erotic aptitudes can only be developed where the right atmosphere for them exists, and where the attitudes of both persons concerned are in harmonious sympathy. That is why the erotic rights of women have been the last of all to be attained.

Yet to-day we see a change here. The change required is, it has been said, a change of attitude and a resultant change in the atmosphere in which the sexual impulses are manifested. It involves no necessary change in the external order of our marriage system, for, as has already been pointed out, it was a coincident and not designed part of that order. Various recent lines of tendency have converged to produce this change of attitude and of atmosphere. In part the men of to-day are far more ready than the men of former days to look upon women as their comrades in the everyday work of the world, instead of as beings who were ideally on a level above themselves and practically on a level considerably below themselves. In part there is the growing recognition that women have conquered many elementary human rights of which before they were deprived, and are more and more taking the position of citizens, with the same kinds of duties, privileges, and responsibilities as men. In part, also, it may be added, there is a growing diffusion among educated people of a knowledge of the primary facts of life in the two sexes, slowly dissipating and dissolving many foolish and often mischievous superstitions. The result is that, as many competent observers have noted, the young men of to-day show a new attitude towards women and towards marriage, an attitude of simplicity and frankness, a desire for mutual confidence, a readiness to discuss difficulties, an appeal to understand and to be understood. Such an attitude, which had hitherto been hard to attain, at once creates the atmosphere in which alone the free spontaneous erotic activities of women can breathe and live.

This consummation, we have seen, may be regarded as the attainment of certain rights, the corollary of other rights in the social field which women are slowly achieving as human beings on the same human level as men. It opens to women, on whom is always laid the chief burden of sex, the right to the joy and exaltation of sex, to the uplifting of the soul which, when the right conditions are fulfilled, is the outcome of the intimate approach and union of two human beings. Yet while we may find convenient so to formulate it, we need to remember that that is only a fashion of speech, for there are no rights in Nature. If we take a broader sweep, what we

may choose to call an erotic right is simply the perfect poise
of the conflicting forces of life, the rhythmic harmony in
which generation is achieved with the highest degree of perfection compatible with the make of the world. It is our part
to transform Nature's large conception into our own smaller
organic mould, not otherwise than the plants, to whom we
are far back akin, who dig their flexible roots deep into the
moist and fruitful earth, and so are able to lift up glorious
heads toward the sky.

Chapter 8

THE PLAY-FUNCTION
OF SEX

WHEN WE HEAR THE SEXUAL FUNCTIONS SPOKEN OF WE commonly understand the performance of an act which normally tends to the propagation of the race. When we see the question of sexual abstinence discussed, when the desirability of sexual gratification is asserted or denied, when the idea arises of the erotic right and needs of women, it is always the same act with its physical results that is chiefly in mind. Such a conception is quite adequate for practical working purposes in the social world. It enables us to deal with all our established human institutions in the sphere of sex, as the arbitrary assumptions of Euclid enable us to traverse the field of elementary geometry. But beyond these useful purposes it is inadequate and even inexact. The functions of sex on the psychic and erotic side are of far greater extension than any act of procreation, they may even exclude it altogether, and when we are concerned with the welfare of the individual human being we must enlarge our outlook and deepen our insight.

There are, we know, two main functions in the sexual relationship, or what in the biological sense we term "marriage," among civilized human beings, the primary physiological function of begetting and bearing offspring and the secondary spiritual function of furthering the higher mental and emotional processes. These are the main functions of the sexual impulse, and in order to understand any further object of the sexual relationship—or even in order to understand all that is involved in the secondary object of marriage—we must go beyond conscious motives and consider the nature of the sexual impulse, physical and psychic, as rooted in the human organism.

The human organism, as we know, is a machine on which excitations from without, streaming through the nerves and brain, affect internal work, and, notably, stimulate the glandu-

79

lar system. In recent years the glandular system, and especially
that of the ductless glands, has taken on an altogether new
significance. These ductless glands, as we know, liberate into
the blood what are termed "hormones," or chemical mes-
sengers, which have a complex but precise action in exciting
and developing all those physical and psychic activities which
make up a full life alike on the general side and the reproductive side, so that their balanced functions are essential
to wholesome and complete existence. In a rudimentary form
these functions may be traced back to our earliest ancestors
who possessed brains. In those times the predominant sense
for arousing the internal mental and emotional faculties was
that of smell, the other senses being gradually evolved subsequently, and it is significant that the pituitary, one of the chief
ductless glands active in ourselves to-day, was developed out
of the nervous centre for smell in conjunction with the mem-
brane of the mouth. The energies of the whole organism
were set in action through stimuli arising from the outside
world by way of the sense of smell. In process of time the
mechanism has become immensely elaborated, yet its healthy
activity is ultimately dependent on a rich and varied action
and reaction with the external world. It is becoming recognised
that the tendency to pluri-glandular insufficiency, with its resulting lack of organic harmony and equilibrium, can be
counteracted by the physical and psychic stimuli of intimate
contacts with the external world. In this action and reaction,
moreover, we cannot distinguish between sexual ends and general ends. The activities of the ductless glands and their
hormones equally serve both ends in ways that cannot be
distinguished. "The individual metabolism," as a distinguished
authority in this field has expressed it, "is the reproductive
metabolism."[1] Thus the establishment of our complete activities as human beings in the world is aided by, if not indeed
ultimately dependent upon, a perpetual and many-sided play
with our environment.

It is thus that we arrive at the importance of the play-
function, and thus, also, we realise that while it extends beyond
the sexual sphere it yet definitely includes that sphere. There
are at least three different ways of understanding the biological
function of play. There is the conception of play, on which
Groos has elaborately insisted, as education: the cat "plays"
with the mouse and is thereby educating itself in the skill necessary to catch mice; all our human games are a training in

[1] W. Blair Bell, *The Sex-Complex*, 1920, p. 108. This book is a cautious
and precise statement of the present state of knowledge on this subject,
although some of the author's psychological deductions must be treated
with circumspection.

qualities that are required in life, and that is why in England we continue to attribute to the Duke of Wellington the saying that "the battle of Waterloo was won on the playing fields of Eton." Then there is the conception of play as the utilisation in art of the superfluous energies left unemployed in the practical work of life; this enlarging and harmonising function of play, while in the lower ranges it may be spent trivially, leads in the higher ranges to the production of the most magnificent human achievements. But there is yet a third conception of play, according to which it exerts a direct internal influence—health-giving, developmental, and balancing—on the whole organism of the player himself. This conception is related to the other two, and yet distinct, for it is not primarily a definite education in specific kinds of life-conserving skill, although it may involve the acquisition of such skill, and it is not concerned with the construction of objective works of art, although—by means of contact in human relationships—it attains the wholesome organic effects which may be indirectly achieved by artistic activities. It is in this sense that we are here concerned with what we may perhaps call the play-function of sex.[2]

As thus understood, the play-function of sex is at once in an inseparable way both physical and psychic. It stimulates to wholesome activity all the complex and inter-related systems of the organism. At the same time it satisfies the most profound emotional impulses, controlling in harmonious poise the various mental instincts. Along these lines it necessarily tends in the end to go beyond its own sphere and to embrace and introduce into the sphere of sex the other two more objective fields of play, that of play as education, and that of play as artistic creation. It may not be true, as was said of old time, "most of our arts and sciences were invented for love's sake." But it is certainly true that, in proportion as we truly and wisely exercise the play-function of sex, we are at the same time training our personality on the erotic side and acquiring a mastery of the art of love.

The longer I live the more I realise the immense importance for the individual of the development through the play-function of erotic personality, and for human society of the acquirement of the art of love. At the same time I am ever more astonished at the rarity of erotic personality and the ignorance of the art of love even among those men and women, experienced in the exercise of procreation, in whom we might most

---

[2] The term seems to have been devised by Professor Maurice Parmelee, *Personality and Conduct*, 1918, pp. 104, 107, 113. But it is understood by Parmelee in a much vaguer and more extended sense than I have used it.

confidently expect to find such development and such art. At times one feels hopeless at the thought that civilisation in this supremely intimate field of life has yet achieved so little. For until it is generally possible to acquire erotic personality and to master the art of loving, the development of the individual man or woman is marred, the acquirement of human happiness and harmony remains impossible.

In entering this field, indeed, we not only have to gain true knowledge but to cast off false knowledge, and, above all, to purify our hearts from superstitions which have no connection with any kind of existing knowledge. We have to cease to regard as admirable the man who regards the accomplishment of the procreative act, with the pleasurable relief it affords to himself, as the whole code of love. We have to treat with contempt the woman who abjectly accepts the act, and her own passivity therein, as the whole duty of love. We have to understand that the art of love has nothing to do with vice, and the acquirement of erotic personality nothing to do with sensuality. But we have also to realise that the art of love is far from being the attainment of a refined and luxurious self-indulgence, and the acquirement of erotic personality of little worth unless it fortifies and enlarges the whole personality in all its aspects. Now all this is difficult, and for some people even painful; to root up is a more serious matter than to sow; it cannot all be done in a day.

It is not easy to form a clear picture of the erotic life of the average man in our society. To the best informed among us knowledge in this field only comes slowly. Even when we have decided what may or may not be termed "average" the sources of approach to this intimate sphere remain few and misleading; at the best the woman a man loves remains a far more illuminating source of information than the man himself. The more one knows about him, however, the more one is convinced that, quite independently of the place we may feel inclined to afford to him in the scale of virtue, his conception of erotic personality, his ideas on the art of love, if they have any existence at all, are of a humble character. As to the notion of play in the sphere of sex, even if he makes blundering attempts to practise it, that is for him something quite low down, something to be ashamed of, and he would not dream of associating it with anything he has been taught to regard as belonging to the spiritual sphere. The conception of "divine play" is meaningless to him. His fundamental ideas, his cherished ideals, in the erotic sphere, seem to be reducible to two: (1) He wishes to prove that he is "a man," and he experiences what seems to him the pride of virility in the successful attain-

ment of that proof; (2) he finds in the same act the most satisfactory method of removing sexual tension and in the ensuing
relief one of the chief pleasures of life. It cannot be said that
either of these ideals is absolutely unsound; each is part of
the truth; it is only as a complete statement of the truth that
they become pathetically inadequate. It is to be noted that
both of them are based solely on the physical act of sexual
conjunction, and that they are both exclusively self-regarding.
So that they are, after all, although the nearest approach to
the erotic sphere he may be able to find, yet still not really
erotic. For love is not primarily self-regarding. It is the intimate, harmonious, combined play—the play in the wide as
well as in the more narrow sense we are here concerned with
—of two personalities. It would not be love if it were primarily
self-regarding, and the act of intercourse, however essential
to secure the propagation of the race, is only an incident, and
not an essential in love.

Let us turn to the average woman. Here the picture must
usually be still more unsatisfactory. The man at least, crude as
we may find his two fundamental notions to be, has at all
events attained mental pride and physical satisfaction. The
woman often attains neither, and since the man, by instinct or
tradition, has maintained a self-regarding attitude, that is not
surprising. The husband—by primitive instinct partly, certainly
by ancient tradition—regards himself as the active partner
in matters of love and his own pleasure as legitimately the
prime motive for activity. His wife consequently falls into the
complementary position, and regards herself as the passive
partner and her pleasure as negligible, if not indeed a thing to
be rather ashamed of, should she by chance experience it. So
that, while the husband is content with a mere simulacrum and
pretence of the erotic life, the wife has often had none at all.

Few people realise—few indeed have the knowledge or the
opportunity to realise—how much women thus lose, alike in
the means to fulfill their own lives and in the power to help
others. A woman has a husband, she has marital relationships,
she has children, she has all the usual domestic troubles—it
seems to the casual observer that she has everything that constitutes a fully developed matron fit to play her proper part in
the home and in the world. Yet with all these experiences,
which undoubtedly are an important part of life, she may yet
remain on the emotional side—and, as a matter of fact, frequently remains—quite virginal, as immature as a school-girl.
She has not acquired an erotic personality, she has not mastered
the art of love, with the result that her whole nature remains
ill-developed and unharmonised, and that she is incapable of

bringing her personality—having indeed no achieved personality to bring—to bear effectively on the problems of society and the world around her.

That alone is a great misfortune, all the more tragic since under favourable conditions, which it should have been natural to attain, it might so easily be avoided. But there is this further result, full of the possibilities of domestic tragedy, that the wife so situated, however innocent, however virtuous, may at any time find her virginally sensitive emotional nature fertilised by the touch of some other man than her husband.

It happens so often. A girl who has been carefully guarded in the home, preserved from evil companions, preserved also from what her friends regarded as the contamination of sexual knowledge, a girl of high ideals, yet healthy and robust, is married to a man of whom she probably has little more than a conventional knowledge. Yet he may by good chance be the masculine counterpart of herself, well brought up, without sexual experience and ignorant of all but the elementary facts of sex, loyal and honourable, prepared to be, fitted to be, a devoted husband. The union seems to be of the happiest kind; no one detects that anything is lacking to this perfect marriage; in course of time one or more children are born. But during all this time the husband has never really made love to his wife; he has not even understood what courtship in the intimate sense means; love as an art has no existence for him; he has loved his wife according to his imperfect knowledge, but he has never so much as realised that his knowledge was imperfect. She on her side loves her husband; she comes in time indeed to have a sort of tender maternal feeling for him. Possibly she feels a little pleasure in intercourse with him. But she has never once been profoundly aroused, and she has never once been utterly satisfied. The deep fountains of her nature have never been unsealed; she has never been fertilised throughout her whole nature by their liberating influence; her erotic personality has never been developed. Then something happens. Perhaps the husband is called away, it may have been to take part in the Great War. The wife, whatever her tender solicitude for her absent partner, feels her solitude and is drawn nearer to friends, perhaps her husband's friends. Some man among them becomes congenial to her. There need be no conscious or overt love-making on either side, and if there were the wife's loyalty might be aroused and the friendship brought to an end. Love-making is not indeed necessary. The wife's latent erotic needs, while still remaining unconscious, have come nearer to the surface; now that she has grown mature and that they have been stimulated yet unsatisfied for so long, they have, unknown to herself, become insistent and sensitive to a sympathetic touch. The friends may indeed grow into lovers, and then some sort of solution, by divorce or intrigue—scarcely, however, a desirable kind of solution—becomes possible. But we are here taking the highest ground and assuming that honourable feeling, domestic affection, or a stern sense of moral duty, renders such solution unacceptable. In due course the husband returns, and then, to her utter dismay, the wife discovers, if she has not discovered it before, that during his absence, and for the first time in her life, she has fallen in love. She loyally confesses the situation to her husband, for whom her affection and attachment remain the same as before, for what has happened to her is the coming of a totally new kind of love and not any change in her old love. The situation which arises is one of torturing anxiety for all concerned, and it is not less so when all concerned are animated by noble and self-sacrificing impulses. The husband in his devotion to his wife may even be willing that her new impulses should be gratified. She, on her side, will not think of yielding to desires which seem both unfair to her husband and opposed to all her moral traditions. We are not here concerned with considering the most likely, or the most desirable, exit from this unfortunate situation. The points to note are that it is a situation which to-day actually occurs; that it causes acute unhappiness to at least two people who may be of the finest physical and intellectual type and the noblest character, and that it might be avoided if there were at the outset a proper understanding of the married state and of the part which the art of love plays in married happiness and the development of personality.

A woman may have been married once, she may have been married twice, she may have had children by both husbands, and yet it may not be until she is past the age of thirty and is united to a third man that she attains the development of erotic personality and all that it involves in the full flowering of her whole nature. Up to then she had to all appearance had all the essential experiences of life. Yet she had remained spiritually virginal, with conventionally prim ideas of life, narrow in her sympathies, with the finest and noblest functions of her soul helpless and bound, at heart unhappy even if not clearly realising that she was unhappy. Now she has become another person. The new liberated forces from within have not only enabled her to become sensitive to the rich complexities of intimate personal relationship, they have enlarged and harmonised her realisation of all relationships. Her new erotic experience has not only stimulated all her energies, but her new knowledge has quickened all her sympathies. She feels, at the same time, more mentally alert, and she finds that she is more alive than before to the influences of nature and of art. Moreover, as others observe, however they may explain it, a new beauty has come into her face, a new radiancy into her expression, a new force into all her activities. Such is the exquisite flowering of love which some of us who may penetrate beneath the surface of life are now and then privileged to see. The sad part of it is that we see it so seldom and then often so late.

It must not be supposed that there is any direct or speedy way of introducing into life a wider and deeper conception of the erotic play-function, and all that it means for the development of the individual, the enrichment of the marriage relationship, and the moral harmony of society. Such a supposition would merely be to vulgarise and to stultify the divine and elusive mystery. It is only slowly and indirectly that we can bring about the revolution which in this direction would renew life. We may prepare the way for it by undermining and destroying those degrading traditional conceptions which have persisted so long that they are instilled into us almost from birth, to work like a virus in the heart, and to become almost a disease of the soul. To make way for the true and beautiful revelation, we can at least seek to cast out those ancient growths, which may once have been true and beautiful, but now are false and poisonous. By casting out from us the conception of love as vile and unclean we shall purify the chambers of our hearts for the reception of love as something unspeakably holy.

In this matter we may learn a lesson from the psychoanalysts of to-day without any implication that psychoanalysis is necessarily a desirable or even possible way of attaining the revelation of love. The wiser psychoanalysts insist that the process of liberating the individual from outer and inner influences that repress or deform his energies and impulses is effected by removing the inhibitions on the free-play of his nature. It is a process of education in the true sense, not of the suppression of natural impulses nor even of the instillation of sound rules and maxims for their control, not of the pressing in but of the leading out of the individual's special tendencies. It removes inhibitions, even inhibitions that were placed upon the individual, or that he consciously or unconsciously placed upon himself, with the best moral intentions, and by so doing it allows a larger and freer and more natively spontaneous morality to come into play. It has this influence above all in the sphere of sex, where such inhibitions have been most powerfully laid on the native impulses, where the natural tendencies have been surrounded by taboos and terrors, most tinged with artificial stains of impurity and degradation derived from alien and antiquated traditions. Thus the therapeutical experience of the psychoanalysts reinforces the lessons we learn from physiology and psychology and the intimate experiences of life.

Sexual activity, we see, is not merely a bald propagative act, nor, when propagation is put aside, is it merely the relief of distended vessels. It is something more even than the foundation of great social institutions. It is the function by which all the finer activities of the organism, physical and psychic, may be developed and satisfied. Nothing, it has been said, is so serious as lust—to use the beautiful term which has been degraded into the expression of the lowest forms of sensual pleasure—and we have now to add that nothing is so full of play as love. Play is primarily the instinctive work of the brain, but it is brain activity united in the subtlest way to bodily activity. In the play-function of sex two forms of activity, physical and psychic, are most exquisitively and variously and harmoniously blended. We here understand best how it is that the brain organs and the sexual organs are, from the physiological standpoint, of equal importance and equal dignity. Thus the adrenal glands, among the most influential of all the ductless glands, are specially and intimately associated alike with the brain and the sex organs. As we rise in the animal series, brain and adrenal glands march side by side in developmental increase of size, and at the same time, sexual activity and adrenal activity equally correspond.

Lovers in their play—when they have been liberated from the traditions which bound them to the trivial or the gross conception of play in love—are thus moving amongst the highest human activities, alike of the body and of the soul. They are passing to each other the sacramental chalice of that wine which imparts the deepest joy that men and women can know. They are subtly weaving the invisible cords that bind husband and wife together more truly and more firmly than the priest of any church. And if in the end—as may or may not be—they attain the climax of free and complete union, then their human play has become one with that divine play of creation in which old poets fabled that, out of the dust of the ground and in his own image, some God of Chaos once created Man.

Chapter 9

WHAT IS FRUSTRATION?

WHAT IS FRUSTRATION? We cannot learn how to deal with it unless we know what it is. Perhaps we may describe it as the failure of a plan in life we had set our heart on, or one to which we believed we were entitled, together with—and this is essential—a hopeless acquiescence in failure. There are thus two stages in a sense of frustration, and until the second is reached it can scarcely be said to exist.

I will illustrate what I mean by an experience of my own. It is trivial and aloof from the larger interests of life. But as an illustration it is significant. It dates from long years ago. I was a student and had just made my first visit to Paris with my nearest friend Angus Mackay, a young poet and critic who later entered the Church and died before gaining the reputation he deserved. At the conclusion of our carefully planned visit we stayed for two days at Rouen on the way back, and were then due to return by the night boat from Dieppe. We awaited the boat train in the waiting room at Rouen but failed to understand the French custom by which the porter comes to the door to announce the train's arrival. When we discovered that we had thus missed the train, Mackay raged and fumed in the full sense of frustration. On my part I simply took out our Baedeker and came to the conclusion that we might spend a pleasant day in exploring Dieppe. Mackay soon came round to the same conclusion and the pleasant day was spent. We had gained rather than lost by our frustration.

I am not claiming that my conduct on this occasion was superior to my friend's. It was simply a matter of difference of temperament, and Mackay quickly overcame his first reaction.

We usually fail to realise that the elements for frustration exist throughout Nature. Indeed I would myself say that life

88

only develops by the conflict of opposing forces, among plants as well as among animals, and into this conflict frustration cannot fail to enter. The seed is engaged in a stimulating struggle against the resistance of the capsule and the ovum against the resistance of the womb. Without opposing pressure there would be no life. "Conflict," as Heraclitus said of old, "is the father of all things." Conflict in this sense does not mean violence. In order to gain the ends of life we need a fine courage, and to succumb at once to opposition is merely a sign of weakness.

But in Nature, as in our human affairs, the obstacles are sometimes impenetrable. How does Nature then proceed? It is enough to observe plants. So long as the conditions permit of the preservation of vitality, there is no yielding to frustration. The plant circumvents the obstacle and vigorously takes a new course. The first stage of frustration occurs, even very commonly, but so long as vitality persists, the second fails to follow. Life and energy persist, but in a new shape or a new direction. That is the natural course of threatened frustration in Nature, and if it fails to occur in the human world we must suspect defective vitality, though possibly only a defect which might be easily overcome by a courageous effort of will.

It may be admitted that the modern frequency of the sense of frustration is not unreasonable. Our age has seen a wider enlargement of the scope of human activities, not only for men but also for women, than any age before. It is inevitable that this enlargement should be a challenge for further enlargements as well as an excuse for the protests of those who fail to achieve them.

The widespread influence of Freud has undoubtedly done much to direct this sense of frustration into the field of sex. This is not altogether Freud's fault, or, if you will, his merit. Freud is an influence over a far larger number of people than have read his books, and those who have read them are aware that he has varied his teaching and is far more cautious than the ignorant Freudian imagines. He has stood for complete openness in the recognition and description of sexual phenomena, and that is perhaps his greatest service, but he is less conspicuous as a revolutionary moralist and by no means eager to destroy the generally accepted sexual morality even though he admits that it is liable to have evil results.

The greater awareness of sexual situations which, in one way or another, we have acquired inevitably makes us more alive to the obstacles which may impede the solution of difficult situations. But the problem of frustration is the same here as in Nature generally. If the sexual impulse is vigorous enough not to perish on meeting an obstacle and if the obstacle is found to be impervious, it must be circumvented. That may be done in many ways according to the circumstance of the case.

The problem of frustration appears in a pronounced shape where there is sexual attraction to a person of the same sex. That of course is common at the school age, and the attraction melts away, or becomes transformed to ordinary friendship, when school days are over. But not always. There are persons who are constitutionally—whether by an exceptional endocrine balance or otherwise—predisposed to homosexuality. Of these some, both men and women, will find a congenial partner with whom they form a sort of marriage. Others will marry in the ordinary way, not always quite happily. For such the frustration problem cannot, however, be said to arise. But there are inevitably some who can find no satisfaction with the opposite sex in the normal way and, on moral and social grounds, feel unable to make any approaches to their own sex. It is here that the question of frustration arises and here that the solution is furnished by the method of Nature. That means, in human terms, that the impulse is directed into permissible channels. This is frequently done by the adoption of a vocation which involves close contact with members of the same sex and the opportunity of devotion to their interests. Various forms of social service lend themselves to this transposed impulse and the teaching profession is frequently followed. I was, for instance, acquainted with a distinguished head master, noted for his originality and success, who had been guided by this secret motive. No scandals, so far as I am aware, ever occurred in his career, and after his retirement he considered the possibility of writing the narrative of his experiences for ultimate publication. I encouraged this plan when he consulted me about it, but he died before he was able to carry it out.

I avoid using the term "sublimation" in this connection, and for two reasons. In the first place when a substantial human relationship, with tangible satisfaction, replaces the abandoned satisfaction, it cannot be said to have been sublimated into a merely vaporous state. In the second place this term "sublimation" is far too commonly and cheaply used. People declare their intention of "sublimating" their desires, or of advising others to do so, without seeming to realise that this is something that cannot be done by a mere act of will. It is a slow process, the outcome of experience under favouring conditions, so that some authorities are even inclined to doubt whether it occurs at all.

The best and surest results of "sublimation" are only

achieved when a threatened "frustration" is met along the natural lines I have described. It is of course a method which, though brilliantly applicable to homosexual tendencies, may be far more widely applied. There are, for instance, the people obsessed by fetichist obsessions, which may be of the most varied kinds: articles of clothing, parts of the body, physiological acts, and so on; there is again the desire to whip or to be whipped. In a mild degree fetichisms are natural and altogether normal, being due to the association of the attractive object with the beloved person; in this way a glove or (even by the great Goethe) a shoe may be cherished. But even when the fetichist obsession is more pronounced there are still outlets which many people have pursued with success. It may sometimes be possible, indeed, for the fetich to be adored even in its extreme form when it is harmless and concealment is possible. But in other cases the personal impulse may be rendered impersonal and the subjective become objective, by giving it an artistic, scientific, or historical direction. It thus becomes possible for a mere personal taste to develop into a work of general value and in the gratification afforded by its pursuit, as well as by the interest it excites, the fetichist finds a satisfaction that compensates him for whatever he may have lost.

I have been drawing illustrations from the more abnormal forms of sex attraction since it is here that the question of frustration is most serious. It is of course far commoner in the normal field but here, with people of healthy mind, it should also be far simpler. Nearly all of us in early life fall in love with an object we are unable to secure and usually soon forget in the prospect of a more assured happy union. The early attraction was frustrated, but since it is nearly always directed to an unsuitable person, this frustration was most fortunate. We may recall how Dickens during many years continued to cherish the memory of the object for whom his early worship was frustrated, and how shocked he was when at last he met her again.

One meets indeed occasionally with persons who not only cherish the memory of an early frustrated love, but brood over it constantly to the exclusion of any other possible object of devotion. But an early chance object of attraction, probably quite unsuitable as a life companion, is very certainly not the only suitable one or the best, and such blind devotion is the sign of a certain degree of mental weakness. Those who experience it are not really entitled to talk about frustration.

The process of frustration is natural and healthy for all

creatures—vegetable, animal or human—that are really in the enjoyment of vital activity. If we turn over the pages of a Dictionary of Biography we find that the eminent man, in the majority of cases, began life in some occupation in which he met with frustration, for either it did not suit him or he did not suit it. He turns to another sometimes quite different occupation, and here it is that his genius eventually becomes manifest.

Whether in the emotional, the practical, or the intellectual life, frustration may be said to be a natural method of development.

Chapter 10

THE INDIVIDUAL AND
THE RACE

THE RELATION OF THE INDIVIDUAL PERSON to the species he belongs to is the most intimate of all relations. It is a relation which almost amounts to identity. Yet it somehow seems so vague, so abstract, as scarcely to concern us at all. It is only lately indeed that there has been formulated even so much as a science to discuss this relationship, and the duties which, when properly understood, it throws upon the individual. Even yet the word "Eugenics," the name of this science, and this art, sometimes arouses a smile. It seems to stand for a modern fad, which the superior person, or even the ordinary plebeian democrat, may pass by on the other side with his nose raised towards the sky. Modern the science and art of Eugenics certainly seem, though the term is ancient, and the Greeks of classic days, as well as their successors to-day, used the word Eugeneia for nobility or good birth. It was chosen by Francis Galton, less than fifty years ago, to express "the effort of Man to improve his own breed." But the thing the term stands for is, in reality, also far from modern. It is indeed ancient and may even be nearly as old as Man himself. Consciously or unconsciously, sometimes under pretexts that have disguised his motives even from himself, Man has always been attempting to improve his own quality or at least to maintain it. When he slackens that effort, when he allows his attention to be too exclusively drawn to other ends, he suffers, he becomes decadent, he even tends to die out.

Primitive eugenics had seldom anything to do with what we call "birth control." One must not say that it never had. Even the mysterious mika operation of so primitive a race as the Australians has been supposed to be a method of controlling conception. But the usual method, even of people highly advanced in culture, has been simpler. They preferred to see the new-born infant before deciding whether it was likely to prove a credit to its parents or to the human race

generally, and if it seemed not up to the standard they dealt
with it accordingly. At one time that was regarded as a cruel
and even inhuman method. To-day, when the most civilised
nations of the world have devoted all their best energies to
competitive slaughter, we may have learnt to view the matter
differently. If we can tolerate the wholesale murder and
mutilation of the finest specimens of our race in the adult
possession of all their aptitudes we cannot easily find anything to disapprove in the merciful disposal of the poorest
specimens before they have even attained conscious possession
of their senses. But in any case, and whatever we may ourselves be pleased to think or not to think, it is certain that
some of the most highly developed peoples of the world have
practised infanticide. It is equally certain that the practise
has not proved destructive to the emotions of humanity and
affection. Even some of the lowest human races—as we commonly estimate them—while finding it necessary to put aside a
certain proportion of their new-born infants, expend a degree
of love and even indulgence on the children they bring up
which is rarely found among so-called civilised nations.

There is no need, however, to consider whether or not
infanticide is humane. We are all agreed that it is altogether
unnecessary, and that it is seldom that even that incipient
form of infanticide called abortion, still so popular among us,
need be resorted to. Our aim now—so far at all events as
mere ideals go—is not to destroy life but to preserve it; we
seek to improve the conditions of life and to render unnecessary the premature death of any human creature that has
once drawn breath.

It is indeed just here that we find a certain clash between
the modern view of life and the view of earlier civilisations.
The ancients were less careful than we claim to be of the
individual, but they were more careful of the race. They
cultivated eugenics after their manner, though it was a
manner which we reprobate.[1] We pride ourselves, rightly
or wrongly, on our care for the individual; during all the past
century we claim to have been strenuously working for an

---

[1] But this statement must not be left without important qualification.
Thus the ancient Greeks (as Moissides has shown in *Janus*, 1913), not
only their philosophers and statesmen, but also their women, often took the
most enlightened interest in eugenics, and, moreover, showed it in practice.
They were in many respects far in advance of us. They clearly realised,
for instance, the need of a proper interval between conceptions, not only
to ensure the health of women but also the vigour of the offspring. It is
natural that among every fine race eugenics should be almost an instinct or
they would cease to be a fine race. It is equally natural that among our
modern degenerates eugenics is an unspeakable horror, however much, as
the psychoanalysts would put it, they rationalise that horror.

amelioration of the environment which will make life healthier and pleasanter for the individual. But in the concentration of our attention on this altogether desirable end, which we are still far from having adequately attained, we have lost sight of that larger end, the well-being of the race and the amelioration of life itself, not merely of the conditions of life. The most we hope is that somehow the improvement of the conditions of the individual will incidentally improve the stock. These our practical ideals, which have flourished for a century past, arose out of the great French Revolution and were inspired by the maxim of that Revolution, as formulated by Rousseau, that "All men are born equal." That maxim was overthrown half a century ago; the great biological movement of science, initiated by Darwin, showed that it was untenable. All men are not born equal. Everyone agrees about that now, but nevertheless the momentum of the earlier movement was so powerful that we still go on acting as though all men are, and always will be, born equal, and that we need not trouble ourselves about heredity but only about the environment.

The way out of this clash of ideals—which has compelled us to hope impossibilities from the environment because we dreaded what seemed the only alternative—is, as we know, furnished by birth control. An unqualified reliance on the environment, making it ever easier and easier for the feeblest and most defective to be born and survive, could only, in the long run, lead to the degeneration of the whole race. The knowledge of the practise of birth control gives us the mastery of all that the ancients gained by infanticide, while yet enabling us to cherish that ideal of the sacredness of human life which we profess to honour so highly. The main difficulty is that it demands a degree of scientific precision which the ancients could not possess and might dispense with, so long as they were able to decide the eugenic claims of the infant by actual inspection. We have to be content to determine not what the infant is but what it would be likely to be, and that involves a knowledge of the laws of heredity which we are only learning slowly to acquire. We may all in our humble ways help to increase that knowledge by giving it greater extension and more precision through the observations we are able to make on our own families. To such observations Galton attached great importance and strove in various ways to further them. Detailed records, physical and mental, beginning from birth, are still far from being as common as is desirable, although it is obvious that they possess a permanent personal and family private interest in addition to their more public scientific value. We do not need, and it would indeed be undesirable, to emulate in human breeding the achievements of a Luther Burbank. We have no right to attempt to impose on any human creature an exaggerated and one-sided development. But it is not only our right, it is our duty, or rather one may say, the natural impulse of every rational and humane person, to seek that only such children may be born as will be able to go through life with a reasonable prospect that they will not be heavily handicapped by inborn defect or special liability to some incapacitating disease. What is called "positive" eugenics—the attempt, that is, to breed special qualities—may well be viewed with hesitation. But so-called "negative" eugenics—the effort to clear all inborn obstacles out of the path of the coming generation—demands our heartiest sympathy and our best co-operation, for as Galton, the founder of modern Eugenics, wrote towards the end of his life of this new science: "Its first object is to check the birth-rate of the unfit, instead of allowing them to come into being, though doomed in large numbers to perish prematurely." We can seldom be absolutely sure what stocks should not propagate, and what two stocks should on no account be blended, but we can attain reasonable probability, and it is on such probabilities in every department of life that we are always called upon to act.

It is often said—I have said it myself—that birth control, when practised merely as a limitation of the family, scarcely suffices to further the eugenic progress of the race. If it is not deliberately directed towards the elimination of the worst stocks or the worst possibilities in the blending of stocks, it may even tend to diminish the better stocks since it is the better stocks that are least likely to propagate at random. This is true if other conditions remain equal. It is evident, however, that the other conditions will not remain equal, for no evidence has yet been brought forward to show that birth control, even when practised without regard to eugenic considerations —doubtless the usual rule up to the present—has produced any degeneration of the race. On the contrary, the evidence seems to show that it has improved the race. The example of Holland is often brought forward as evidence in favour of such a tendency of birth control, since in that country the widespread practise of birth control has been accompanied by an increase in the health and stature of the people, as well as an increase in their numbers to a remarkable degree, for the fall in the birth-rate has been far more than compensated by the fall in the death-rate, while it is said that the average height of the population has increased by four inches. It is, indeed, quite possible to see why, although theoretically a random application of birth control cannot affect the germinal possibilities of a community, in practise it may improve the somatic conditions under which the germinal elements develop. There will probably be a longer interval between the birth of the children, which has been demonstrated by Ewart and others to be an important factor not only in preserving the health of the mother but in increasing the health and size of the child. The diminution in the number of the children renders it possible to bestow a greater amount of care on each child. Moreover, the better economic position of the father, due to the smaller number of individuals he has to support, makes it possible for the family to live under improved conditions as regards nourishment, hygiene, and comfort. The observance of birth control is thus a far more effective lever for raising the state of the social environment and improving the conditions of breeding, than is direct action on the part of the community in its collective capacity to attain the same end. For however energetic such collective action may be in striving to improve general social conditions by municipalising or State-supporting public utilities, it can never adequately counter-balance the excessive burden and wasteful expenditure of force placed on a family by undue child-production. It can only palliate them.

When, however, we have found reason to believe that, even if practised without regard to eugenic considerations, birth control may yet act beneficially to promote good breeding, we begin to realise how great a power it may possess when consciously and deliberately directed towards that end. In eugenics, as already pointed out, there are two objects that may be aimed at: one called positive eugenics, that seeks to promote the increase of the best stocks amongst us; the other, called negative eugenics, which seeks to promote the decrease of the worst stocks. Our knowledge is still too imperfect to enable us to pursue either of these objects with complete certainty. This is especially so as regards positive eugenics, and since it seems highly undesirable to attempt to breed human beings, as we do animals, for points, when we are in the presence of what seem to us our finest human stocks, physically, morally, and intellectually, it is our wisest course just to leave them alone as much as we can. The best stocks will probably be also those best able to help themselves and in so doing to help others. But that is obviously not so as regards the worst stocks. It is, therefore, fortunate that the aim here seems a little clearer. There are still many abnormal conditions of which we cannot say positively that

they are injurious to the race and that we should therefore
seek to breed them out. But there are other conditions so
obviously of evil import alike to the subjects themselves and
to their descendants that we cannot have any reasonable
doubt about them. There is, for instance, epilepsy, which is
known to be transformed by heredity into various abnormali-
ties dangerous alike to their possessors and to society. There
are also the pronounced degrees of feeble-mindedness, which
are definitely heritable and not only condemn those who reveal them to a permanent inaptitude for a full life, but constitute a subtle poison working through the atmosphere in all directions and lowering the level of civilisation in the community.
Nowhere has this been so thoroughly studied and so clearly
proved as in the United States. It is only necessary to mention Dr. C. B. Davenport of the Department of Experimental
Evolution at Cold Spring Harbor (New York) who has carried on so much research in regard to the heredity of epilepsy
and other inheritable abnormal conditions, and Dr. Goddard
of Vineland (New Jersey) whose work has illustrated so fully
the hereditary relationships of feeble-mindedness. The United
States, moreover, has seen the development of the system of
social field-work which has rendered possible a more complete
knowledge of family heredity than has ever before been possible on a large scale.

It is along such lines as these that our knowledge of the
eugenic conditions of life will grow adequate and precise
enough to form an effective guide to social conduct. Nature,
and a due attention to laws of heredity in life, will then rank
in equal honour to our eyes with nurture or that attention to
the environment conditions of life which we already regard as
so important. A regard to nurture has led us to spend the
greatest care on the preservation not only of the fit but the
unfit, while meantime it has wisely suggested to us the desirability of segregating or even of sterilising the unfit. But the
study of Nature leads us further and, as Galton said, "Eugenics rests on bringing no more individuals into the world
than can be properly cared for, and these only of the best
stocks." That is to say that the only instrument by which
eugenics can be made practically effective in the modern world
is birth control.

It is not scientific research alone, nor even the wide popular
diffusion of knowledge, that will suffice to bring eugenics
and birth control, singly or in their due combination, into
the course of our daily lives. They need to be embodied in
our instinctive impulses. Galton considered that eugenics must
become a factor of religion and be regarded as a sacred and

virile creed, while Ellen Key holds that the religions of the past must be superseded by a new religion which will be the awakening of the whole of humanity to a consciousness of the "holiness of generation." For my own part, I scarcely consider that either eugenics or birth control can be regarded as properly a part of religion. Being of virtue and not of grace they belong more naturally to the sphere of morals. But here they certainly need to go far deeper than the mere intelligence of the mind can take them. They cannot become guides to conduct until their injunctions have been printed on the fleshy tablets of our hearts. The demands of the race must speak from within us, in the voice of conscience which we disobey at our peril. When that happens with regard to ascertained laws of racial well-being we may know that we are truly following, even though not in the letter, those great spirits, like Galton with his intellectual vision and Ellen Key with her inspired enthusiasm, who have pointed out new roads for the ennoblement of the race.

II

It may be well, before we go further, to look a little more closely into the suspicion and dislike which eugenics still arouses in many worthy old-fashioned people. To some extent that attitude is excused, not only by the mistakes which in a new and complex science must inevitably be made even by painstaking students, but also by the rash and extravagant proposals of irresponsible and eccentric persons claiming without warrant to speak in the name of eugenics. Two thousand years ago the wild excesses of some early Christians furnished an excuse for the ancient world to view Christianity with contempt, although the extreme absence of such excesses has furnished still better ground for the modern world to maintain the same view. To-day such a work as *Le Haras Humain* ("The Human Stud-farm") of Dr. Binet-Sanglé, putting forward proposals which, whether beneficial or not, will certainly find no one to carry them out, similarly furnishes an excuse to those who would reject eugenics altogether. Utopian schemes have their value; we should be able to find inspiration in the most modern of them, just as we still do in Plato's immortal *Republic*. But in this, as in other matters, we must exercise a little intelligence. We must not confuse the brilliant excursion of some solitary thinker with the well-grounded proposals of those who are concerned with the sober possibilities of actual life in our own time. People who are incapable of exercising a little shrewd commonsense in the affairs of life, and are in the habit of emptying out the baby with the bath, had better avoid touching the delicate problems connected with practical eugenics.

There is one prejudice already mentioned, due to lack of clear thinking, which deserves more special consideration because it is widespread among the socialistic democracy of several countries as well as among social reformers, and is directed alike against eugenics and birth control. This prejudice is based on the ground that bad economic conditions and an unwholesome environment are the source of all social evils, and that a better distribution of wealth, or a vast scheme of social welfare, is the one thing necessary, when that is achieved all other things being added unto us, without any further trouble on our part. It is certainly impossible to overrate the importance of the economic factor in society, or of a good environment. And it is true that eugenics alone, like birth control alone, can effect little if the economic basis of society is unsound. But it is equally certain that the economic factor can never in itself suffice for fine living or even as a cure-all of social and racial diseases. Its value is not that it can effect these things but that it furnishes the favorable conditions for effecting them. He would be foolish indeed who went to the rich to find the example of good breeding and, as is well known, it is not with the rich that the future of the race lies. The fact is that under any economic system the responsible personal direction of the individual and the family remains equally necessary, and no progress is possible so long as the individual casts all responsibility away from himself on to the social group he forms part of. The social group, after all, is merely himself and the likes of himself. He is merely shifting the burden from his individual self to his collective self, and in so doing he loses more than he gains.

Thus there is always a sound core in that Individualism which has been preached so long and practised so energetically, especially in English-speaking lands, however great the abuse involved in its excesses. It is still in the name of Individualism that the most brilliant antagonists of eugenics and of birth control are wont to direct their attacks. The counsel of self-control and foresight in procreation, the restriction necessary to purify and raise the standard of the race, seem to the narrow and short-sighted advocates of a great principle an unwarrantable violation of the sacred rights of their individual liberty. They have not yet grasped the elementary fact that the rights of the individual are the rights of all individuals, and that Individualism itself calls for a limitation of the freedom of the individual.

That is why even the most uncompromising Individualist must recognise an element of altruism, call it whatever name you will, Collectivism, Socialism, Communism, or merely the vague and long-suffering term, Democracy. One cannot assume Individualism for oneself unless one assumes it for the many. That is a great truth which goes to the heart of the whole complex problem of eugenics and birth control. As Perrycoste has well argued,[2] biology is altogether against the narrow Individualism which seeks to oppose Collective Individualism. For if, in accordance with the most careful modern investigators, we recognise that heredity is supreme, that the qualities we have inherited from our ancestors count for more in our lives than anything we have acquired by our own personal efforts, then we have to admit that the capable man's wealth is more the community's property than his own, and, similarly, the incapable man's poverty is more the community's concern than his own. So that neither the capable nor the incapable are entitled to an unqualified power of freedom, and neither, likewise, are justly liable to be burdened by an unqualified responsibility. It is the duty of the community to draw on the powers of the fit and equally its duty to care for the unfit. In this way, Perrycoste, whose attitude is that of the Rationalist, is led by science to a conclusion which is that of the Christian. We are all members each of the other, and still more are we members of those who went before us. The generations preceding us have not died to themselves but live in us, and we, whom they produced, live in each other and in those who will come after us. The problems of eugenics and of birth control affect us all. In the face of these problems it is the voice of Man that speaks: "Inasmuch as ye did it not unto the least of these my brethren, ye did it not unto me." However firmly we base ourselves on the principles of Individualism we are inevitably brought to the fundamental facts of eugenics which, if we fail to recognise, our Individualism becomes of no effect.

But it is the same with Socialism, or by whatever name we chose to call the Collectivist activities of the community in social reform. Socialism also brings us up against the hard rock of eugenic fact which, if we neglect it, will dash our most beautiful social construction to fragments. It is the more necessary to point this out since it is on the Socialist and Democratic side, much more frequently than on the Individualist side, that we find an indifferent or positively hostile attitude towards eugenic considerations. Put social

[2] F. H. Perrycoste, "Politics and Science," *Science Progress*, Jan., 1920.

conditions on a sound basis, the people on this side often say, let all receive an adequate economic return for their work and be recognised as having a claim for an adequate share in the products of society, and there is no need to worry about the race or about the need for birth control, all will go well of itself. There is not the slightest ground for any such comfortable belief.

This has been well shown by Dr. Eden Paul, himself a Socialist and even in sympathy with the extreme Left.[3] After setting forth the present conditions, with our excessive elimination of higher types, and undue multiplication of lower types, the racial degeneration caused by the faulty and anti-selective working of the marriage system in modern capitalist society, so that in our existing civilisation unconscious natural selection has largely ceased to work towards the improvement of the human breed, he proceeds to consider the possible remedies. The frequent impatience of the Socialist, and Social Reformers generally, with eugenic proposals has a certain degree of justification in the fact that many evils thoughtlessly attributed to inferiority of stock are really due to bad enviornment. But when the environment has been so far improved that all defects due to its badness are removed, we shall be face to face, without possibility of doubt, with bad inheritance as the sole remaining factor in the production of inefficient and anti-social members of the community. A socialist community must recognise the right to work and to maintenance of all its members, Eden Paul points out, but, he adds, a community which allowed this right to all defectives without imposing any restrictions in their perpetuation of themselves would deserve all the evils that would fall upon it. It is quite clear how intolerable the burden of these evils would be. A State that provided an adequate subsistence for all alike, the inefficient as well as the efficient, would encourage a racial degeneration, from excessive multiplication of the unfit, far more dangerous even than that of to-day.[4] Ability to earn the

[3] In an essay on "Eugenics, Birth Control and Socialism" in *Population and Birth Control: A Symposium,* edited by Eden and Cedar Paul.

[4] This is here and there beginning to be recognised. Thus, not long ago, the Hereford War Pensions Committee resolved not to issue a maternal grant for children born during a prolonged period of treatment allowance. Such a measure of course fails to meet the situation, for it is obvious that, when born, the children must be cared for. But it shows a glimmering recognition of the facts, and the people capable of such a recognition will, in time, come to see that the right way of meeting the situation is not to neglect the children, but to prevent their conception. Mothers' Clinics for instruction in such prevention are now being established in England, through the advocacy of Mrs. Margaret Sanger and the actual initiative of Dr. Marie Stopes.

minimum wage, Eden Paul argues in agreement with H. G. Wells, must be the condition of the right to become a parent. "Unless the socialist is a eugenist as well, the socialist state will speedily perish from racial degradation."

Thus it is essential that the eugenist, dealing with the hereditary factor of life, and the social reformer or socialist, dealing with the environmental factor, should supplement each other's work. Neither can attain his end without the other's help, for the eugenist alone cannot overcome the environmental factor, even perhaps increases it if he is an individualist in the narrow sense, and the socialist alone cannot overcome the bad hereditary factor, and will even increase it if he is no more than a socialist. The more socialist our State becomes the more essential becomes at the same time the adoption of eugenic practices as a working part of the State. "Socialism and eugenics must go hand in hand."

Perrycoste from his own point of view has independently reached the same conclusions. He is not, indeed, concerned with any "Socialist" community of the future but with the dangerous results which must inevitably follow the already established methods of social reform in our modern civilised States unless they are speedily checked by effective action based on eugenic knowledge. "If," he observes, "the community is to shoulder half or three-quarters of the burden of sustaining those degenerates who, through no fault of their own, are congenitally incompetent to maintain themselves in decent comfort, and is to render the life-pilgrimage of these unfortunates tolerable instead of a dreary nightmare, if it is to assume paternal charge of all the tens or hundreds of thousands of children whose parents cannot or will not provide adequately for them and is to guarantee to all such children as much education as they are capable of receiving, and a really fair start in life: then in sheer self-preservation the community must insist on, and rigidly enforce, its absolute claim to secure that no degeneracy or inheritable congenital defects shall persist beyond the present generation of degenerates, and that the community of fifty or seventy years hence shall have no incubus of mentally, or morally, or even physically, degenerate members—none but a few occasional sporadic morbid 'sports' from the normal, which it, in turn, may effectively prevent from handing on their like." Unless the problem is squarely faced, Perrycoste concludes, national deterioration must increase and a permanently successful collectivist society is inherently impossible.

We are not now concerned with the details of any policy of eugenics and of birth control, which I couple together because although a random birth control by no means involves much, if any, eugenic progress, it is not easy under modern conditions to conceive any practical or effective policy of eugenics except through the instrumentation of birth control. We here take it for granted that in this field the slow process of scientific knowledge must be our guide. Premature legislation, rash and uninstructed action, will not lead to progress but are more likely to delay it. Yet even with imperfect knowledge, it is already of the first importance to evoke interest in the great issue here at stake and to do all that we can to arouse the individual conscience of every man and woman to his or her personal responsibility in this matter. That is here all taken for granted.

It seems necessary to consider the political aspect of eugenics because that aspect is frequently invoked, and a man's attitude towards this question is frequently determined beforehand by what he considers that Individualism or Socialism demands. We see that when the question is driven home our political attitude makes no difference. It is only a shallow Individualism, it is only a still more shallow Socialism, which imagines that under modern social conditions the fundamental racial questions can be left to answer themselves.

III

Many years before the Great War, in all the most civilised countries of the World, there were those who raised the cry of "Race-Suicide!" In America this cry was more especially popularised by the powerful voice of Theodore Roosevelt, but in European countries there were similar voices raised in tones of virtuous indignation to denounce the same crime. Since the war other voices have been raised in even more high-pitched and feverish tones, but now they are less weighty and responsible voices, since to those who realise that at present there is not food enough to keep the population of the world from starvation it seems hardly compatible with sanity to advocate an increased rate of human production.

Now, though it is easy to do so, we must not belittle this cry of "Race-Suicide!" It is not usually accompanied by definite argument, but it assumes that birth control is the method of such suicide, and that the first and most immediately dangerous result is that one's own nation, whichever that may be, is placed in a position of alarming military inferiority to other nations, as a step towards the final extinction. It is useless to deny that it really is a serious matter if there is danger of the speedy disappearance of the human race from the earth by its own voluntary and deliberate action, and that within a measurable period of time—for if it were an immeasurable period there would be no occasion for any acute anxiety—the last man will perish from the world. This is what "Race-Suicide" means, and we must face the fact squarely.

It can scarcely be said, however, that the meaning of "Race-Suicide" has actually been squarely faced by those who have most vehemently raised that cry. Translated into more definite and precise terms this cry means, and is intended to mean: "We want more births." That is what it definitely means, and sometimes in the minds of those who make this demand it seems also to imply nothing more. Yet it implies a great number of other things. It implies certain strain and probable ill-health on the mothers, it implies distress and disorder in the family, it implies, even if the additional child survives, a more acute industrial struggle, and it further involves in this case, by the stimulus it gives to over-population, the perpetual menace of militarism and war. What, however, even at the outset, more births most distinctly and most unquestionably imply is more deaths. It is nowadays so well known that a high birth-rate is accompanied by a high death-rate—the exceptions are too few to need attention—that it is unnecessary to adduce further evidence. It is only the intoxicated enthusiasts of the "Race-Suicide" cry who are able to overlook a fact of which they can hardly be ignorant. The model which they hold up for the public's inspiration has on the obverse "More Births!" But on the reverse it bears "More Deaths!" It would be helpful to the public, and might even be wholesome for our enthusiasts' own enlightenment, if they would occasionally turn the medal round and slightly vary the monotony of their propaganda by changing its form and crying out for "More Deaths!" "It is a hard thing," said Johnny Dunn, "for a man that has a house full of children to be left to the mercy of Almighty God."

If, however, we wish to consider the real significance of the facts, without regard for the wild cries of ignorant cranks, it is scarcely necessary to point out here that neither the birth-rate taken by itself, nor the death-rate taken by itself, will suffice to give us any measure even of the growth of the population, to say nothing of the progress of civilisation or the happiness of humanity. It is obvious that we must consider both gains and losses, and put one against the other, if we wish to ascertain the net result. We may roughly get a notion of what that result is by deducting the death-rate from the birth-rate and calling the remainder the survival-rate. If we are really concerned with the question of the alleged suicide of the race, and do not wish to be befooled, we must pay little attention to the birth-rate, for that by itself means nothing: we must concentrate on the survival-rate. Then we may soon convince ourselves, not only that the human race is not committing suicide, but that not even a single one of the so-called civilised nations of which it is mainly composed is committing suicide. Quite the contrary! Every one of them, even France, where this peculiar "suicide" is supposed to be most actively at work, is yearly increasing in numbers.

It is interesting to note, moreover, that the French have been increasing faster, that is to say the survival-rate has been higher in recent years just before the war, when the birth-rate was at its lowest, than they were twenty years earlier, with a higher birth-rate. And if we take a wider sweep and consider the growth of the French population towards the end of the eighteenth century, we find the birth-rate estimated at the very high figure of 40. But the death-rate was nearly as high, the average duration of life was only half what it is now. So that the survival-rate in France at that time, with widely different rates of birth and death, was not much unlike what it is now. The recent French birth-rate of 19 and less, which automatically causes the "Race-Suicide" marionette to dance with rage, is producing not far from the same result of growth of the population—we are not here concerned with the enormous difference in well-being and happiness—as the extremely high rate of 40 which sends our marionettes leaping to the sky with joy. In war-time England, in 1917, the birth-rate sank to 17.8, yet the death-rate was at 14 and the increase of the population continued. The more the human race commits this kind of suicide, one is tempted to exclaim, the faster it grows!

It is, however, in the New World—as in Canada, Australia, and New Zealand—that we find the most impressive evidence of the real criteria of the growth in population set up for judgment on the race-suicide cranks. Canadian statistics bring out many points instructive even in their variation. Here we see not only unusual curves of rise and fall, but also pronounced differences, due to the special peculiarities of the French population, most clearly in the Province of Quebec but also in some parts of the Province of Ontario. In Quebec the birth-rate some years ago was 35, and the death-rate 21, both rates high, and the survival-rate high at 14; recently the birth-rate has risen to 37 and the death-rate fallen to 17, with the result that the survival-rate of 20 is the highest in the world, though it must be noted that the high birth-rate is not likely to last long, since in Quebec, as elsewhere in the world, increasing urbanisation causes a decreasing birth-rate. In mainly English-speaking Ontario the birth-rate is much lower, about 24, but the death-rate is also lower, about 14, so that the fairly considerable survival-rate of 10 is obtained. But we note the highly significant fact that some thirty years or more ago the birth-rate was much lower, about 19, and yet the survival-rate was almost 9, nearly as high as to-day! The death-rate was then at 10, and nothing could be more instructive as to the real relationship that holds in this matter. There has been a great rise in the birth-rate and the only result, as someone has remarked, is a great increase in the population of the grave-yards. Equally instructive is it to compare various cities in this same Province, living under the same laws, and fairly similar social conditions. In the report of the Registrar-General of Ontario for 1916 I find that highest in birth-rate of cities in the Province stands Ottawa with a very considerable French population. But first also stands the same city for infant mortality, which is three times greater than in some other cities in the Province with a low birth-rate. Sault Ste Marie, again with an enormous birth-rate, stands third for infant mortality. Canada shows us that, even if we regard the crude desire for a large growth of population as reasonable—and that is a considerable assumption—a high birth-rate is an uncertain prop to rest on.

Canada is an instructive example because we have some ground for believing that the differences between the English-speaking and French-speaking populations—the greater care of the former in procreation and the more recklessly destructive methods of the latter in attaining the same ends—are due to their different attitudes towards the use of methods of birth control. What the result of a general use of such methods is we know from the example already mentioned of Holland, where they are taught, officially recognised, and in general use, not only among the rich but among the poor. The result is that the birth-rate has been falling slowly and steadily for forty years. But the death-rate has also been falling and at a greater rate. So that the more the birth-rate has fallen the higher has been the rate of increase among the population.

It is perhaps in Australia and New Zealand that we find the most satisfactory proofs of the benefits of a falling birth-rate in relation to "Race-Suicide." The evidence may well appeal to us the more since it is precisely here that the race-suicide fanatic finds freest scope for his wrath. He looks gleefully at China with its prolific women, at Russia with its magnificent birth-rate before the War of nearly 50, at Roumania with its birth-rate of 42, at Chile and Jamaica with nearly 40. No nonsense about birth control there! No shirking by women of the sacred duties of perpetual maternity! No immoral notions about claims to happiness and desires for culture. And then he turns from those great centres of prosperity and civilisation to Australia, to New Zealand, and his voice is choked and tears fill his eyes as he sees the goal of "Race-Suicide" nearly in sight and the spectre of the Last Man rising before him. For there is no doubt about it, Australia and New Zealand contain a population which is gradually reaching the highest point yet known of democratic organisation and general social well-being, and the birth-rate has been falling with terrific speed. Sixty years ago in the Australian Commonwealth it was nearly 44, only forty years ago in New Zealand it was 42. Now it is only about 26 in both lands. Yet the survival-rate, the actual growth of the population, is not so very much less with this low birth-rate than it was with the high birth-rate. For the death-rate has also fallen in both lands to about 10 (in New Zealand to 9) which is lower than any other country in the world. The result is that Australia and New Zealand, where (so it is claimed) preventives of conception are hawked from door-to-door, instead of being awful examples of "Race-Suicide," actually present the highest rate of race-increase in the world (only excepting Canada, where it is less firmly and less healthily based), nearly twice that of Great Britain and able at the present rate to double itself every 44 years. So much for "Race-Suicide."

The outcry about "Race-Suicide" is so far away from the real facts of life that it is not easy to take it seriously, however solemn one's natural temperament may be. We are concerned with people who arrogantly claim to direct the moral affairs of the world, even in the most intimately private matters, and who are yet ignorant of the most elementary facts of the world, unable to think, not even able to count! We can only greet them with a smile. But this question has, nevertheless, a genuinely serious aspect, and I should be sorry even to touch on the question of birth control in relation to "Race-Suicide" without making that serious aspect clear.

"Race-Suicide," we know, has no existence. Not only is the race as a whole increasing in number, especially its White branches, but even among the separate national groups there is not even one civilised people anywhere in the world that is decreasing in number. On the contrary they are all, even France, increasing at a more or less rapid rate. In England and Wales, for example, where the birth-rate has steadily fallen during the last forty years from 36 to 23 (I disregard the abnormal rates of War-time) the population is still increasing, and even if the present falls in birth-rate and death-rate continue, it will for years still go on increasing by an excess of over 1,000 births a day. When we realise that this is merely what goes on in one corner of the world and must be multiplied enormously to represent the whole, we shall find it impossible even to conceive the prodigious flow of excess babies which is being constantly poured over the earth. If we are capable of realising all the problems which thereby arise we must be forced to ask ourselves: *Is this state of things desirable?*

"Be ye fruitful and multiply." That command was, according to the old story, delivered to a world inhabited by eight people. It has been handed down to a world in which it has long been ridiculously out of place, and has become merely the excuse for criminal recklessness among a race which has chosen to forget that the command was qualified by a solemn admonition: "At the hand of man, even at the hand of every man's brother, will I require the life of man." The high birth-rate has meant a vast slaughter of infants, it has meant, moreover, a perpetual oppression of the workers, disease, starvation, and death among the adult population; it has meant, further, a blood-thirsty economic competition, militarism, warfare. It has meant that all civilisation has from time to time become a thin crust over a volcano of revolution, and the human race has gone on lightly dancing there, striving to forget that ancient warning from a soul of things even deeper than the voice of Jehovah: "At the hand of man will I require the life of man." Men have recklessly followed the Will o' the Wisp which represented mere multiplication of their inefficient selves as the ideal of progress, quantity before quality, the notion that in an orgy of universal procreation could consist the highest good of humanity.

The Great War, that is scarcely yet merged into an only less war-like Peace, has brought at least the small compensation that it has led men to look in the face this insane ideal of human progress. We see to-day what has come of it, and the further evils yet to come of it are being embodied beneath our eyes. So that at last the voice of Jehovah has here and there been faintly heard, even where nowadays we had grown least accustomed to hear it, in the Churches. It is Dr. Inge, the Dean of London's Cathedral of St. Paul's, a distinguished Churchman and at the same time a foremost champion of eugenics, who lately expressed the hope that the world,

especially the European world, would one day realize the
advantages of a stationary population.[5] Such a recognition,
such an aspiration, indicates that a new hope is dawning on
the world's horizon, and a higher ideal growing within the
human soul. The mad competition of the industrial world
during the past century, with the sordid gloom and wretch-
edness of it for all who were able to see beneath the surface,
has shown for ever what comes of the effort to produce a growing population by high birth-rates in peace-time. The Great
War of a later day has shown, let us hope in an equally decisive
manner, what comes to a world where men have been for
long generations produced so copiously and so cheaply that
it is natural to regard them as only fit to sweep off the earth
with machine guns. And the whole world of to-day—with its
starving millions struggling in vain to feed themselves, with
most of its natural beauty swept away by the ravages of man,
and many of its most exquisite animals finally exterminated—
is likely to become merely the monument to an ideal that
failed. It was time, however late in the day, for a return to
common sense. It was time to realise that the ideal of mere
propagation could lead us nowhere but to destruction. On that
level we cannot compete even with the lowest of organised
things, not even with the bacteria, which in number and in
rapidity of multiplication are inconceivable to us. "All hope
abandon, ye that enter here" is written over the portal of
this path of "Progress."

There are definite reasons why real progress in the supreme
tasks of civilisation can best be made by a more or less stationary population, whether the population is large or small, and
it need scarcely be added that, so far as the history of mankind
is yet legible, the great advances in civilisation have been made
by small, even very small populations. Where the population
is rapidly growing, even if it is growing under the favourable

---

[5] This has long been recognised by men of science. Even anyone with
the slightest knowledge of biology, Professor Bateson remarked in a
British Association Presidential address in 1914, is aware that a population
need not be declining because it is not increasing; "in normal stable conditions population is stationary." Major Leonard Darwin, the thoughtful
and cautious President of the Eugenics Education Society, has lately stated
his considered belief ("Population and Civilisation," *Economic Journal*,
June, 1921) that increase in numbers means, ultimately, relative reduction
of wealth per head, with consequent lowering of the standard of civilisation;
that it also, under existing conditions, involves the production of a smaller
proportion of men of ability; and, further, a depreciation of our traditions; he concludes that, whatever element in civilisation we regard—
wealth, or stock, or traditions—"any increase in the population *such as that
now taking place* will be accompanied by a lowering in the standard of
our civilisation."

conditions that hardly ever accompany such growth, all its energy is absorbed in adjusting its perpetually shifting equilibrium. It cannot succeed in securing the right conditions of growth, because its growth is never ceasing to demand new conditions. The structure of its civilisation never rises above the foundations because these foundations have perpetually to be laid afresh, and there is never time to get further. It is a process, moreover, accompanied by unending friction and disorder, by strains and stresses of all kinds, which are fatal to any full, harmonious, and democratic civilisation. The "population question," with the endlessly mischievous readjustment it demands, must be eliminated before the great House of Life can be built up on a strong solid human foundation, to lift its soaring pinnacles towards the skies. That is what many bitter experiences are beginning to teach us. In the future we are likely to be much less concerned about "race-suicide," though we can never be too concerned about race-murder.

When we think, however, of the desirability of a more or less stationary population, in order to insure real social progress, as distinct from that vain struggle of meaningless movement to and fro which the history of the past reveals, we have to be clear in our minds that it may be far from desirable that the present overgrown population of the world should be stationary. That might indeed be better than further increase in numbers; it would arrest the growth of our present evils; it might open the way to methods by which they would be diminished or eliminated. But the process would be infinitely difficult, and almost infinitely slow, as we may easily realise when we consider that, with a population even smaller than at present, the human race has not only ravished the world's beauty almost out of existence, but so ravaged its own vital spirit that, as was found with some consternation during the Great War, a large proportion of the male population of every country is unfit for military service.

So often we hear it assumed, or even asserted, that greatness means quantity, so that to look forward to the replacement of the present teeming insignificant human myriads by a rarer and more truly greater race is to be a pessimist! Oh, these "optimists!" To revel in a world which more and more closely resembles all that the poets ever imagined of Hell, is to be an "optimist!" One wonders how it is that in no brief moment of lucidity it occurs to these people that the lower we descend in the scale of life the greater the quantity in a species and the poorer the quality, so that to reach what such people should really regard as the world's period of supreme greatness in life we must go back to the days, before animal life appeared, when the earth was merely a teeming mass of bacteria.[6]

To-day, we are often told, the majority of human beings belong either to the Undesired Class or the Undesirable Class. To realise that this is so, we are bidden to read the newspapers or to walk along the streets of the cities—whichever they may be—wherein dwell the highest products of our civilisation. In the better class quarters it is indeed the Undesirable Class that seems to predominate, and in the poor quarters, the Undesired. Yet, viewing our species as a whole, the two classes may be seen to walk hand in hand along the same road, and in proportion as our nobler instincts germinate and develop, we must doubtless admit that it ought to be our active aim to make that road for both of them—socially though not individually—the Road to Destruction.

To stem the devastating tide of human procreativeness, however, easy as it may seem in theory, is by no means so easy as some think, especially as those think who believe that the human race stands on the brink of suicide. For there is this about it that we must never forget: the majority of those born to-day die before their time, so that by diminishing the production of the unfit, as well as by the progressive improvement of the environment that automatically accompanies such diminution, we may make an imposing difference in the appearance of the birth-rate, whilst yet the population goes on increasing rapidly, probably even more rapidly than before. It needs a most radical and thorough attack on the birth-rate before we can make any real impression on the rate of increase of the population, to say nothing of its real reduction. There is still an arduous road before us.

True it is that we have two opposing schools of thought which both say that we need not, or that we cannot, make any difference by our efforts to regulate the earth's human population. According to one view the development of population, together with the necessity for war which is inextricably mixed up with a developing population, cannot be effected without, as one champion of the doctrine is pleased to put it, "shattering both the structure of Euclidean space and the psychological laws upon which the existence of self-consciousness and human society are conditional."[7] In simpler words, populations tend to become too large for their territories, so that war ensues, and birth control can do nothing because "it is doubtful whether a group in the plenitude of vigour and self-con-

[6] See, for instance, H. F. Osborn, *The Origin and Evolution of Life*, 1918, Ch. III.

[7] B. A. G. Fuller, "The Mechanical Basis of War," *Hibbert Journal*, 1921.

sciousness can deliberately stop its own growth." The other school proclaims human impotence on exactly opposite grounds. There is not the slightest reason, it declares, to believe that birth control has had any but a completely negligible influence on population. This is a natural process and fertility is automatically adjusted to the death-rate. Whenever a population reaches a certain stage of civilisation and nervous development its procreativeness, quite apart from any effort of the will, tends to diminish. The seeming effect of birth control is illusory. It is Nature, not human effort, which is at work.[8]

These two opposing councils of despair, each proclaiming, though in a contrary sense, the vanity of human wishes in the matter of procreation, might well, some may think, be left to neutralise each other and evaporate in air. But it seems worth while to point out that, with proper limitations and qualifications, there is an element of truth in each of them, while, without such limitations and qualifications, both are alike obviously absurd and wrong-headed. Undoubtedly, as the one school holds, in certain stages of civilisation, even at a fairly advanced stage, nations tend to break out over their frontiers with resulting war; but the period when they reach "the plenitude of vigour and self-consciousness" is exactly the period when the birth-rate begins to decline, and the population, deliberately or instinctively, controls its own increase. That has, for instance, been the history of France since the great expansion of population, roughly associated with the Napoleonic epopee—which doubtless covered a web of causes, sanitary, political, industrial, favourable to a real numerical increase of the nation—had died down slowly to the level we witness to-day.[9] Similarly, with regard to the opposing school, we must undoubtedly accept a natural fall in the birth-rate with a rising civilisation; that has always been visible in highly civilised individual couples, and it is an easily ascertainable

[8] Sir Shirley Murphy some years ago (*Lancet*, 10 Aug., 1912) argued that the fall of the birth-rate, as also that of the death-rate, has been largely effected by natural causes, independent of man's action. Mr. G. Udney Yule (*The Fall in the Birth-rate*, 1920) also believes that birth control counts for little, the chief factor being natural fluctuations, probably of economic nature. Recently Mr. C. E. Pell, in his book, *The Law of Births and Deaths* (1921), has made a more elaborate and systematic attempt to show that the rise and fall of the birth-rate has hitherto been independent of human effort.

[9] The reader may point to the renewal of Militarism and Imperialism in France since the Great War. That, however, has been an artificial product (in so far as it exists among the people themselves) directly fostered from outside by the policy of England and the United States, just as the same spirit in Germany before the war, in the face of a falling birth-rate, was artificially fostered from above by a military and Imperialistic caste.

zoological fact that throughout the evolution of life procreativeness has decreased with the increased development of species. We may agree that a natural factor comes into the recent fall in the human birth-rate. But to argue that because a natural decline in birth-rate is the essential factor in the slowing down of procreative activity with all higher evolution, therefore deliberate birth control counts for nothing, since exactly the same result follows when voluntary prevention is adopted and when it is not, seems highly absurd. We must at least admit that voluntary birth control is an important contributory cause, in some sense indeed, of supreme importance, because it is within man's own power and because man is thus enabled to guide and mould processes of Nature which might otherwise work disastrously. How disastrously is shown by the history of Europe, and in a notable degree France, during the four or five centuries preceding the end of the eighteenth century when various new influences began to operate. During all these centuries there was undoubtedly a very high birth-rate, yet infant mortality, war, famine, insanitation, contagious diseases of many and virulent kinds, tended, as far as we can see, to keep the population almost or quite stationary,[10] and so ruinous a method of maintaining a stationary population necessarily used up most of the energy which might otherwise have been available for social progress, although the stationary population, even thus maintained, still placed France at the head of European civilisation. The more firmly we believe that the diminution of the population is a natural process, the more strenuously, surely, we ought to guide it, so that it shall work without friction, and, so far as possible, tend to eliminate the undesirable stocks of man and preserve the desirable. Clearly the theory itself calls for much effort, since it is obvious that along natural lines the decline, if it is the result of high evolution, will affect the fit more easily than the unfit.

Thus there seems, on a wide survey of the matter, no reason

[10] See especially Mathorez, *Histoire de la Formation de la Population Française*, Vol. I, 1920, *Les Etrangers en France*. The fecundity of French families, even among the aristocracy, till towards the end of the eighteenth century, was fabulous; in the third quarter of the seventeenth century the average number of children was five in Paris. But the mortality was extremely high; under the age of sixteen, Mathorez estimates, it was 51 per cent, and infant mortality was terrible in all classes, small-pox being specially fatal. Then there were the various diseases termed plagues, with famine sometimes added, while war, emigration, and religious celibacy all counteracted the excessive fecundity, so that from the thirteenth century to the third quarter of the eighteenth, the population seems to have been stationary, about twenty-two millions. Then the size of the family fell in Paris to 3.9 and in France generally to 4.3, while also there were fewer marriages. Therewith there was an increase of prosperity.

whatever to quarrel with that conviction, which is gradually over-spreading all classes of human society in all parts of the world, and ever more widely leading to practical action, that the welfare of the individual, the family, the community, and the race is bound up with the purposive and deliberate practice of birth control, whether we advocate that policy on the ground that we are thereby furthering Nature, or on the opposite, and no doubt equally excellent, ground that we are thereby correcting Nature.

Along this road, as along any other road, we shall not reach Utopia; and since the Utopia of every person who possesses one is unique that perhaps need not be regretted. We shall not even, within any measurable period of time, reach a sanely free and human life fit to satisfy quite moderate aspirations. The wise birth-controller will not (like the deliciously absurd suffragette of old time) imagine that birth control for all means a New Heaven and a New Earth, but will, rather, appreciate the delightful irony of the Biblical legend which represented a world with only four people in it, yet one of them a murderer. Still, it may be pointed out, that was a state of things much better than we can show now. The world would count itself happier if, during the Great War, only twenty-five per cent. of the population of belligerent lands had been murderers, virtually or in fact. There is something to be gained, and that something is well worth while.

Still, whether we like it or not, the task of speeding up the decrease of the human population becomes increasingly urgent.[11] To many of our Undesirables it may seem mere sentiment to trouble about the ravishing of the world's beauty or the ravaging of the world's humanity. But certain hard facts, even to-day, have to be faced. The process of mechanical invention continues every day on an ever increasing scale of magnitude. Now that process, however necessary, however beneficial, involves some of the chief evils of our present phase of what we call civilisation, partly because it has deteriorated the quality of all human products and partly because it has enslaved mankind, and in so doing deteriorated also his quality.[12] Now we cannot abolish machinery, because machinery

[11] Professor E. M. East, a distinguished biologist and lately President of the American Society of Naturalists (*Nature*, 23 Sept., 1920), has estimated that, for all the fall in the birth-rate the present rate of increase in the population of the world, chiefly of whites, who are increasing most rapidly, will, in the lives of our grandchildren, lead to a struggle for existence more terrible than imagination can conceive.

[12] This has been set forth with admirable lucidity and wealth of illustration by Dr. Austin Freeman in his *Social Decay and Regeneration* (1921), already mentioned.

lies in the very essence of life and we ourselves are machines. But, as the largest part of history shows, there is no need whatever for man to become the slave of machinery, or even for machinery to injure the quality of his own work; rightly used it may improve it. The greatest task before civilisation at present is to make machines what they ought to be, the slaves, instead of the masters of men; and if civilisation fails at the task, then without doubt it and its makers will go down to a common destruction. It is a task inextricably bound up with the task of moulding the human race for which birth control is the elected instrument. Indeed they are but two aspects of the same task. We have to accept the rugged fact that every step to render more nearly perfect the mechanical side of life correspondingly abolishes the need for men. Thus it is calculated to-day that whenever, in accordance with a growing tendency, coal is superseded by oil in industry two men are enabled to do the work of twelve. That is merely typical of what is taking place generally in our modern system of civilisation. Everywhere a small number of men are being enabled to replace a large number of men. Not to avoid looking ahead, we may say that of every twelve millions of our population, ten millions will be unwanted. Let them do something else! we cheerfully exclaim. But what? No doubt there are always art and science, infinite in their possibilities for joy and enlightenment, infinite also, as we know, in their possibilities of mischief and shallowness and boredom. Let it only be true science and great art, and one man is better than ten millions. To say that is only to echo unconsciously the ancient saying of Heraclitus, "One is ten thousand if he be the best."

The vistas that are opened up when we realise the direction in which the human race is travelling may seem to be endless; and so in a sense they are. Man has replaced the gods he once dreamed of; he has found that he is himself a god, who, however realistic he seeks to make his philosophy, himself created the world as he sees it and now has even acquired the power of creating himself, or, rather, of re-creating himself. For he recognises that, at present, he is rather a poor sort of god, so much an inferior god that he is hardly, if at all, to be distinguished from the Lords of Hell.

The divine creative task of man extends into the future far beyond the present, and we cannot too often meditate on the words of the wisest and noblest forerunner of that future: "The whole world still lies before us like a quarry before the master-builder, who is only then worthy of the name when out of this casual mass of natural material he has embodied with all his best economy, adaptability to the end, and firmness, the image which has arisen in his mind. Everything outside us is only the means for this constructing process, yes, I would even dare to say, also everything inside us; deep within lies the creative force which is able to form what it will, and gives us no rest until, without us or within us, in one or the other way, we have finally given it representation." The future, with all its possibilities, is still a future infinitely far away, however well it may be to fix our eyes on the constellation towards which our solar system may seem to be moving across the sky.

Meanwhile, every well-directed step, while it brings us but ever so little nearer to the far goal around which our dreams may play, is at once a beautiful process and an invigorating effort, and thereby becomes in itself a desirable end. It is the little things of life which give us most satisfaction and the smallest things in our path that may seem most worth while.

PART TWO:

More Essays of Love and Virtue

PREFACE

IN PUTTING FORTH a further series of such *Little Essays of Love and Virtue* as I published nine years earlier I must begin with a warning. I do not regard this book of *More Essays* as addressed to the same class of readers as the *Little Essays.* That volume, I stated in the Preface, was specially intended for young people on the threshold of mature life, and I proposed to leave to them the delicate question of its suitability for older people. My feeling about the present volume is the reverse of that. It seems to me that I have been here writing, in the main, less for the young than for those who have passed the stresses of youth and its ardours and are able to take a wide and serene view of the facts of the present and the limited possibilities of the future. For though in the past the young were too often left in ignorance of the things that belonged to their fate, it is possible that there may be limits to the consciousness it is desirable for us to possess in youth of the processes going on within us and of the direction in which we are moving.

Perhaps it may be asked how it comes about that, after writing a book with a primary desire for readers who are young, only a few years later I desire to write for those no longer young. Do I pretend to put myself at the point of view of both? The two viewpoints seem, as we look round us to-day, so different. On the one hand are the young, with their impulse to question, perhaps to shatter, all the things presented to them for reverence, and to set up for worship new images as unlike as possible the idols of their elders. On the other hand, we find the old clinging with tenacity to the new ideals they had set up in youth and vituperating the young for doing precisely what they themselves had once done, denouncing in consequence the irreverence, the disorder, the immodesty, the obscenity, the immorality, of the literature, the art, and the life of the younger generation. "How insolent is youth!" sighed Benjamin

Constant more than a century ago; "age seems to it an unpardonable offence." He might have added that we have but
to wait a few years to see what had been the youth of to-day
finding unpardonable offence in the youth of to-morrow.

It so happens that I do pretend to take the two points of
view. I chance to have been much alive in youth, and to retain
in consequence a vivid memory of that youth and of my revolutionary irreverence at the acme of the Victorian period. I
even recall how as a boy I once accidentally saw the revered
Queen Victoria herself—from a gallery at an International
Exhibition which she was visiting unannounced—and (I have
heard) told my family afterwards that she was "just like a fat
cook." In my independent irreverence towards the idols of
Victorian literature and art, I scarcely deigned to read their
poems or look at their pictures, while I eagerly searched for
the things that pleased myself, things, some of them, which
afterwards also pleased other people so much so that they have
since left me tired. As one grows older, indeed, one may observe with intelligent interest, and if one is sensitive also
share, the perpetual slight change which taste is always undergoing, the perpetual slight novelty in which all life, and indeed
all art, consists. So it is possible to be young and to be old
many times, even in the course of the same life.

That may be how it comes about that I feel with the young,
when I find them falling into the same attitude I assumed in
youth, and with the same arrogance dismissing the generation
which immediately preceded; and I can therefore afford to
smile when I find that among the things they so dismiss are
many that under different circumstances I had cherished, and
even that I am myself thus dismissed. For it should be among
the precious gifts of age that it releases us from the solemnity
of youth, and that we learn to hold loosely and lightly and
playfully the things that once we had persistently clung to;
and this not alone because they must soon fall from our hands
altogether, but because we have learnt to know them better,
and perhaps to realise how much nearer were our loves to our
hates, and our hates to our loves, than at the outset we had
assumed. That process of age is—as it should be—a movement
in the direction of dissolution and death; but meanwhile it is
a phase of sweetness and mellowness, the fruit's one moment of
ripeness, or of what, more or less foolishly, men call "wisdom."

In thus putting myself alike at the standpoint of youth and
of age, I am not, I hope, adopting a literary artifice but keeping within the sphere of facts. Whether falling in with the
rhythm of youth or of age, I would desire still to keep close to
the facts of life. In a certain sense, indeed, literature is, as

Milton felt it to be, life itself. I would desire to say everything I have to say as well as I can—as precisely and as clearly—but never to pass beyond the orbit of life. Therein all great literature moves. Homer and Virgil and Dante and Shakespeare and Cervantes and Racine and Goethe are all concerned with life, even though in different senses or on different aspects; and life means for us, at the beginning and at the end, no abstracted formula, no "society," but this human organism, with its desires and its satisfactions, its ardours and its weariness, its endless mysteries, its strange possibilities, its curious loveliness, not yet fully explored and known.

"Love" and "Virtue," the lines along which, here and before, I have tried a little to explore and to know, I regard as two main paths along which the human organism seeks to find for itself development and expression. I am not likely, I think, to be accused of meaning by "love" merely a mild euphemism for the physical explosion of sex, or by "virtue" merely the namby-pamby convention of "goodness." If when I speak of "love" I may sometimes seem to recall Freud's *libido* and its sublimations. there is also an echo of the love that Dante celebrated as one with the force that moves the stars; and when I speak of "virtue," it is more often the sort of virtue which Nietzsche proclaimed, free from all "moralic acid," the sort which men sometimes mistake for vice, while they bow down to the hollow image of an outworn virtue, and smugly mistake their own feebleness for "the will of God." It is the old heroic "virtue," firm alike in the discipline of self-control, and thereby in the strength to control the world, that we need to-day, whatever may have been needed in the days when men gathered together to listen to the Sermon on the Mount and thereupon went forth to slay and steal and lie and make the world a hell. The love I have in mind is that which secretly inspires a virtue which refuses to yield weakly to the circumstances of a world moulded by the dead heroisms of a past it has outgrown. It comes forward with its own heroisms to guide life into new forms, even if in so doing it must sweep away the old moralities to set up other moralities more in accordance with the increased knowledge of our own days. I belong to a land where all who are truly alive are to-day specially called upon to live daringly, and where virtue, in the antique and genuine sense, as the impulse to demand things that are great and rare, becomes a prime duty. For I am surrounded by traditions that once were living and now are dead, not only in the spiritual world but even in the industrial and commercial world, and yet are clung to with a passionate tenacity which blinds those who hold them to the fate they are bringing down on themselves. I see government entrusted to men of no virtue, by the votes of men and women made of the same stuff, and guided by principles—if they deserve the name—that may once have been those of sanity but in the light of a later age are imbecility. To-day virtue is an adventure.

I am well aware that in setting forth, here and elsewhere, the claims of Love and Virtue, as I conceive them, it will seem to many that I carry them to the point of extravagance and make demands that are at present impossible. But anyone who realises that in every ancient and firmly established social order the forces of inertia are of immense weight will realise also that we cannot strike too hard or make our demands too large. In such an impermeable world we can only gain much by having asked more. To do so is the only course open to men of reason and moderation who are pioneering the future. This is life. Even if I sometimes dream, I do not dream beyond the circumference of life and the aptitudes of the human organism.

When, indeed, I come to think of it, that may be the reason why my "dreams" are at first regarded as shocking and after-wards as commonplace. They are within the orbit of life, even though they seem to present some new vision of life. My first book, *The New Spirit,* was greeted on publication with howls of execration, as outrageous or perverse or ridiculous. On re-issue, thirty years later, it was, with scarcely a dissenting voice, called sane and reasonable. When the volume of *Little Essays of Love and Virtue* was published less than ten years ago, one at least of those included had seemed so alarming that the editor who had originally commissioned it could not dare to publish it himself and found no other editor who would do so. Now I am told that the truth of those *Little Essays* is "obvious." Well! I can only hope that, if not to-day, at all events to-mor-row, these new essays on Love and Virtue will also be found to contain nothing that is not "obvious."

H. E.

Chapter 11

THE NEW MOTHER

A FEW YEARS AGO it was the fashion to discuss the modern girl and her imperfections. The flapper, as some insisted upon calling her, had, it appeared, many imperfections. The scantiness of her hair and her skirts was more than matched by the scantiness of her morals. We need not deny the reality of many of the imperfections revealed in the course of this discussion. Every generation has its own vices, and many others as well, for every generation includes individuals of opposite temperaments.

That has now probably been realized by most people, and the agitation over the modern girl—who is now indeed no longer "modern"—has died down. It begins to be seen that our views of the present are falsified by our imaginative ideas of the past. In the depth of our unconscious we ingeniously construct a picture of the past, and then we are horrified or delighted—according to our individual tastes—by its contrast with the present. In this matter the picture of the past is constructed out of rags and tags of what we call "Victorianism." There was an amusing satire on this tendency of the human mind in a brilliant Revue not long ago played in London and New York, *This Year of Grace*. Here we were given a glimpse of the Victorian bride and bridegroom of 1890 arriving in all their primness and prudery at seaside lodgings (in, it so chances, the coast resort where I write these lines), and then a glimpse of a similar couple of 1928 in all their easy familiarity. One scarcely needs to be old enough and privileged enough to know how these things happened in 1890 to be able to state with assurance that the real bride of that date was far more like that of 1928 than like her imaginary self. The real differences are in things not essential, in dress and in social conventions.

Those differences, it is true, strike deep. They do not affect the great central situations of life, where the eternal human impulses speak as clearly in one generation as in another. If no woman of the public stage in the nineteenth century, or even in the eighteenth, wrote of her own life so frankly as Isadora Duncan, that was not because they were less apt to live daringly, or more apt to be hypocritical, but simply because the social conventions were different. Mrs. Inchbald, one of the most interesting Englishwomen of the eighteenth century, wrote frank memoirs, but she was persuaded to destroy them; Byron's were solemnly burnt in manuscript; Trelawney's *Adventures* were at once carefully expurgated by his friend Mrs. Shelley. Always, close at a writer's elbow, was some fierce and potent incarnation of Social Conventions. More than a thousand years ago the poems of Sappho, greatest of women artists and the most poignantly naked, were so rent to pieces by this same fury that only a few fragments have reached us. Even the little conventions regarding what may or may not be done in public are often the expression of profound impulses, and exert a widespread influence which could not be foreseen. That is so, for instance, as regards fashions of dress. The new tendency of feminine dress in our own day seemed at first merely a phase of the seesaw of fashion, as affected by the economies rendered necessary in wartime. But it was found to be influenced by, and in its turn to influence, many elements of our civilised life that are deeper than the changing fashions of the day: sport, hygiene, the immensely improved health of women, as witnessed by the disappearance of disorders like chlorosis, formerly considered to be inevitably bound up with the feminine sex, a new fellowship of equality with men in work and in play. The new physical aptitudes were found to be associated with new psychic aptitudes. There was a new directness of vision, a new downrightness of speech, a new spirit of adventure, a resolve to experiment even in fields ostensibly prohibited. These new conventions involved an often open disregard of old conventions. They have proved of far-reaching significance. They do not touch the deep springs of human action which operated in 1890 as they do now. They are scarcely even new in those manifestations which have most exercised the minds of moralists; and "petting," if we could recover the prehistoric evidence, might be traced back to origins in the Garden of Eden. They are none the less far-reaching, and the modern girl of yesterday leads up to the new mother of to-day.

The conventions of the past, however superficial, were, as conventions are apt to be, sometimes rigid and almost unbreakable. That was especially so—as still it is apt to be—when they took the form of sexual taboos. These are far from being distinctive of so-called "Victorianism." They go much further back, and they exist in countries completely outside Victorian influence, even in France, which is by some ignorantly supposed to be a land free from sexual taboos. I know a Frenchwoman who can still be called young, belonging to a bourgeois family of superior ability, and the mother was a typically admirable and devoted housewife. But she never gave her daughter the slightest instruction concerning any natural sex function, and no other sources of knowledge were open. The young girl, being highly intelligent, succeeded in forming for herself some general ideas on the subject, infusing them with a poetic spirit, so that she gave the impression to those around her that she was well informed in these matters, and her mother, realising at last that instruction of this kind is desirable yet still unable to overcome her own inhibitions, asked her daughter to instruct her younger sister. This was done to the apparent satisfaction of the pupil, yet the teacher herself remained so ignorant that when some years later she was about to have a child of her own she believed, even to the very day when the child was born, that birth would take place through the navel. Such ignorance is not uncommon even in France. A woman of such distinguished intellect as Madame Adam believed in girlhood that a kiss on the lips from a man produced a child, and many French girls, until recently and perhaps to-day, have had the same belief, which is also found in the United States. The taboo on sexual speech is ancient and has no national frontiers.

It is because it is ancient, passed on by tradition from generation to generation, that it still subsists to-day, even among parents who regard themselves as emancipated and who are fully aware of the duty to train their children in a wholesome knowledge of the vital facts of sex. There is now indeed a widespread conviction among parents, who were themselves brought up amid the old conspiracy of silence in the home, that this is wrong and that they must inaugurate in their own homes a new and better era of sexual enlightenment. But how are they to do it? And what ought they to tell their children? They do not know. The result is that in a large proportion of cases they do nothing, although still retaining an uneasy conscience, in this indeed unlike their own parents, who had similarly done nothing, but on principle, with the virtuous conviction that they were "preserving the innocence" of their children.

Even if they make the plunge the results may not be satisfactory. I recall an English mother of some years ago—but she was not unlike many more recent mothers—who was firmly convinced that it was her duty to impart sexual enlightenment to her daughters when they had reached the age of puberty. She was an intellectual woman of advanced ideas for her time, the friend of some of the leaders in women's movements, and fervent in her convictions. But her excursions into the field of sexual enlightenment must be counted a failure. She had never prepared the way for her exposition; she had not acquired the tact, the sympathy, the insight, needed to give, so suddenly, a lesson her daughters were neither expecting nor desiring. They were simply repelled and disgusted; perhaps the impression thus made was never entirely effaced. Quite recently another mother, an American university woman, has recorded her attempts at the sexual enlightenment of her daughter, aged five. She had herself been brought up, like many other mothers, in a strict middle-class Victorian home, where the word "sex" was unknown, and all her knowledge of it before marriage was acquired from the walls of public-school toilet rooms in New York, and similar tainted sources. She resolved to be "modern and sensible" in the sex education of her own children. She timed the operation at a more reasonably early age than the English mother, but, again, the results were not satisfactory. The child was told an idyllic tale of the planting of little seeds. There was a barrage of questions: "How?—When?—May I see it done?—Please let me see a baby seed!—Does anyone plant seeds in the kindergarten teacher?" And so on. Moreover, the child began to be alarmingly communicative of her new knowledge to friends and visitors. Finally her mother angrily shouted to the child that if she talked any more about the subject she would be whipped. That is one of the possible results of sexual enlightenment. But in both these instances—that of the English mother and that of the American mother—the really significant point to be noted is that from the first the mother was hardly in harmonious rapport with the children on whom she suddenly and injudiciously sprung her "revelations"; nor was she adequately prepared for the ways in which the minds of children react to revelations. Such parents are not really to be accounted among the "new mothers." They are the outcome of the old order, according to which all the facts of procreation were outside the openly accepted order of things and never mentioned. Mothers could not cultivate with their children the simple and open footing on which the natural facts come gradually and almost insensibly into sight, without the shock of any morbid or startling novelty.

It has, of course, to be realised that children may react in various ways that cannot always be foretold, but of necessity it is largely affected by the way in which the "revelation" comes to them. Dr. G. V. Hamilton in his elaborate *Research in Marriage,* among 200 men and women of superior character and ability, found that 37 per cent. of the men and 29 per cent. of the women felt proud and gratified when their curiosity about sex matters was first satisfied; 20 per cent. of the men and 17 per cent. of the women accepted it as a mere matter of fact; there were also as many as 23 per cent. of the men and 31 per cent. of the women who were necessarily shocked and repelled by the unfortunate way in which the revelation came to them.

The subject was investigated also by Dr. Katharine B. Davis among one thousand married women of much above the average in education and of an average age of thirty-eight, so that their youth belonged to a period when the new mother had not yet arrived. They were asked to answer the question: Had you been at all adequately prepared by instruction for the sex side of marriage? To this 55.8 replied that they had. But many of these affirmative answers revealed how inadequate were the notions concerning "adequate preparation." Some thought a knowledge of contraception all that was needed; others an expectation of pain; a few were quite content with "duty of wife to submit to husband." Most of those who had no "preparation" at all (there were 438 of these) regretted that they went into marriage blindfold and felt that preparation would greatly have helped them in adjusting their lives; as a matter of fact, a much larger proportion of those who considered themselves happy had received instructions than of those who considered themselves unhappy. Some suggestive and significant remarks were, however, made by women who had received information of the usually approved kind and found it inadequate: "Mere knowledge of facts is of very little value"; "I knew nothing about *emotions*"; "Fanciful explanations by means of birds and flowers did not help"; "The factor of passion was left out"; "Books deal with things as they should be, not as they are."[1] These are the opinions of the new mother, but they are based on the bitter experience of an order of things which, we may hope, is now passing away.

The new mother, as I have from time to time seen her, neither shrinks in alarm from the subject of sex nor attempts

[1] Katharine B. Davis: "A Study of the Sex Life of the Normal Married Woman:" *Journal of Social Hygiene,* 1922-1923; also the same author's *Factors in the Sex Life of Twenty-Two Hundred Women,* 1920, p. 67.

any heroic feat of "sexual enlightenment" with her children. She has no need to. She regards motherhood as a relationship of loving and natural intimacy, and she differs from any ordinary affectionate mother of old mainly through being guided by intelligence, and not by obedience to outworn traditions. She has learnt how to become the friend of her children. The relationship thus becomes more, and not less, simple, for our traditions had introduced an unnatural artificiality with endless complications. It was inevitable that any sudden attempt to be "modern and sensible" in matters of sex within that artificially woven web must often prove disturbing and unsatisfactory. And even if the mother's ideas may claim to be modern all through, if she fails to establish the fundamental basis of friendship with her child she has failed altogether. The new mother is learning to be "modern and sensible," not in sudden spasms, but from the first, in the whole relationship of motherhood.

There is nothing here meant to suggest that motherhood is so alarming and formidable a vocation that a woman should not venture to approach it without much special preparation. Such preparation is certainly desirable. But the new mother is not always, or indeed usually, the outcome of formal training, or the creature of dogmas, whether her own or of others. That is what is so interesting about her; that is why I have so much faith in her reality. Again and again I find her in all sorts of places, without any expert preparation for her maternal tasks, often herself springing from an old-fashioned home of unwholesome type. But there seems to be a subtle change in the atmosphere to-day, and as it were instinctively, by natural impulse, the new mother often follows a course which might well have been the outcome of the finest teaching by experience.

The functions of sex are just as natural as the other human functions, the main natural difference being, not that they are more obscene or more sacred but that they develop at a slower pace. They seem equally natural to the child when they come before him naturally, and it is because they so seldom come before him naturally that his attention is apt to be concentrated on them with a secret and morbid intensity. We can scarcely wonder when we realise that, as Dr. Hamilton has found even among superior persons, only 2 per cent. of the men and the same proportion of the women had received from any source "full and adequate information." There are innumerable children who, when they have first come in contact with some fact or word of sex, have asked an innocent and perhaps even casual question about it and received an unexpected snub which is not to be forgotten. Never again is any question asked, but beneath the surface the young mind works at unravelling the mystery.

That need not happen. It can scarcely happen when the relationship between mother and child is so simple and natural that the germs of such morbid mysteries find no place to develop in the child's mind. There can be no point at which any mysterious "forbidden" subject is enabled to take shape. The child's natural reactions are naturally met, and when these reactions touch the region of sex and reproduction or of excretion the child is not carefully headed off. That ancient conspiracy between parents, teachers, and social environment to persuade the child that everything to do with sex and with excretion is disgusting, and the simple words describing them so "filthy" that they must be replaced by cumbersome euphemisms, if not abolished, is now at least rendered harmless. The origin of babies thus comes to appear to the child at an early age as simple as the origin of kittens, however more wonderful by being brought home to him as a fact of personal experience. Nor is there room left for those unwholesome curiosities concerning the physical form of the opposite sex which so often tormented the child of a former age when he approached puberty and grew conscious of sexual differences. The social convention in regard to the body has changed so much during recent years that the path has been rendered easy for the new mother. She puts no barriers in the way of boys and girls seeing each other naked when circumstances render it simple and natural, and her children from early age sometimes see their parents in the bath. Adult nakedness can thus never become that occasion for the shock of fascination or repulsion which it has often been for those children from whom this sight is hidden until they are approaching puberty or later. It is largely an unnatural physical attitude which fosters the "castration complex" of the psychoanalysts, just as it is largely an unnatural emotional attitude which fosters their "mother-fixation"; although it is scarcely possible for either to develop in any intense degree except on a hereditarily neurotic foundation.

I have said that the method of the new mother, as I have seen it in action, is nothing if not simple and natural. But I do not deny that it is often, at the same time, difficult and troublesome. What is simple is not always easy. The mother of old time by whom so many adults of to-day were brought up—and they will often be prepared to say well brought up—was affectionate but severe. The child's part was to obey and to respect, and it was not encouraged to be intimate, so that it seldom felt any impulse to be intimate, and the mother seemed, on her side, to have found it difficult to be intimate with her children, thus soon becoming as shy with them as they were with her. Dr. Hamilton finds that nearly half of the men and women he has so carefully investigated report that their relations with their parents in early life had been either "undemonstrative" or "very undemonstrative." A system of artificial taboos ruled both parties in the relationship; it was not a simple relationship, but it evaded many difficulties. The child of to-day is less easily moved to obey his parents and still less to treat them with respect. He treats his mother with a familiarity which sometimes seems shocking to those of us whose attitude in childhood was so different, though we realise, as years go on, how much this method achieves that the old method could never attain. The new mother was often herself brought up by the old method, and she suffers sometimes from the freedom she leaves unchecked. But she has realised that it is but a poor preparation for life that lies in a gospel of *Don'ts*. And when that freedom becomes too extravagant she gently explains that great truth, lying at the foundation of society, which children never understand spontaneously—nor always, indeed, adults— that, however free we may be, we are not free to do the things which interfere with the equal freedom of other people.

The troubles of the new mother do not end there. She has soon to realize that new mothers are at present a small minority, scattered through the community and unorganised, although there is a remarkable similarity in their methods. They are surrounded by the old mothers bringing up the old sort of children and still feeling that they have on their side the primitive herd instinct which encourages intolerance of novelty. A new mother had familiarised her little daughter of six with the elementary facts of sex and the origin of babies. But one day the child, having received a different statement from other sources, came questioningly to her mother: "Babies come out of eggs!" Her mother gently explained that there are people who think that children are not old enough to understand the truth about these things and so make up stories to tell them. The little maiden drew herself up and said: "I will never believe anything but what *you* tell me." In such a way a beautiful relation of intimacy and trust is established for the enlightenment and development of the child, and the tainted influences of the external world are sterilised beforehand.

It should, however, be clear to parents at the outset that they have to reckon with this external world and to guard themselves and their child against it, though this should not be done before an actual clash has occurred, and only then to meet the case in hand. Undue haste in forewarning the child might be as harmful as was the deliberate attempt to thrust upon him sex revelations he had not asked for. It would prematurely destroy the child's spontaneity. The new mother has no wish to protect the child unduly and rob him of initiative. If she holds the child's friendship, she knows no fear and goes joyfully ahead, extending to the external world the same trust as at first does the child, though hers is often based on merely a smiling tolerance. She knows that if any clash occurs between the world and the child, he will come to her, and she will then effect the necessary adaptations to the world for the protection of the child. In thus encouraging self-reliance, and not unduly sheltering him beforehand, the new mother finds no great harm resulting from any clash, since she is always the friend to whom the problem is brought for solution, and any germs of secrecy and distrust, such as the child may naturally possess as part of his human inheritance, she has an opportunity of training in the right direction, tempering them with her own tolerance.

At puberty the new mother will still find further problems to face, not now from without, but from within her children. For at puberty the developing impulses from within bring to the boy's or girl's consciousness elements which are strange to it and seem to demand as their natural right a secrecy which, where the earlier questionings were concerned, was, if it existed, imposed rather than natural. It is no longer easy, it may no longer be natural, for the pubescent boy or girl to confide completely even in the new mother. So that she may sometimes be doubtful at this stage as to what is going on within the rapidly growing organism, and what problems it may be secretly facing. But even here the new mother may contain herself in patience. If she has so far guided her children wisely, no great harm is likely to ensue. The developing son or daughter, when secrecy no longer seems important, or when it becomes unendurable, will most naturally turn to his parents if he is assured that their guidance in the past has been sound. And even if they do not, the old guidance will still have left its traces. If the developed child is now training himself, the sound tradition of training he has known will still remain with him. And if in this evolution a new instinct of reserve appears —as it most probably will appear—in the adolescent mind, the new mother will recognise that that is not really a turning away from herself, but a necessary accident of the development of individuality, and by that recognition she will the more deeply win the love and gratitude, as well as the confidence, of her child. We have always to remember that an education which is not a discipline, and a self-discipline, can scarcely be considered a preparation for life.

The question of discipline, which comes in here, cannot be passed over, for it is the essence of the whole matter. At first sight it might seem that the attitude of the new mother towards her child deprives him of discipline. She allows him the utmost amount of freedom compatible with other claims. She treats him as an equal rather than as an inferior, apparently extending to children the same kind of equality which has only of recent years been accorded to women themselves. When that means indulgence, with an artificial protection against the natural results of indulgence, it may well be unfavourable to any sort of discipline for life. "The Garden of Eden," it has been said, "is a poor preparation for toiling in the sweat of one's brow." But it is necessary to point out that the old system, now decaying, was in its extreme form still more ill-adapted as a disciplinary preparation for life. A famous author of the nineteenth century, Ruskin, wrote an autobiography, called *Praeterita,* which deserves to live when his books on art are forgotten; in this he tells how he was brought up in his very Victorian middle-class home by loving parents who shielded him from every harm and allowed him absolutely no freedom of action. Looking back on this training in old age, he realised how sadly it unfitted him for the discipline of life and became the direct cause of misfortune when he was cut loose from his mother's apron-strings. If the new mother leaves a large scope for freedom to her child, and encourages him to act for himself instead of acting for him, he may have to suffer for his actions, but he is learning responsibility and is being trained in the home for the discipline of the world.

It is not to be assumed that the mother of old days was entirely wrong and the new mother of to-day entirely right. The task is difficult for any kind of mother, and the one may fail as well as the other. Motherhood is an art, a rarer art than is commonly supposed, and while every woman has sometimes wanted to be a mother, she may well think twice before she decides that she is fitted to become one, for she may be unfitted spiritually even if she is physically fitted. The old-time mother was capable of producing splendid children; where the material was good, her methods were brilliantly successful; but her failures were many, and when the child was of poor material he remained undeveloped or deviated in morbid directions, becoming the victim of "mother-fixation" or the "Œdipus Complex," a suitable patient for the psychoanalysts who flourish on the failures of old-world training.

Whether for good or for evil, however, we cannot carry over the methods of the past into the present. Every age must deal with its own problems in its own way. The new generation demands the new mother. How finely successful she can prove—especially when herself inspired by a happy love-life—some of us are already able to testify.

Chapter 12

THE RENOVATION OF
THE FAMILY

THE DECAY OF THE FAMILY has long been a favourite theme of social alarmists. Looking back on the conventions which in their own early days were held to be sacred, whether or not they were actually observed, elderly people exclaim on the "bankruptcy" of those marriage conventions to-day and the consequent dissolution of home life.

In a sense they are completely justified. The conventions they were brought up in are really changing; marriage is not the same thing as it was in their early days; the new home is certainly different from the old. It is true. It has, indeed, been more or less true ever since social life began. Yet, under all modifications, there has always been some form of marriage, and the home in some shape has still persisted.

It is, therefore, only the shallow and the ignorant who can mistake the changes that take place in their own little day and environment for the obliteration of great landmarks—that is, when we have put aside those well-meaning people who like to play with the idea of the "bankruptcy of marriage" in order to startle their fellows into a more lively concern with social problems. As a matter of fact, it is necessary to take a wide view of human history, such as may be gained from Westermarck's *History of Human Marriage* or Briffault's *The Mothers* —I purposely choose two works widely opposed in their temper and conclusions—in order to realise that the family and the home, even under the most divergent social conditions that we can well conceive to be possible for Man, have still persisted.

We may go further still. It is not only a truth for the human species that marriage is omnipresent; it is also found among the higher mammals. This is not only so, as far as our imperfect knowledge extends, among the closely related anthropoid apes; it is so among the superior quadrupeds; the elephants lead a conventional life of the type familiar among ourselves, of which, with its related education of the young, adventurous camera hunters are now revealing the details; while among birds, who are phylogenetically so remote from ourselves, the resemblances are often still closer. It is vain for even the most conservative of human beings to lament the failure of marriage; it is futile for even the most light-hearted of radicals to hope to get beyond it. The family is at the root of our bisexual constitution, and needs no formal institution.

"The abolition of marriage in the form now practised," wrote Godwin, "will be attended with no evils. It really happens in this, as in other cases, that the positive laws which are made to restrain our vices irritate and multiply them." It is more than a century since those wise words were spoken. But the great pioneer who uttered them exerted no influence on legislation, and their truth has now had time to be illustrated by thousands of prohibition laws against all sorts of real or imaginary vices.

There are at least three tendencies which we may term biological, common to Man and the animals immediately below Man, which constitute for the family foundations we cannot conceive as being overthrown: (1) the impulse of sexual attraction which leads to mating; (2) the tendency to close comradeship, even apart from the sex of the comrade, within the herd or community;[1] (3) the instinctive impulse of mates to care for their offspring.

Yet it is true that new social factors, developed during the lifetime even of those of us still of middle age, are causing a greater modification on the conventions of marriage and the home than we can easily find traces of in our past history.

The ever increasing approach to social and industrial equality of the sexes, the steady rise and extension of the divorce movement, the changed conceptions of the morality of sexual relationships, the spread of contraception—all these influences are real, probably permanent, and they have never been found at work before in combination, seldom even separately. Not one of them, however, when examined with

[1] Dr. M. A. Bigelow ("Biological Foundations of the Family," *Journal of Social Hygiene*, March, 1930) calls this tendency to pairing of comrades, who may or may not be of the same sex, "comrade-instinct." He remarks: "I have made some unpublished observations on herds of common domesticated animals in which I have found a surprising number of pairs of comrades associating for months and years while they live freely in what appeared to be herds." Apart from herds, we may frequently observe a close comradeship between two animals often of the same sex and even of different species.

care, bears within it any necessary seeds of destruction. On the contrary, they are adapted to purify and fortify, rather than to weaken, the family as we know it, to enable it to work more vigorously and effectively rather than to impair its functions as what has been termed "the unit of civilisation." It is true that the younger women of to-day are often dissatisfied with marriage, but that attitude is a belated recognition that they are entitled to satisfaction, and we may accept it as wholesome. The greater economic independence of women assists them in the task of sexual selection and is found to be conducive to marriage, though it is also favourable to divorce when marriage is disrupted.

The greater facility of divorce aids the formation of the most satisfactory unions. A greater freedom between the sexes before marriage, even if it has sometimes led to license, is not only itself beneficial but the proper method of preparing for a more intimate permanent union. And the exercise of contraceptive control is the indispensable method of selecting the best possibilities of offspring and excluding from the world those who ought never to be born. As a matter of fact, marriage, so far from dying out, tends in various countries of the West to increase in frequency. Even the Great War, which was expected to make marriage more difficult for women, had no such effect; thus in England, in 1921, out of every 1,000 women over fifteen years of age 520 were married, though ten years earlier (1911) only 506 were married. While as regards the production of children through the agency of the family, the danger that faces Western civilisation to-day is not of a deficient production but of an enormous excess. So that, whatever changes of form it may undergo, we clearly have to reckon with the persistence of the family, whether that is a prospect which causes our hearts to sink or whether it fills us with satisfaction.

We might reach the same conclusion even without any close examination of the sociological data of to-day. It is enough to survey the fundamental biological facts on which all human or other societies must rest, or to glance at the history of marriage and the family from the earliest period at which our knowledge begins.

Not that that may be easy. We find many people doing it, with an air of the greatest self-confidence, and reaching exactly opposite conclusions, or, at all events, conclusions that seem to themselves to be opposite. On the one hand are those who start from promiscuity and regard the clan and the mother (with perhaps her brother thrown in) as the most solid facts of the primitive situation. On the other hand are those who, in extreme reaction from that view, put the biological fact in the foreground and are inclined to discount any modification of it by cultural influences, so that the human family continues from the point reached by the animal family, in father, mother and offspring.

To-day it is perhaps possible to see that both these views have elements of truth, but that either of them is wrongly held if it is believed to exclude elements of the opposite view. That is the standpoint which I have myself for many years tried to indicate as probably the most correct, though I could not feel that I had the right to do so emphatically. Now I am more prepared to do so in the light of conclusions which have been reached by one who is perhaps, to-day, second to none as a profound investigator of these problems and an intimate student of the sex-life of savages as it at present is carried on. Dr. Malinowski sees the elements of soundness and truth in each of the two hitherto rival doctrines, which have flourished side by side during the last century, and, except when they are stated in an extreme form, he denies that they are contradictory. They both present aspects of the big procreative institution of mankind; biological or animal marriage is the core but it is capable of more or less transformation into culturally socialised forms.[2] What mainly concerns us here to observe is that, whatever view of the family we adopt, we are still constrained to admit, that, under all changes of form, it has always persisted, so that its existence may even be said to be woven into the texture of the species.

It has too often been forgotten that the family possesses this many-sided flexibility and has in different ages and lands shown endless variations of shape in adjustment to varying social conditions. Those who overlooked this essential fact have frequently cried out in rebellion against the whole conception of the family. Because they themselves have chanced to come out of an unhappy family life—though the excellent qualities they have notwithstanding often displayed go far to show that even an unhappy family life may have happy results—they impetuously demand the complete abolition of the family. An anonymous German correspondent, who

[2] In the important essay here referred to on "Parenthood the Basis of Social Structure" (published in *The New Generation,* New York and London, 1930) Professor Malinowski sets forth what he describes as "the first full statement of my theory of kinship, the result of over twenty years' work on a subject to which I have devoted most of my attention."

opposes my acceptance of the family as a suitable home for the young and refers to the certainly deplorable fact (to be matched also in other countries) that in all Germany and Austria during the last sixteen years only four Schools for Mothers have been founded or planned, has lately sent me a long and imposing series of quotations from eminent writers, ancient and modern, denouncing the family. I quote a few at random: "I reject family education altogether; public education is better" (Fichte); "Give me other mothers and I will give you another world" (St. Augustine); "Of ten blows which a child receives nine are from its mother" (T. Hippel); "Maternal love easily becomes pernicious, and animal affection, overlooking, forgiving, and sparing all the child's faults, immensely injuring the child itself, and imparting at the outset the germ of future illusions in life" (Forel); "Many women wish to abolish war; but these very same women, in the sphere of education, cannot give up those methods of force which call out rough passions and unworthy ideas of right, and are the counterpart of war" (Ellen Key); "Babies need better education than the individual mother gives them" (Mrs. Perkins Gilman); "Poor child! Your father is tied to his office, your mother is vexed to-day, to-morrow she has a visitor, the day after, her moods" (Pestalozzi); "The family, the Hell of the child, the home of all social vices!" (Strindberg); "If the punishment of the criminal is justified we must first ask: How did he become a criminal? What was his mother like?" (Brockhaus's *Hours with Bismarck*).

Such outbursts have their significance. They show us that the family, however fundamental, will not fit everyone and that not all are worthy of the privileges it offers. They clearly indicate that those who are not fitted, by nature or by training, for marriage and parenthood would be well advised to follow some other career. They are a warning that every institution must perpetually grow and change if it is not to prove pernicious. Above all, they impress on us how deeply founded the family must be when it can evoke such hearty condemnation even from the most eminent personages without in the slightest degree endangering its stability.

There is one important change which must be recognised at the outset. Hitherto the question of the family has been mainly, if not even altogether, the question of marriage. To a large extent it must continue to be so. But it is a distinguishing characteristic of our Western civilisation, in all the countries it has touched, that this is no longer necessarily the case. In the history of mankind in general marriage has meant a family, and when no children appeared the marriage has often been dissolved, sometimes almost automatically. With us, not only is the absence of children considered no adequate ground for the dissolution of the marriage, but the marriage may at the outset be planned to avoid procreation, whether temporarily or permanently. That is becoming the central characteristic of our marriage system, and it is of immense significance in relation to the family. Not that it can affect the existence of the family, since that rests on a biological foundation which cannot be destroyed. But it furnishes an altogether new control over the forms the family may assume, and it renders the family adjustable, in a way that has never before been possible, to the developing direction of our general social organisation.

This is notably conspicuous in relation to the changing economic position of women. In the phase of civilisation out of which we are growing, a phase which persisted unimpaired until the Industrial Revolution at the end of the eighteenth century, the economic position of woman was as wife and mother at the head of the home. That was no small position to occupy, and it required most diverse gifts, since the home was a centre of industrial activity for a large part of its own needs. But woman to-day occupies a totally different position. She has lost her industrial activities in the home, but has regained them in the wider world, and added to them the freedom to adopt, if she so chooses, most of the activities formerly reserved to men.[3] At the same time she tends more and more to accept, at all events as an ideal, the principle of complete economic independence, even in the exercise of her functions as wife and mother, since she no longer considers that as wife and mother she becomes the servant of a man and entitled to wages as such, but holds that she is gratifying her own desires. That principle, however, though it may be reasonable, leads to a great conflict if pushed to its logical extreme in practice. If a woman, when she becomes a wife, is to follow the example of the woman of the old world and spend her time and strength in bearing perhaps a dozen children, of

[3] The part played by women in industry is steadily increasing, and the restrictions often imposed for their protection (in my opinion unquestionably beneficial, as may be seen in my book *Man and Woman*) have had no effect in limiting that increase. The English evidence is clear on this point (*Home Office White Paper*, Cmd. 3508, 1930). In textile industries women have always played a large part; it is now about 64 per cent. of the whole; in non-textile industries women's part has risen in recent years from 15 to 27 per cent. There is a tendency for women to be engaged in the more unskilful processes, as they mostly look upon factory work as a temporary career to fill up the interval between school and marriage.

whom not half may survive, she cannot possibly be economically dependent on her own exertions. She must remain unmarried or renounce her independence in becoming wife and
mother. The difficulty is always real, but it has now become,
in some measure at all events, adjustable. It has become clear,
that is to say, that the number of children and the times when
they are to be born may be arranged according to the circumstances in which the two parents are situated, and it is
also seen to be reasonable that, since the mother must necessarily devote a larger share of time and care to the child, the
father may be called upon to take a larger financial share,
without the economic equality of the two parents being thereby
injured.

The desirability of controlling the appearance of children
in the family brings us to the question of contraception. That
is a question around which in the immediate past much controversy raged. It cannot even yet be said that it has ceased
to rage. And since in some countries of the West there are
still legal disabilities to be remedied in order to bring the law
into harmony with custom and opinion, propaganda is artificially stimulated. There is, however, no longer the shadow of a
doubt that both the principle and the practice of birth control
are now firmly established in all civilised lands, and gradually
becoming accepted by every class of the community, so that
before long the only matter of dispute will be concerning the
best method by which it can be carried out. It is estimated that
at the present rate birth control will become practically universal in our civilisation within from twenty-five to fifty years,
and it may be that with better conditions of sexual initiation,
increased medical study of the difficult problems involved, and
the cultivation of self-control, mechanical methods of contraception will become less necessary. There are three main
lines along which this development has proceeded. In the
first place there has been the insistence of women that they
will no longer be mere breeding machines, destroying alike
themselves and their excessive progeny. In the second place,
the economic conditions of life for all social classes in the
modern world tend to render caution and foresight necessary
in family life, and there are now but few parents who can
afford to disregard so completely these conditions, and the
responsibilities of bringing up children in the world of to-day,
as to have an unlimited family. In the third place, scientific
demographers and statisticians are now, with ever greater
decision, pointing out that the enormous increase in the earth's
population, which up to about a century ago was practically

stationary, cannot be much longer continued, since even another century may suffice to reach the limit of possible expansion. Each of these lines of argument is legitimate. When combined, they are of irresistible force.[4]

Another modern condition which has an important bearing or the family in our Western civilization is constituted by the increase of divorce and the ever greater legal facilities for securing it. Speaking generally (there are always exceptions) it may be said that in savage societies, as probably in the primitive world, matings, provided they are formed with members of the group with which mating is permitted, are easily formed and rather easily ended. In more advanced barbarous societies, in which property becomes a chief factor in society, masculine influence is more predominant than before over feminine influence, the marriage bond grows more rigid and is especially rigid in favour of the husband. In the later civilised social states this rigidity is relaxed, divorce becomes easier and more frequent, and the rights of the sexes tend to be equalised.

[4] It is sometimes supposed that the Catholic Church is opposed to contraception and that Catholics refuse to practise it. Both these suppositions involve some misapprehension. It is certain that Catholics practise contraception. France, a largely Catholic country, has been the leader in the movement, and in Germany the Catholic birth-rate is falling; in the United States it is found at Mrs. Margaret Sanger's clinic in New York that the proportion of Catholic women who apply for advice is about 32 per cent., that is to say, nearly as large as the proportion of Protestant women, which is 33 per cent. In some countries, it is true, statistics show a higher birth-rate among the Catholics than among the Protestants, but in those countries the Catholics usually belong to a lower and less educated social class which would inevitably show a higher birth-rate whatever religion they professed. Dignitaries of the Catholic Church have sometimes distinguished themselves by denunciation of contraceptive measures. But those of them who have to speak with a sense of responsibility are cautious in their statements. Thus the most conspicuous English ecclesiastic of the Catholic Church, Cardinal Bourne, Archbishop of Westminster, has lately ascribed the condemnation of birth control as "unnatural sin" to "Christian tradition" (*The Times*, October 6, 1930). That view, it may be added, is also accepted by the chief ecclesiastic of the Church of England, Dr. Lang, Archbishop of Canterbury, who regards the opposition to birth control as due to "the influence of a long church tradition," but Dr. Lang is careful to add that that tradition receives "no clear direction or even guidance" from the New Testament, and that there is no reason to regard birth control as "sinful" (*The Times*, November 14, 1930). No advocate of birth control need complain of this ecclesiastical attitude. And so far as the Catholic Church is concerned, it is hardly possible for a Church which venerates chastity and maintains the celibacy of the clergy to be fundamentally opposed to contraception, since chastity and celibacy themselves involve contraception. The only dispute possible is with regard to methods, and that is a comparatively trivial matter. There would appear to be no dogma of the Church incompatible with contraception, nor could there be so long as the celibacy of the clergy is maintained.

We may see that process in classic Rome. Beginning, it may well be, in a social state of more or less matriarchal constitution, when the Roman social order became patriarchal, marriage in some of its forms was almost indissoluble, and divorce, so far as it existed, was usually a privilege confined to the husband, except in a "free" marriage, where the wife did not fall under the *manus* of her husband. But in the later developments the privileges of free marriage were extended to *manus* marriages, and Roman law became equally liberal to husbands and wives in the matter of divorce. That represents approximately the stage that we have to-day reached in Western civilisation.

The frequency of divorce has much increased since the Great War, but it was steadily if more slowly increasing long before, though in France the frequency of divorce increased up to 1921 and since then has somewhat decreased. The post-war so-called "epidemic of marriage" was naturally followed by an "epidemic of divorce," which is now subsiding, although we may still expect the rate to rise slowly as the impediments are removed. In Japan, it may be remarked, which comes next to the United States in frequency of divorce, there was no post-war rise. The United States holds the record; in 1923 there were 360 divorces to 100,000 of married population (or 149 to 100,000 of the whole population). And in some States this means one or more divorces to every five marriages, though, according to the later (1928) American results of Groves & Ogburn, there is one divorce to every seven marriages, actors and musicians constituting the most divorcing professional class. In Europe, Austria and Switzerland stand high, and England (1922) very low with only 6.8 divorces to 100,000 of population. In Russia divorce may be obtained at the wish of either party (and at the wish of both it may be arranged before the Registrar, without recourse to the Courts), yet divorce is far less frequent than in the United States, and the younger generation cultivate the ideals of self-discipline and self-control on which Lenin insisted.[b] Such differences represent differences of social opinion and of religion, as well as discrepant facilities for obtaining divorce. The general advance of divorce corresponds to the normal condition of advanced civilisation and represents a necessary and healthy adjustment to the complex social conditions. Divorce by mutual consent (and even on the demand of either party) is the goal towards which we are moving, and it has already been reached in some countries.

[5] Anne L. Strong; *Marriage and Morals in Soviet Russia*, 1927. The position in Russia is discussed by M. Hindus: *Humanity Uprooted*.

It is reasonable that a contract formed by mutual consent should be dissolvable by mutual consent, and so far from divorce being destructive to the family, we may agree with Westermarck that it is a necessary means of preserving the dignity of marriage by ending such marriages as have ceased to be worthy of the name.

The tendency to diminish the rigidity of marriage ties is being carried further, it may be added, than an increased legal facility for divorce can carry it. There is undoubtedly a tendency in our Western civilisation to recognise the existence of sexual relationships outside marriage altogether, always provided that such relationships are not for the procreation of children. It may be said that such extra-marital manifestations of the sexual life are no novelty. Prostitution has flourished in secret and even been defended in public, while what is called "seduction" has everywhere been taking place. But the novelty lies in the fact that both prostitution and seduction are diminishing. Prostitution is becoming less attractive and seduction less possible. The palmy days of prostitution (which seems to have begun as a religious rite) were before syphilis entered civilisation, and its prestige has been gradually falling ever since. Seduction in the legitimate sense of the word (as "seduced" is often merely the expression used by women of low social class to describe their first act of sexual intercourse) is only possible when the woman is unduly ignorant of the nature of sexual relations, and that state of affairs is coming to an end. But when prostitution and seduction are, so far as may be possible, eliminated, the objections to the formation of sexual relationships—in the absence of higher ethical or religious considerations and provided off-spring are not contemplated—largely fall away. There can be no doubt that this new condition is becoming appreciated by the younger generation. Young people of both sexes are now in a position to view a larger proportion of the facts involved than were open to the generations preceding them, and they are acquiring the courage to act in accordance with the facts. That means that many mistakes are being made, for the deepest facts of the sex life can only be learnt by experience, and experience can only come slowly. But it is perhaps better to make the mistakes of facing life than to make the mistakes of running away from life. For those mistakes may enrich and enlighten, while these are apt to prove futile. The paths of the sex life are beset by difficulties; but so is the whole of life. If we are to live in any true sense at all we are compelled to live dangerously.

A large proportion of the men and women of to-day form sexual relationships outside marriage—whether or not they ultimately lead to marriage—which they conceal, or seek to conceal, from the world. This has always been so[6]; what is new is the attitude taken towards such relationships, leading to the conception of the "companionate marriage," that is, an openly acknowledged and recognisable relationship less binding than ordinary marriage, though liable to become ordinary marriage should children be born. This conception has not been put forward as a method of relaxing morals, but rather of supporting them, since the open recognition of a kind of relationship which already exists secretly on a large scale cannot but be a steadying and ennobling influence.[7]

The preceding considerations represent conditions which are modifying marriage in our Western civilisation. But they are far from overthrowing marriage or threatening the life of the family. On the contrary, they help to strengthen them. It is the rigid institution that is broken; the institution that cannot change is dying. By its flexibility and its adaptation to changing conditions, the family reveals its stability and its power of growth.

But marriage, it may once more be repeated, rests fundamentally on biological instincts and the facts of constitutional organisation; it is not strictly an institution. The flexibility and the adaptation are limited, and if they sometimes seem extreme, that is simply because we happen to be dealing with individual cases of constitutional variation, such as we can statistically estimate. Even in Soviet Russia, where the legal flexibility of sexual unions has been carried to an extent unusual in the European world, the fundamental facts of human nature remain the same as well as the ordinary human valuations of those facts.

This seems to come out clearly in a recent study of "the psychology of the monandric and the polyandric woman in modern culture," that is to say in Moscow, by Professor Blonsky.[8] He finds that there are two types of women: the monan-

[6] Sexual intercourse outside marriage, as Malinowski truly remarks, is no "anomaly," nor does it contravene marriage. In prenuptial licence we even have, he adds, "an institutionalised method of arranging marriage by trial and error."

[7] M. Knight: "The Companionate and the Family," *Journal of Social Hygiene*, May, 1924. Judge Ben Lindsey, with his wide experience of social conditions, has vigorously advocated this conception in his *Companionate Marriage*, 1927.

[8] Pawel Petrovitch Blonsky: *Zeitschrift fur Sexualwissenschaft*, May, 1930.

dric woman, who is only drawn into serious relationship with one man, and the polyandric woman, who tends to form numerous relationships with men, either successively or simultaneously. There is, as we should expect, between these two types an intermediate group. The women in question were teachers, between the ages of thirty and forty, and they were investigated with the help of women, friends or pupils of Blonsky, themselves teachers, who had been intimately acquainted with them for some years. It was found that the monandric women were nearly twice as numerous as the polyandric women, and each type presented characters concerning which the observers (with whom Blonsky also is in complete agreement) concur to a remarkable extent. They all asserted that egoistic individualism was the most prominent characteristic of the polyandric woman; they tend to act on their own, making no attempt to win the support of their fellows, with whom they are often in conflict; they have no genuine talent for organisation, but at the same time wish to assert themselves, overestimating their own abilities (which do not carry them beyond the average in their own profession, though they may be highly accomplished), and are apt to show morbid susceptibility when they fail to secure recognition. They tend, indeed, to be restlessly nervous, and frequently pass on this nervosity to their offspring. At the same time they are often attractive, and they pay much attention to their appearance.

The monandric woman shows totally different traits. She is sincere, faithful, not externally formal, but devoted to her professional duties. (And Blonsky remarks incidentally that it is a mistake to suppose that the monandric woman is unfitted for public life, or that for such life the polyandric woman is better suited.) She possesses energetic organising capacity and is usually able to deal effectively with both her private and her public life, aided in this by the stability and balance of her character. She is guided less by vanity than by honour and the sense of her own inner worth. Blonsky concludes that the moral characteristics of the monandric woman are mostly positive, while those of the polyandric woman are mostly negative. As we are, he affirms, so we love; our way of love is not a thing in itself, but related in the most intimate manner to the whole of our character.

This analysis is instructive. It is interesting, that is, to find even under the revolutionised social conditions of Soviet Russia not only that the woman of what some would consider the old-fashioned type is still predominant, but that she is regarded with as much admiration as we might expect to find in a conservative country like France. It would almost seem indeed that the polyandric woman whom, in the opinion of some Western persons, Soviet conditions favour, is there unduly depreciated.

There is really more to be said for her than Blonsky is inclined to admit. That may in part be due to the fact that the investigators were women. Blonsky points out, however, that the depreciation of the polyandric women is shared by men, even the men who form temporary relationships with them, for men are inclined to look on such women as convenient means of satisfying sexual needs, simply as substitutes for prostitution, and feel for them no high regard. That, Blonsky considers, is an influence making for the degradation of polyandric women, whose life-courses are not usually happy. It is unnecessary to add that the monandric woman, who is peculiarly adapted for motherhood and family life, will not easily be deprived of that career.

So we still have, notwithstanding all the modifications that we can regard as within the limits of probability, the family persisting, essentially, in its primitive form: father, mother, offspring. The impulses that make these three units a trinity are all primordial: the desire of the parents for each other, the desire of each for the child, and the dependence of the child on its parents, rightly considered on both its parents, for even where there is no material need of a father there is yet a spiritual need.

It is interesting to observe that this trinity is so fundamental in human societies that it is even found in communities of a low degree of culture where ethnographers have independently given it this identical name, finding that by such peoples themselves the family is regarded as strictly a trinity, even when consisting of more than three persons. Radcliffe-Brown who, following Lyons, sets forth this conception, states that it "is found in a great many primitive societies, probably in all." In some such societies the family does not really exist until the birth of the first child, the relationship between husband and wife not being directly created by marriage but indirectly through the birth of the child. The conception of a trinity is sometimes preserved by regarding the children of a family as multiples of a single personality, and in a polygynous household by regarding the wives as multiples of one personality. Sometimes the family trinity is solidified by the imposition of a special taboo in which all three members share.[9]

It is true, that, in the supposed interests of the child, the

[9] A. R. Radcliffe-Brown: "Father, Mother, and Child," *Man*, Sept., 1926.

idea has been put forward (first of all by Plato in the famous fifth book of his *Republic*) that the infant should be removed from its natural parents and placed in the hands of nurses skilfully trained in all the science and art of modern hygiene in general and puericulture in particular. Certainly it is possible to find innumerable parents who are completely and lamentably ignorant of this science and this art. This may be especially so in those lands of Communistic tendency, like Soviet Russia, where the Platonic ideal is most commended. But to be content to leave the mothers in ignorance and to train up in the knowledge of the duties of maternity a body of women who are not intended to be mothers, except for other women's children, seems a perverted attempt to escape the difficulty. It is not calculated to benefit, and still less to render happy, the real mothers, the artificial mothers, or the children. An institution on so unreal a foundation cannot possibly compete with one on a sound biological basis which is just as susceptible to any necessary cultivation and development as the other. As Malinowski well says, "social and cultural influences always endorse and emphasise the original individuality of the biological fact." It is scarcely surprising that we find little indication that this artificial method is likely to be followed on any large scale, if at all. It seems only in place when we are concerned with motherless waifs and strays. The legitimate method of approaching the problem—as is constantly becoming more widely recognised—lies in training the real mothers, and, so far as possible, before they have begun to be mothers. In our world motherhood has ceased to be the inevitable fate of every woman who enters marriage and many who remain outside it. It may be said to have become a vocation. It is true that nearly every woman, at some period in her life, desires to become a mother, and that most men desire to become fathers, sometimes indeed without clearly realising that fatherhood implies motherhood and that it is a vastly more difficult task to be a mother than to be a father. But this is a vocation which not all who feel called to it ought to follow. Only those who are fitted by nature, and also by training, should attempt to follow it. In various countries now, and on an ever larger scale, efforts are being made to provide this training. The establishment of Schools for Mothers, in some countries facilitated by law, constitutes a notable step along this path.[10] In England Nursery Schools for the pre-school

[10] Dr. Miele of Ghent has sometimes been credited with initiating this step, which, however, naturally grew out of the insistence on puericulture by Budin and Pinard in France. An early pioneer in the establishment of Schools for Mothers seems to have been Dr. E. S. Goodhue, of California and Hawaii, who is still active in this field.

child are slowly increasing, and with most of them are formed Clubs for Mothers, which are readily attended and furnish advice and instruction to mothers in the care of children. By such measures it is found that the sense of parental responsibility is not diminished but increased.[11]

So far we have been viewing the family as a domestic fact. As such it is the central core of all human and even animal life. In the most primitive conditions, before any wide social bonds were formed, or any compact community existed, we must postulate the family, for we cannot conceive how any creature with the prolonged helpless infancy of human beings could otherwise survive in this dangerous world. But with the formation of communities, with the multiplication of social ties, the family ceases to be a merely domestic fact, and it is possible, and even probable, that the family became more complex in its relationships even at a fairly early period of human prehistory. It is certainly complex to-day among those peoples whom we are pleased to regard as "primitive."[12]

With the development of civilisation the form assumed by the family becomes again more simple and independent in appearance, but the family remains in an intimate relationship with the community to which it is constantly furnishing new members. Beyond its elementary domestic functions, the family thus necessarily enters into reciprocal functions of responsibility with the community. The community undertakes duties —which may vary to a wide extent—towards the family, and the family, in return, is called upon to contribute, to the best of its abilities, to the community. There are wide variations in the conception of the duties on either side, and this leads to-day to a frequent conflict in opinion and practice. On the one hand, there is the tendency to diminish the duties of the family and of the state towards each other to a minimum; on the other hand, the tendency to increase them to a maximum. The former tendency may be called Individualism, the latter Socialism. It is common for those who associate themselves with one of these tendencies to sneer at the other or denounce it as dangerous. From the social point of view, however, as is fairly obvious to an impartial observer, both tendencies are

[11] *Annual Report of the Chief Medical Officer of the Board of Education for 1928*, London, 1929.

[12] See, for instance, the fascinating books, based on intimate knowledge, of Professor Malinowski concerning the social and sexual life of the Trobriand Islanders of New Guinea. See especially his study of "Parenthood the Basis of Social Structure" (*The New Generation*, 1930), in which the two aspects of the human procreative institution, the marriage aspect and the social aspect, are admirably balanced.

necessary. A society without socialist impulses could not co-here; a society without individualist impulses could not survive. But with regard to the limits to be set to each group of impulses opinions are bound to vary. We may believe that with regard to many elementary requirements, of which all have an equal and common need—such as provisions of open spaces in cities, a pure water supply, and a sanitary system—the collective activity of the community is rightly invoked; and that in regard to religion, to opinion in general, and to the higher branches of education, a large scope must be left to the individual. But there are many spheres in which arguments clash. In this special question of the family, for instance, we may ask how far children are reared for their parents or for themselves, and how far for the community. And if, as we are bound to hold, children have a value as future members of the community, should the community, in addition to other services, contribute financially to the upbringing of the children? In this way we have the question of mothers' pensions.

It appears that the idea of "family endowment" was first put forward by Thomas Paine, that great fertilising genius whose suggestions on so many subjects, Utopian when he formed them, are now becoming embodied in our Western civilisation; and he was followed by Condorcet, who was also the pioneer in publicly advocating the use of contraceptive measures, for there is no opposition between birth control and family endowment. On the contrary, it may be said that the prevention of unwanted children and the proper care of wanted children (whether or not that should be aided by the State) are closely related measures.

There is still dispute as to whether children should be subsidised by the State, and although the principle is becoming widely transformed into practice, the implications of mothers' pensions (for it is generally held that the payment should go direct to the mother) are not yet always fully understood or realised. In France such assistance is given partially, especially to the families of State employees, in various ways, from anxiety to increase the growth of population on militaristic and other grounds, and with no regard to the quality of the children who may thus be produced; nearly half of the wage earners in France, it is said, now benefit in some way or other by these measures. Both in France and Belgium it seems to be found (*The Times*, March 26, 1930) that a system of family allowance slightly increases the number of children and diminishes infantile mortality. In Germany, modifications of the same methods, on a more socialistic basis, have been put into action but do not seem to flourish. In Russia, which aims at becoming a Paradise for children, mothers receive state aid and special funds. In Australia the problem of family endowment has been approached in a logical and systematic manner, and a government commission was set up to investigate its feasibility. Every political party is said to favour it, but the cost of a thoroughgoing scheme is so vast that no Australian state has yet ventured to set it up, except (1927), on a comprehensive but modest basis, New South Wales. New Zealand had previously adopted the plan on a small scale.

There are, however, many convinced opponents to any scheme of this kind. They hold, on the one hand, that there is not the slightest need to assist maternity since the population is nearly everywhere increasing already at too rapid a rate, and, even if there appeared to be such need, maternity is not a suitable function for State endowment, since it is not essential to a woman's life to become a mother, and there are ample recompenses in maternity itself. Even among those who are not opposed to a State subsidy there is severe criticism of the motives and methods of the schemes usually adopted or proposed. Nationalistic and militaristic motives are here out of place, nor can they often appeal to the mothers it is proposed to assist. On the other hand, the real interests of the community demand a discriminate selection of population, and for the State to offer to assist the procreation not merely of the highest and best—who scarcely need such assistance—but the lowest and worst, is to stultify itself and to work for its own decadence. A wiser and more reasoned scheme than has yet been devised is needed, if the present tendency to maternal endowment is to prove of substantial benefit to the community.[13]

In England, even the Labour party, notwithstanding its strong Socialist trend, has not tried to carry out, or so much as put on its programme, any system of family allowance, or any alternative system of greatly increased social services. The question has been carefully investigated by a joint committee

[13] The cause of family endowment is ably and persuasively stated, and the present position of such schemes in various countries set forth in detail, by Miss Eleanor Rathbone in her *Disinherited Family* and *Ethics and Economics*, 1927. She fails to insist adequately on the need of birth control and eugenical safeguards, but argues that to help the mother is to aid "orderly and self-respecting living which is the best cure for indiscriminate and dysgenic breeding." She considers that family aid in France has done nothing to increase the birth-rate, though introduced for that purpose, and points out that grants may be limited to the early children of the family and refused altogether where the heredity is bad. An argument on which she forcibly insists is that equal payment to men and women for equal work is not practicable unless in association with family endowment.

of the Labour party and the Trades Union Congress, and it was felt that the enormous sums required might have the effect of dislocating the wage system, and that even the simplest alternative of increasing the cost of social services by the one hundred million pounds that would be required might have an unfavourable reaction on the wage rates of industry. To the wisest Labour leaders the experiment still seems too hazardous.[14]

When the question of mothers' pensions arises, and the function of the community in supplying financial aid towards the production of children, we are faced by a problem which is often ignored when this measure is adopted or advocated. That is the problem of how far the community really needs its production of children to be subsidised, and how far it is desirable to afford that aid without regard to the probable quality of the children produced. The measures adopted or advocated for maintaining or increasing the population of a state have so far been confused, unintelligent, and even maleficent. The old feverish anxiety to increase the population at all costs has ceased to be reasonable. The growth of the world's population has become during the past century so enormously rapid, being doubled every hundred years, that we are approaching a period when the strongest country will be that which increases most slowly or not at all.[15] Even among the nations concerned in the Great War, Russia, with the largest population and the highest birth-rate, was almost the first to succumb, for the size of a population is not the measure of its strength. The two countries of the Old World which to-day display the greatest anxiety to stimulate their own growth in population, France and Italy, both illustrate the methods which should not be adopted. In France the growth of the population is small, but the country has reaped many benefits from that slow growth, which is not, however, due to a low birth-rate but to a high rate of infantile mortality. Yet the official policy of France is directed much less to the task of better caring for the children born than to the encouragement, by all sorts of small benefits,

[14] *The Times*, March 10, 1930.

[15] The whole question of the rapid growth of population in modern times and its bearing on the future of the world is discussed in a masterly manner by Professor E. M. East, *Mankind at the Crossroads*, 1924. For a more recent discussion of fundamental population problems from various points of view, by leading scientific authorities of Europe and America, see *Proceedings of the World Population Conference*, 1927, edited by Margaret Sanger. And for a clear and authoritative statement, in a concise form, see Sir George Knibbs, "The Fundamental Elements of the Problems of Population and Migration," *Eugenics Review*, Jan., 1928; he concludes that the great problem before Man now is "how best to *control the rate at which he multiplies.*"

of still more births, without any regard for the quality of the children thus to be born. In Italy, where the rate of population growth is already high, the energetic encouragement to further increase for which the Fascist government is responsible can only lead to internal suffering and discontent or to external trouble, due to difficulties with other countries refusing to accept immigrants and to the resulting temptation to risk war, which form of old has been the method for arresting internal rebellion and reducing superfluous populations. A wiser course is being pursued in the New World. The United States, in view of the growing perfection of technical processes and the increasing tendency to unemployment, realises that the desirable limits of population are being reached, and is slackening its own rate of growth (it once doubled its population in twenty-three years), and excluding all but a small proportion of foreign immigrant peoples, whose rates of increase are usually higher than its own. To the United States thus belongs the honour of being first among great nations to assert, virtually, the international importance of birth control. In Australia, also, though in a less definitely formulated manner, the same attitude prevails, and while internal expansion has not yet reached its limits, although at the present rate of increase it is rapidly drawing near them, the tendency is now towards hostility to immigration.

We thus approach the problem of the desirable size of the family. It is a problem which has only in recent years become practical. In old days children were "given by God," and God who gave them often took them back again with extreme rapidity. The population was practically stationary, and yet families were frequently of enormous size. Many were called into the world, but few were chosen to live. In old family records we see two or even three brothers of the same name. "John" was christened and "John" died, so the name was available for a later "John," and, if he too died, for a third. Nowadays the progress of medicine and hygiene has rendered life safer; when a child is born there is a reasonable probability that he will live, and we can afford to be more economical in child production. The old methods, indeed, become impracticable; they produced too large an excess of population.[16] If we desire to retain that almost stationary population which has, on the whole, been normal for mankind, we can no longer

[16] The old methods are not extinct. In 1927 Friedjung gave the history of 100 working-class women of Vienna who had borne six or more children, the average being over ten. But only about half the children were alive a few years after birth; one mother lost sixteen out of twenty-four children born alive, and many others more than half.

effect it by the method of large gross production and small net results.

The optimum number of children in a family has often been exaggerated, especially by those who have not realised how greatly in modern times the conditions of life have changed in the direction of diminishing wastage. Thus Grotjahn in Germany has stated that an average of 3.8 children is required per marriage in order to maintain the population in equilibrium. But this is, as a general rule, certainly too high. In England, it is calculated, an average of about 2.5 children per marriage now amply suffices to do more than maintain a stationary population, by ensuring a considerable increase. The optimum size of the family now therefore oscillates between two and three. To many marriages we find more children, and to many we find fewer or none.

We cannot yet attempt to calculate all the benefits arising to the community from the diminution in the size of the family which has now become possible owing to new hygienic and medical conquests in the economy of life. There is far more in it than the simple ascent to a higher level of well-being inevitably resulting from a diminution of our excessive procreation, our excessive diseases, and our excessive deaths. The family has been called the "unit of civilisation."[17] But in so far as the family is merely an isolated unit, civilisation still remains primitive. It is by its capacity for inter-penetrating contacts with the community that family and community are alike enabled to develop a fine civilisation. It is largely because the family has been so much a self-centred unit, absorbed in the constant stress and strain of self-reproduction, that our civilisation is still, on the whole, so crude. An important factor in this development is the liberation of women who are mothers from an undue absorption in maternal functions. It is estimated that a healthy woman in a healthy environment, when left to

---

[17] In using this old phrase I by no means wish to imply that I unconditionally accept it. There is excellent reason for regarding the family as the *biological* unit, and, as such, essential and permanent. But there is no such good reason for considering the family as the sole *cultural* unit. Civilisation needs more than the family before it can be built up. It is inconceivable without assuming the close interaction of a whole community. Indeed, the family itself as a trinity seems only to become a conscious unit in relation to a realised community. That may be indicated by the word "family" itself, which in Latin, and even in English law and custom, does not refer to the biological trinity. (This is pointed out in a paper by Lord Raglan, *Man*, Jan., 1931.) The "familia" was the whole number of slaves belonging to one master, and was therefore a small community. In many languages there is no word for the family as a trinity. The family is clearly the biological unit, but, as such, it may be originally unconscious; it is not strictly an "institution," and we must be cautious in defining its cultural relationship to the systematised clan.

nature, produces on an average fifteen children. Apart from the fact that the world nowadays has no use for such women, it is obvious that a woman whose life was thus occupied had little time or strength left over for the wider functions of social life. She could not exercise a profession, and she could not bring her knowledge and experience to bear on the life of the world outside her own home. Moreover, her knowledge and experience were so limited from lack of contact with that larger world that, unless rarely gifted, she was not fitted even to conduct her small domestic life wisely. The affairs of the world, so far as women are concerned, were left to the unmarried, often, by the limitation on another side of their experience, narrow and prejudiced, and to a few fine exceptional women who, when the period of sexual activity was over, still had the strength and ability for wider activities. These conditions are responsible for the severe criticisms (some I have already quoted) mistakenly directed against the activities of women in the family life of the community, mistakenly because it is not women, but a special and untypical class of women, whose activities arouse this criticism.

The proper fulfilment of all that maternity means involves, even for the average 2.5 children, the devotion of a large slice of a woman's life. But it is very far from demanding the whole of it, and by a due appointment of her time and energy between her family and the world a woman may enrich both to an extent in previous times impossible. In Russia, where the social equality of women is established in accordance with the original intention of Lenin, who declared that "every kitchen maid must learn to rule the State," it is found practicable for women to work and even to occupy high posts without prohibiting maternity, the woman being released from work and provided for by the State for two months before and two months after her confinement, assisted in her maternal duties by communal nurseries and kindergartens, and not mulcted in salary for the time spent in suckling her infant. That is a step, however inadequate, in the right direction. The obstacles that in many countries are only slowly being overcome are due less to any inherent difficulty in combining work and motherhood than to effete traditions and blind prejudices.

This is well illustrated in the special and important case of teachers. A large proportion of teachers are to-day women, often not only for children of their own sex but for boys. There cannot be the smallest doubt that women who have had sex experience of their own and children of their own are incomparably better fitted to deal with the special difficulties of children than those who have not. A few gifted women may be found who can make up for personal inexperience by insight and artificially acquired knowledge, but they are rare exceptions. This is a fact that should be fairly obvious even to one who knew nothing about schools and education. But it becomes conspicuous when we observe the actual conditions that prevail. The teacher who has had children of her own is seen to possess an almost instinctive comprehension of children which is seldom present in her unmarried colleagues. Their scholastic attainments may be of the highest, and yet they may be unable to meet even the slightest emergencies of child life, themselves little more than children, and sometimes—indeed often—more ignorant of the facts of human life, and more afraid of them, than are their pupils, whom they are supposed to be competent to "educate." Children to-day are apt to be acute critics of the abilities of their teachers, and if children had a voice in the selection of teachers the level of education would certainly soon be raised. At present a large majority of elementary teachers (in England nearly 80 per cent.), and a considerable proportion in secondary schools, are women. Yet how many of them are encouraged by the official authorities, or even allowed, to acquire, in or out of marriage, the essential experiences of sexual pleasure and motherhood? In spite of the recent progress of science, the depths of human imbecility have not yet been plumbed.

But the family is not only a domestic question, not only a social question, as the almost tragic failure to recognise it in the great function of education brings home to us. It is, finally, a racial question. The well-being of the individual in the home, his due equipment in the community, and, ultimately, his fate in the species, must rest on the sound organisation of the family. The increasing recognition of this fact on a scientific foundation is one of the most notable features of our Western civilisation.

In an almost instinctive and unconscious manner it has been recognised and acted on ever since human society became organised. Equally among savages and among the founders of the classic cultures of Greece and Rome, from whom we inherit so much, it was recognised, without question and without discussion, that the population must sometimes be restricted, and that only the best children should be allowed to live. The method of infanticide has everywhere been the most usual method of attaining this end.[18] Then a new ideal, sup-

[18] The various methods which Man throughout his history has practised in order to reach the ends now possible through birth control and eugenics are fully set forth by Professor Carr-Saunders in his elaborate work, *The Population Problem.*

ported by Christianity and emphasising the value of every human being as a soul, began to be developed, and finally to be carried out in an extreme form, owing to the modern advances in medicine and hygiene. That movement has meant much for the growth of human sympathy and solidarity. But it was unbalanced, for it failed to perceive the precious elements that had been lost in the decay of the earlier ideal. Our civilisation to-day is marked by an increased perception of the fundamental conditions of racial well-being. We have gained the ability and the will to cherish every human creature, however feeble, that is brought into the world. But we also see the cruelty of bringing into the world human creatures that are maimed, physically or spiritually, merely that we may prolong or alleviate their sufferings. And we realise how heavy is the burden that we thus place on the race, not only of to-day but of to-morrow, by cherishing the feeblest specimens of humanity and enabling them to increase and multiply. We further realise—and that is our main discovery—that it is unnecessary. The advance in medicine and hygiene which enables us to preserve the defective members of our kind also enables us to prevent, in large measure, their production, by methods which, unlike those practised in the early world, are humane.[19]

There are two lines along which these measures for the eugenic good of the race are being embodied in our general life: by legislation and by education. The first has often been resorted to, because for the ordinary mind it is the easier. But it is futile without the second. Many eugenical laws have been passed, especially in the United States, merely to be evaded or become a dead letter because they are not in accordance with the general sentiment of the community. On the other hand, when a line of action is spontaneously carried out by the community without penal sanction, legislation became unnecessary, save ultimately in order to whip into line a small recalcitrant minority. It is by the growth of scientific knowledge, by the spread of education, and by an increased sense of personal responsibility—all now slowly permeating civilised communities—that alone we can expect any sound advance in the eugenic field. By a reasonable regard for the probabilities of heredity, and a well-directed attention to personal fitness or unfitness for paternity or maternity, we are moving, even though at present slowly, in the right direction. Certificates of

[19] For the history of contraception, see M. C. Stopes, *Contraception: Its Theory and Practice*, 2d. ed., London, 1928, and for discussion of all its aspects—medical, eugenic, religious, moral and international—see *Proceedings of the Sixth International Neo-Malthusian and Birth Control Conference*, edited by Margaret Sanger, New York, 1926.

fitness for marriage—more accurately for fatherhood and motherhood—are now actively advocated or projected in various countries.[20] But they cannot be effectively introduced by legislation; they must first become the imperative demand of each individual for himself and herself, and his or her partner. When they become that, all is effected that we need trouble about, and legislation becomes a matter of comparative indifference, except to set the seal on a social custom of the first importance for the purification of the race.

It used sometimes to be asked: What has posterity done for me that I should do anything for posterity? The question was wrongly put. "Posterity" is only another name for Mankind, and when we pose the question rightly there can be no dispute about the answer. If we put aside the part that belongs to Nature or to God, we owe everything to Mankind. All that we are, and all that we possess in civilisation, we owe to the everlasting aspiration and struggle of Mankind before us, and to the slow accumulation of knowledge and art on the topmost level of which we now stand. Our immense debt to Mankind in the past can only be repaid to Mankind in the future. It is our privilege, if we do not regard it as our duty, to pass on, in ever finer shapes, the great traditions which have been handed to us.

These traditions in the matter of the procreation of the race—we may repeat at the end what I said at the beginning—take the form generally termed *marriage*. It is a form which from the first has been constantly varying its shape, but its most frequent shape has been throughout that of father, mother, and child, all three which units, as well as the community to which they belong, have generally found it suits them well to continue through the early life of the child, while even when the offspring is able to take care of itself the two parents have frequently found it to be to their own comfort and joy to continue living together. Here we have, in a fairly permanent form, marriage, even if by no means necessarily indissoluble, the family, and the home, even if by no means

---

[20] See, for instance, the *World's Health*, in which the question of prenuptial medical examinations has frequently been discussed, as in a paper by Professor J. A. Lopez del Valle, Sept., 1927. Mrs. Sidonie Gruenberg stated in 1930 that there are in the United States alone now sixty-one national, State, and private educational organisations concerned with parental education (*Journal of Social Hygiene*, March, 1930). The churches are also giving attention to the matter, and at a conference of the Ministers' Association on Marriage and the Home, held in Buffalo, in 1930, it was resolved to urge on theological seminaries a thorough training of divinity students in mental hygiene, family case work, and sex instruction. The general establishment, on a combined medical and religious basis, of Marriage and Home clinics was also advocated.

hermetically closed. For the evil of the home has been, in part, that it was closed to currents of fresh air, and in part that we had too much of it; of precious things one must not have too much.

All these related phenomena—marriage, the family, the home—have been in recent years, as we know, the subject of fierce and brilliant attack. As I write, there comes into my hand a little book by Dr. Eden Paul (containing much with which all may heartily agree) where I find it stated that "it is almost a commonplace to say that such an institution as the family is not necessarily a permanent part of human social life," and that soon "marriage in the present meaning of the word as the foundation of family life will have ceased to exist." [21]

I will not again repeat that the variations, ancient or modern, in marriage, the family, or the home do not in the slightest degree indicate any destruction of any of them; that the very conditions which Dr. Eden Paul and others regard as disrupting and undermining marriage and the family are really calculated to support and stabilise both; and that, as a matter of fact, so far from any decay of marriage being visible, all precise and reliable evidence points in the opposite direction.

It is enough to refer to so great an authority as Professor Malinowski, who, in the already quoted study of "Parenthood the Basis of Social Structure," has so luminously shown that the procreative institution of mankind is many-sided and welds all the facts of sexuality, marriage, family and clanship into "one integral institution," without abolishing any, however great the scope left for flexibility. From a very difficult point of departure Keyserling comes to a similar conclusion. When writing from Japan in his *Travel Diary of a Philosopher*, and referring with approval to the growing sexual freedom of our West and the increasing ability of women to follow their own personal law, he adds: "The old forms of social life will not on this account become extinct but will continue to exist as before; they will in fact hardly suffer even quantitatively." And writing in a more popular style, Professor Sapir of Chicago, while quite willing to sweep away the family in its old form, says that when we have recovered from our dizziness at its apparent disappearance and our gasps of horror have subsided, and we open our eyes again, "the family will be seen to be still there, a little cleaner, a little more truthful, a little happier." [22]

[21] Eden Paul, *Chronos or the Future of the Family*, 1930, pp. 5, 44.

[22] E. Sapir, "What Is the Family Still Good For?" *Journal of Social Hygiene*, Dec., 1930.

We may observe the progress now being made in the renovation of marriage and the family if we note what is taking place in Soviet Russia, where we find an immense social laboratory, highly instructive for our civilisation to-day. No doubt there are political and economic matters for which most people of the West would regard Russia as the last place to seek inspiration. But that aversion cannot be brought into action where social matters are concerned. Here, in the opinion of the most competent judges from other lands—those whose knowledge of the language and familiarity with the corresponding institutions of other countries best entitle them to speak—much has been attained that the rest of the world is still only striving to attain. The progress reached is along our lines, but it has gone ahead of us.[23] There has been an erroneous idea abroad in the world that the Bolsheviks believe in sexual intemperance and promiscuity in sex relations, an idea no doubt based on the chaos which inevitably resulted at first when the new regime was so suddenly inaugurated. That disorder much distressed Lenin himself, who was entirely opposed to promiscuity and all merely physical indulgence, and held that the highest human elements entered the love relationship. It is Lenin's doctrine which now permeates Soviet society. This doctrine, maintained by the young men and women of Russia to-day, Dr. Yarros describes as "sincerely idealistic." Indeed, one might add that so far from there being, as some people imagine, too little idealism in Russia to-day, there is probably too much, and of too fanatical a sort, more, for instance, than is now frequently manifested, as regards sex relationships, in America. The Bolsheviks, as "social idealists," tend to minimise sex as an important part of life indeed, but still only a part. There is complete facility of divorce, but, as in the countries of the West where divorce most tends to prevail, that is a purifying rather than a corrupting influence on marriage, and in Russia the majority of people still prefer the formal civil union to the freer relationships which also are recognised, nor is any effort made to separate children from their parents. It is felt that in the past the family has been too much an enclosed unit, but that is what so many of us are feeling also in the West. Dr. Reynolds similarly could see no evidence of any break-up of the family as a permanent institution in Russia, though, on account of the housing difficulty, a certain

[23] See a notable paper by Rachelle S. Yarros, M.D., of Chicago, on "Social Hygiene Observations in Soviet Russia," published in the *Journal of Social Hygiene*, Nov., 1930; also an article in the same number by Ralph A. Reynolds, M.D., on "Social Hygiene in Soviet Russia," and an interesting sketch of personal impressions by Scott Nearing, "The Child in Soviet Russia," *The New Generation*, p. 232.

amount of communal family life exists, while there is immense
development of the hygienic, educational, and recreational elements. Among the peasantry the new laws have had little
effect at all on the stability of marriage. Scott Nearing similarly writes, after a visit, that "the family in the Soviet Union
impresses the visitor as being very much like the family anywhere else in Central or Western Europe." Thus, on the most
advanced practical side, the marriage situation to-day presents
an aspect harmonious with that which it has long presented
in the West on its more theoretical aspect.

Among the writers of to-day who have most broadly and
most judiciously approached these questions, it is easy to find
a recognition of that aspect.[24] Thus Walter Lippmann, in a
lucidly written book which has found a wide and appreciative
audience, while considering that the difficulty of a successful
marriage in the modern world has been doubled, and that in
the future there will be no compulsion on sexual unions except
the inner compulsion to find a true adjustment, still holds that
"the convention of marriage, when it is clarified by insight into
reality, is likely to be the hypothesis upon which men and
women will ordinarily proceed."[25] Similarly Mary Messer, in
her historic sketch *The Family in the Making,* concludes that
the falling away of the outworn conventions of marriage still
leaves a form admitting of the highest measure of freedom
and supporting rather than constricting the rich life of to-day.
From a very different standpoint, that of a Freudian psycho-
analyst of the more cautious and balanced sort, Flügel, in a
thoughtful psychological study of the family, concludes that
not only are marriage institutions so deeply rooted in Man's
nature as to be essential, but that, in spite of their rather
archaic character, "it is almost certain that they still perform
a necessary and beneficial part in the process of psychical development—a part for which no adequate substitute could
easily be found."[26]

Flügel, it may be seen, would agree with those students of
early institutions who regard marriage, whatever its various
forms, as "archaic." The investigators who maintain the view
that marriage is somehow less primitive in origin are even
more convinced of its immense present and future importance.
Thus F. Müller-Lyer, who held that the clan so dominated
primitive man that the family, though existent, was unim-

[24] For a full statement of this position, as it appears to me, I may refer
to "The History of Marriage," in Vol. VII of my *Studies in the Psychology of Sex,* 1929, pp. 508-532.

[25] W. Lippmann, *A Preface to Morals,* 1929, p. 312.

[26] J. C. Flügel, *The Psycho-Analytic Study of the Family,* 1921, p. 220.

portant, and sexual relationships polygamous, yet proclaimed (in his *Phasen der Liebe,* translated under the title of *The Evolution of Modern Marriage*) a great future for sexual unions when men and women can face each other in equal economic independence and all motives for marriage have fallen into the background, with the exception of love, which "will be more and more the only determining motive that can induce a man and woman to deny their freedom and bind themselves permanently to one another." We may not regard love as the self-sufficient motive for marriage in so far as marriage involves procreation. Yet if the foundation of marriage seems so solid, even to one who regards it as a denial of freedom and a bondage, how much more for those who find in it no such denial and no such bondage!

Chapter 13

THE FUNCTION OF TABOOS

WHEN PEOPLE TALK NOWADAYS of the social aspects of modern life, and especially of its sexual aspects, they are sure to refer to what they call the disappearance of taboos. They proceed to enumerate a number of things which in our society were formerly forbidden (and presumably not done) and now are not forbidden, together with a corresponding list of things which were formerly prescribed (and presumably carried out) but now are regarded as unnecessary, indifferent, or even undesirable, to use no stronger term.

It seems true to anyone whose memory goes back for half a century that these people may be justified in their statements, and as one who has sometimes been execrated or eulogised for playing a part in the change I have no wish to deny its existence. It even seems to me that the time has come for taking a broad view of this change. I think I am competent to take that view, for my attitude is really impartial, since if, on the one hand, I had done my best to destroy some taboos, on the other, I not only have a firm faith in taboos, but I regard them as absolutely an indestructible element of social life, and not of human life alone.

A taboo, speaking roughly, simply indicates something that is "not done." [1] The reason why it is not done may be, and often is, unknown to those who observe the taboo. So that all sorts of reasons—often very unreasonable reasons—are invented to explain the taboo. But below the surface there always are reasons for taboos. Among wild birds in a special phase of bird-existence it is taboo to remain close to human beings. That taboo is strictly analogous to human

[1] See the article "Tabu," by R. R. Marett, in Hastings' *Encyclopedia of Religion and Ethics*. "Taboo" was a word first met with by Captain Cook at the island of Tonga in 1777, as meaning "things not to be touched," though Cook clearly understood and expressed the more comprehensive meanings of the term, and that it was both spiritual and temporal in its nature and effects.

taboos; it is an adopted custom. It is not found everywhere among birds. When men first visit virgin islands of the southern seas there are birds who do not regard human beings as taboo. The taboo is introduced later when human beings have become destructive to the bird society. It is, of course, completely unnecessary to be aware of the reason for the taboo, and if birds ever acquired speculative minds they would invent reasons. That is, as we know, exactly what human societies do. The distinction of human taboos lies largely in their high imaginativeness, alike as regards their nature and the supposed reasons assigned for them, and in the comparative swiftness with which they may change.

Yet taboos remain as essential in human life as in life generally. They are a part of tradition, and it is difficult to say that tradition, though always growing and changing, is anywhere non-existent or that life would be possible without it. Among lower forms of life we commonly talk of an adaptation to the environment. The adoption of a taboo, whether or not by modifying it, is exactly such an adaptation to the environment, in accordance with tradition.[2] In the British Isles it is usually taboo for men and women to go about naked. But it is not invariably so. In the seventeenth century, as Fynes Moryson testifies, high-born ladies could go about naked in some districts of Ireland, and, as Pepys testifies, occasional eccentric individuals could do so even in the streets of London. It is quite likely that this taboo will shift again—it is indeed already beginning to do so—and become less stringent. Taboos are constantly liable to shift backwards and forwards over the threshold between prohibition and permission. We witness similar shifting taboos in Nature, and it might not be too fanciful to trace them even in the plant world. We are often so obsessed by our own modes of activity that we fail to

---

[2] Taboos, as thus understood, correspond to what Walter Lippmann, in his remarkable and in many ways admirable *Preface to Morals*, 1929, less happily terms "conventions." "Although it may be," he states (p. 300), "that no convention is any longer coercive, conventions remain, are adapted, revised, and debated. They embody the considered results of experience: perhaps the experience of a lonely pioneer or perhaps the collective experience of the dominant members of a community. In any event they are as necessary to a society which recognises no authority as to one which does. In the modern world the function of conventions is to declare the meaning of experience. Just because the rules of sexual conduct by authority is dissolving, the need of conventions which will guide conduct is increasing." While the term "convention" brings out some aspects of taboo, it fails to indicate the quasi-religious element which gives the weight of a taboo (which cannot be violated so easily and cheerfully as a convention), and it conceals the fact that new taboos, while more in accordance with new social conditions, are not different in nature and quality from the outworn taboos made authoritative by tradition.

realise that we are, after all, a part of Nature and that the same movements which occur in us also occur, however widely different the forms, in other vital phenomena.

Unthinking people sometimes talk as though taboos were effete relics of the past which it is in our power to cast away altogether. A little reflection might serve to show not only that they are far too numerous and too deeply rooted to be torn up at will, but that we should be in a sad case without them; indeed, that human society could not survive their loss. It is certain that property—which from neolithic times and no doubt earlier has been an important element of human society—could not exist without the taboo against stealing. Law and the police struggle against the violations of that taboo; but they do so very ineffectually; they could not do it at all in the absence of the taboo, for we all of us every day possess the opportunity to steal. Among savages nearly everywhere it is taboo which binds the members of the clan together and ensures that they shall behave one to another in a decently social manner.[3] We have lost the word, but we have the bond under other names. To-day, a distinguished English lawyer, Lord Buckmaster, calls it "social opinion." He is strongly opposed to capital punishment and to any form of vengeance wreaked on the criminal. "It is my belief," he said, giving evidence before a Select Committee of the House of Commons (March 26, 1930), "that the real deterrent against crime is social opinion. It is not the police nor the laws. It is the healthy public opinion which affects and surrounds a man from his youth." In other words, it is the existence of taboos.

It is indeed only the existence of such taboos which enables us to possess any sacredness of personality at all. It is taboos that preserve our more refined sensibilities from the people who wipe their mouths with the tablecloth and blow their noses with the serviette, and it is taboos that preserve us from being murdered outright. If we were objects of complete indifference to our fellows, or of no more concern than stones or trees, we should soon be driven up to or over the verge of suicide. Life is livable because we know that wherever we go most of the people we meet will be restrained in their

---

[3] The word "savagery," now that we know more about savages, is losing its old meaning. For the most part, as Dr. Haddon, who has known them well, remarks, "savages are gentlemen." Among the Papuans, K. E. Williams, who has specially studied their moral code (*Orokaiva Society,* Chapter XVIII, 1930), finds no supernatural sanction of morality; the fear of hurting the feelings of one's fellow men is the real "moral sanction," though it is associated with, as minor motives, the fear of retaliation, and still more, the fear of public reprobation. Williams terms it "the sympathetic sanction," as it involves a constant consideration for all the members of one's "sympathy-group."

actions towards us by an almost instinctive network of taboos. We know that they will allow us the same or nearly the same degree of freedom and privilege that they claim for themselves; if we take our place in a queue at a railway station or a theatre they will not thrust themselves in front of us; if we claim a seat by placing our suitcase on it they will not fling the article aside and place themselves there; if they desire to perform any of the intimate natural excretory functions which are commonly regarded as disgusting they will not spontaneously do it before our faces; if—to come to the sphere with which taboos are to-day for most persons specially associated —they chance to experience an impulse of sexual attraction they will not lay lustful hands on us but either conceal their feeling or strive to find delicate methods of expressing it. No published laws and regulations—even when such exist—are needed to restrain them. They are held back by almost instinctive taboos.[4]

The pronounced growth of a new taboo in a whole nation is seen in the change of attitude towards drunkenness which has taken place in England during the lifetime of those past middle age, and clearly demonstrated alike by the statistics of the consumption of alcohol and police-court convictions for drunkenness. Among the upper classes drunkenness had disappeared as a prominent social phenomenon at the beginning of the nineteenth century. It was in the previous century that a great statesman like Pitt could openly relieve himself of the results of excessive drink by going behind the Speaker's chair in Parliament to vomit, and that men of good society after dinner, when the ladies had retired, could drink port till they fell beneath the table. But such scenes among the populace in the streets of that country, as depicted by Hogarth, were much slower to pass away. Within living memory, however, there has been a great change in this respect among the lower social classes, and those of us who knew London fifty years ago can bear witness to the frequency of the signs of drunkenness then compared with their rarity now. The change is reflected in police-court convictions for drunkenness; comparing even so recent a year as 1905 with

---

[4] I would endorse the observations recently made in a leading article by the London *Times:* "Manners, especially among the young, did indeed incline to be rough and ready as the too much and too little discipline of the War time took to shaking down together; but the patient and self-effacing elder seems now to be reaping his reward in the new gentleness, new consideration, new attention to social forms and refinements of behaviour which he cannot help observing among his young acquaintance. As for their morals, it is certain that any man who was even suspected of committing the offences of which the Restoration gallants and the Regency bucks made a boast would be cut by everyone."

1928, there was a drop of 73 per cent. in the convictions during those twenty-three years. To some extent the change is due to diminished facilities for obtaining drink, and its higher price. The young man of to-day has a new social ideal; he does not want to spend his evenings in a public house, like the men of an elder generation now dying out; "he puts on a nice suit of clothes," as an ex-chief constable of police remarks, "and nicely cleaned boots, with the other accessories of a tidy turnout, and takes his young lady to cinema, dance, or wherever fancy may lead them; she is smartly dressed, and he has to live up to her standard. The shillings that used to go in drink are saved up for clothes and to spend on amusement; and the young man is so far different from his predecessor of another generation that he has acquired the necessary amount of self-respect to feel it a disgrace to be seen drunk." In other words, a new taboo has come into existence.

Such taboos are typical in our own society and are cherished even by the person who professes the strongest contempt for taboos, if he is a fairly normal member of our society. We may even say that he is—whether or not he knows it—actually engaged in increasing and strengthening them. The whole tendency of our society to-day is to increase and strengthen the taboos which preserve the freedom and enlarge the activities of the individual in moving about in a civilised environment. Several even of those taboos which I have just mentioned as to-day "almost instinctive" had little or no force half a century ago; I can myself recall the time when some of them had not come into being, or were not commonly recognised, and I can therefore realise the benefits they confer. There is no doubt that the growth of urban life and the associated collectivistic activities which are for the benefit of all, but belong to no individual, demand for their full enjoyment a system of taboos, either automatic and instinctive or self-imposed by an effort of discipline. It is only so that the municipal organisation of books and pictures and music and gardens and fountains, and all the privileges and the conveniences of urban life, become possible. The individual in whom the taboos necessary for such organisation are not either automatic or self-imposed are an anti-social individual, and his elimination would be for our benefit. For while some of the taboos in question are objectified in rules and regulations with penalties for their violation, many could not be carried out by force, even with an army of officials, unless supported by the general taboo-observance of the community.

The recognition of the permanence of the taboo-observing impulse, and the constant tendency to develop new taboos, may enable us to face with calmness the counterbalancing fact of the falling away of taboos which have served their purpose and are no longer needed under changed social conditions. That is a process always going on, and in some spheres it has during recent years moved with unusual rapidity. The reality of the changes that have thus taken place, whether they are to be approved or condemned, we may thus all accept. As often happens, it is small things— small yet significant—which enable us to grasp the reality of change. When we read Pepys's *Diary* it is the minute points which fascinate us, for they enable us to realise profound differences in the attitude of seventeenth-century people compared with our own; as when Pepys found lice in a strange bed he slept in, "which made us merry." I always recall as significant (so that I noted it in my *Impressions and Comments* for June 15, 1918) the first occasion on which I observed a young woman in a London street pausing a moment to adjust her stocking without embarrassment and without going a step out of her way. I had been brought up in the Victorian period when, if a woman even of the poorest class (though, for the matter of that, it is women of low social class who are most prudish) wished to pull up her stocking, she retired into the darkest alley she could find with her face to the wall. The difference is typical of a revolutionary change in the whole attitude of women.

That was wartime, and the Great War undoubtedly had its influence in the movement we are here considering, not indeed by generating but by accelerating it. All the social changes which were witnessed during the war in the belligerent countries would have taken place without it. But they would have taken place more gradually and unevenly, not in so dramatic and spectacular a shape.

The whole series of changes, so far as women have been concerned—and it is in connection with women that the violated taboos have caused most uproar—were the outcome of a single movement: the movement for making women the companions of men. They were not that in mediæval theory; woman for that theory was either above man or below him; as Miss Eileen Power remarks, she was Janus-faced: in one of her aspects she was Mary, the mother of God and the Saviour of men; in the other, Eve, the seducer of man and the cause of all his woe. By the nineteenth century this theory had become reduced to an empty shell of convention, but it still retained influence, even though within the shell new conceptions were germinating and causing it to crack.

The woman moulded according to these new conceptions is no longer the angel-devil which her predecessor seemed to imaginative eyes, but obviously made to be—as witnessed even by her hair and her skirts and the simple fashion of her garments—the social equal and companion of man, whether in work or play, even perhaps the play of sex.

That has meant the falling away not only of deliberately broken taboos, but of a greater number that have disappeared almost unconsciously and automatically. The girl who without thought stopped in the middle of the pavement to adjust her stocking was the typical pioneering figure. She was introducing a new kind of simple directness into life, a new sort of modesty, a new courage. Naturally, it is in the sphere of sexual emotions and habits that these attributes become most conspicuous, for men and even more for women, whose sphere is by constitution so largely that of sex, whether for good or evil. The new freedom and directness are obviously shown in public speech and the world of journalism. In private speech, of course, things have always been spoken of—often ignorantly and unwholesomely, and seldom between people of opposite sex even when married to each other—which were regarded as indecorous to speak of in public, even when they were of most vital concern to society. Venereal disease is such a subject. It concerns everyone, because, however austerely the individual may live, he or she is always liable to come into contact with a venereally infected person or even to enter into a lifelong relationship with such a person and so to risk the prospects of health and happiness. Yet all of us who are past youth once lived in a time when the taboo on discussion was so strict that only in professional or highly specialised quarters was it possible to discuss frankly the issues of venereal disease, and such a word as "syphilis"—which is merely the simple and correct name for the most potently dangerous venereal disease—was for public purposes prohibited. Even to-day, so strong has been the hold of the old taboo, we find a tendency to disguise these subjects under the vague and fumbling name of "social hygiene," although that term, so far as it has any meaning at all, has no special connection with the subject in question.

The necessity for plain speaking about venereal disease, now universally admitted, was first felt as a gradual extension of that great organised movement for "Public Health" which we owe to the enthusiasm for materialistic progress of the so-called "Victorian" epoch. It was inevitable that an important aspect of public health should soon be felt to lie in the spread of information to young people concerning the exact nature of the danger of venereal diseases. Thus was reached the idea of a sort of "sexual education." But it was obvious that an education in sex which merely meant the imparting of information necessary as a warning against disease was absurdly inadequate and might even sometimes prove mischievous. There thus came into view, not indeed for the first time, but in a more urgent and generally acceptable fashion, the whole question of education in matters of sex. This is now being more or less systematically carried out in all countries. In Russia it may be found here and there developed with relentless thoroughness and with the aid of the cinema to illustrate the various actual phases of the sex life. In Germany also, which has long been a centre of sexological science, the cinema is largely employed. But even in the most conservative and the most puritanic countries (though conservative and puritanic are by no means necessarily identical) the need of education in matters of sex is generally accepted, and, here and there, more or less cautiously carried out, though all its implications are yet far from being generally accepted.

Yet this innovation alone represents an enormous change in the incidence of taboos. Of all the taboos in civilisation up to recent years none has been stronger than that against speech on matters of sex. It is all the more powerful because it is one of the taboos which have been inherited by civilisation from savagery, and in the transfer grown even stronger. Even in the early books of the Bible, when we read of "feet" they are not always the part of the body which we are thereby to understand, and thousands of years later, when I was a child in London, I was told that America was the land where it was indelicate to speak of "legs"; the word "limbs" was used instead. There is no doubt about the progress made during the present century. But we must not be surprised that even those who no longer believe in the taboo often still observe it in practice. The taboo had always involved private revolts, with outbursts of what even those who thus revolted felt to be filthy and disgusting language, so that they were all the more anxious to keep them secret from the young. It was the most difficult thing in the world to speak to children, their own children, of what they themselves still instinctively felt to be filthy and disgusting. It could only be done rightly and naturally when the parents had undergone more than mere intellectual conviction, something which religious people used to call "a change of heart"; and that change itself, to be really operative, should take place early in life. So that still to-day the child is too easily allowed to follow the old paths, and a vicious circle remains established.

Undoubtedly a change is slowly taking place. The new mother is gradually being moulded to match the new child. We are less and less called upon to witness the amusing yet rather pathetic spectacle of the well-informed child carefully tempering his or more often her enlightenment to the virginal sensitiveness of a Victorian parent. The literature of recent times is alone enough to create a new atmosphere in this matter, since the taboos that are falling off life are at the same time falling off the literature of life. A double stream is indeed here at work, the stream of science and the stream of art: on the one hand a flood of scientific and pseudo-scientific books aiming at the enlightenment of the public in matters of sex, and from the other side a flood of novels in which sexual situations are set forth with a freedom, or a nonchalance, unknown, at all events in English literature, since the robustious mediæval romanticism of Scott and the elegant drawing-room manners of Jane Austen put the eighteenth century to shame, Victor Hugo with his fellows and followers performing the same purgation in French literature. No doubt the supporters of the old traditional taboos revolt at moments, and spasmodic attempts at suppression occur from time to time, but they are not only ineffectual, but capricious, for what offends tradition in one country passes without protest in another.

We are not here, however, concerned with protests or with the censorship. They represent the last convulsive movements of a generation which still possesses a measure of official power but is rapidly dying. Disregarding them altogether, we easily distinguish a modern stream in imaginative literature which arose about the middle of the last century and gradually gained full strength and influence towards the beginning of the present century, while at the same time as that stream arose an older stream was failing. Victor Hugo, already mentioned, was the supreme European representative of the earlier stream; Ibsen may be said to represent the later stream. Zola stands as the world-famous representative of the transition between the two, springing out of the romantic movement and unconsciously retaining much of its spirit, while at the same time he consciously—however mistakenly—aimed at scientific veracity, and vigorously displayed a grasp of real things which disdained any charge of crudity.

Even within the nineteenth century we may see the whole process in the English novel. Dickens belongs to the early stream and Hardy to the later stream, while Meredith, starting from romanticism and reaching towards the modern spirit, represents the transition. In America the two movements are just as distinct. No one doubts to which stream belong Hawthorne and James, and to which Dreiser and Sherwood Anderson. Whatever their comparative rank as artists, these two groups, in both countries, show a different social outlook, different conventions and ideals, different taboos, different values of life. The earlier writers, if springing from the higher social environment, observe ostentatiously a great number of traditional decorums, and if from a lower, they are gushing over with a respectable sentimentality which brought tears to the faces of their contemporaries and smiles or yawns to ours. The decorums of the first group have disappeared from the later group, and their taboos may be said to be almost reversed. Henry de Montherlant, one of the younger poets and novelists of France, finds it natural to begin a book (*La Petite Infante de Castille*) with the simple and homely (but incorrect) statement that there is only one public urinal in Barcelona. Imagine Henry James, or, for the matter of nationality, Victor Hugo, thus preluding a book! In the opening chapter of *All Quiet on the Western Front*, the Iliad, maybe, of our latest European war, Remarque discusses latrines as clearly a subject of the first importance; yet it does not seem to have been thought so when the Homeric account of the first great European war was written, nor (except in Ireland in relation to Queen Medbh) was it a recognised aspect of great warlike exploits. It may seem a small matter, but it is probably significant of a different attitude towards life. The classical tradition, as well as the Christian, is here reversed, and the old champions of Greek literature (like Mr. Gilbert Murray) are even more shocked than the archbishops. This new attitude involves not a single point only, but at all points a closer grasp of real facts, with a more negligent, or a more playful, attitude towards pretensions. It means, very significantly, a greater disregard for the prettinesses of life and a greater regard for its austerities. What is called "vice" is no longer made charming, and what is called "virtue" no longer easy and comfortable. To the people of the nineteenth century it was shocking to make vice anything but prettily elegant and virtue anything but comfortably happy. They considered it immoral, even punishable. Our view to-day is more nearly the opposite of that; the taboos are not so much abolished as inverted. And there can be little doubt that, being nearer to the facts, the new attitude is in reality the more moral attitude.

Life, as we live it to-day, is more highly socialised, more urbanised, more—so far as external relationships are concerned—standardised than it used to be. The world has become uncomfortably small; we have not yet gained a complete control of our excessive procreational activity; so that there are far too many of us, and, being so closely crowded together, we have to adopt all sorts of new precautions to avoid friction and permit of the greatest amount of mutual freedom available within our unduly narrow frontiers. So many of the old traditional social taboos having become antiquated or no longer adequate, there has been a furious activity in making new laws and regulations, without a due recognition of the fact that old taboos can only be replaced by new taboos, and that mere legal enactments, enforced, or left unenforced, by paid officials or the police, to be effective must themselves become taboos, printed on the fleshy tablets of the individual citizen's heart. If they are thus to become of the nature of taboos they must be few in number, indisputable in value, and so urgent that they are felt to be on the way to become instinctive. No society can live wholesomely by any other sort of regulation, and State legislatures stultify themselves when they fail to realise that their part is merely to formalise, and record, and support, the growth and the decay of taboos.

Sex taboos are at the centre of this process, not only because it so happens that sex is a sphere in which change has of late taken place with unusual rapidity, but because sex is at once an extremely important region—so that it becomes a training ground for the social activities generally—and yet a region in which most of the essentials do not lend themselves to direct external control, and so its taboos must be both made and maintained, at all events in the first place, privately.

During recent years, a half of this truth, the more destructive half, has become widely realised. It is realised, that is to say, that many of the family and other social restrictions which were once inculcated on youth are outworn and no longer correspond to the facts of the modern situation. The discovery was made with enthusiasm by many who jumped to the conclusion that a go-as-you-please policy—a naïve obedience to the crude and uninformed impulse of the moment—was henceforth right and justifiable. As Mr. Aldous Huxley, who has interspersed his delineation of some aspects of contemporary life with a wise criticism, well remarks in a thoughtful essay, the modern reaction against Victorian respectability, by taking the cheap form of promiscuity, has too often "exchanged the bad features of the nineteenth for the bad features of the eighteenth century"; it has bartered, he acutely points out, the Puritanical repression of sex for another form of repression, just as full of hatred and contempt as the Puritanic, but effected by the "deadening influence of promiscuous indulgences."

It seldom takes long, however, for those who follow this line of conduct, to find where it inevitably leads. They have failed to see that in throwing away the old worn-out taboos they had still retained the licence that those taboos assumed. The taboos, having largely become merely external restraints, had the function of keeping within bounds an impulsive licence which was always tending to break those bounds, and demanded, perhaps rightly, an occasional orgy. The two, on the whole, balanced each other and were necessary to each other; the external taboo was functionless without the licence, and the licence was mischievous without the taboo. To cast aside the one without casting aside the other merely produces confusion.

The old licences are just as much out of place under present conditions as the old taboos. Life under the former conditions were certainly a discipline, but a discipline mainly imposed from without, whence the rebellion against it as soon as its prohibitions were found to be dead. Life, however, is always a discipline, even for the lower animals as well as for men; it is so dangerous that only by submitting to some sort of discipline can we become equipped to live in any true sense at all. The disappearance of the discipline of the old external taboos thus imposes upon us, inescapably, the creation of a new self-discipline of internal and personal taboos. If we are not responsible to an outside order which we no longer regard as valid, then we are responsible before the inner tribunal of the self, which cannot but be valid for us so long as we are alive.[5]

That really is the task for all who are young to-day. And so far from it being an easy and pleasant task, as some may at first have thought when they saw the old taboos melting away, it involves difficulties which their grandparents never knew.

[5] When the above was written I had not in mind the writings of Dr. Marett. But it is a satisfaction to me to record that my conception of "taboo" is in essential respects the same as that maintained by so distinguished a student of this group of psychological phenomena. See, for instance, Chap. III of his *Threshold of Religion*, where he shows how taboo is a breach of customary rule, "with a sanction in the shape of some suggestion of mystic punishment," which yet is never a measurable quantity. There are, he repeats, "always penalties of a distinctively social kind to be feared by the taboo-breaker," in extreme cases death and always more or less what the Australian natives call "growling." All social disapproval borrows the tone of religious aversion, but the sanctioning power remains social in the sense that society takes forcible means to remove the curse from its midst. More recently, in the article "Taboo" already mentioned, Marett writes still more clearly: "The primitive institution of taboo will be found to embody elemental principles of order that are to-day as active as ever beneath the surface of a changed custom." Similarly Professor Radcliffe-Brown declares (*Man*, Sept., 1926) "that the same general principle underlies taboos in all parts of the world; however such customs may vary in detail in different cultures, the same fundamental sociological laws underlie them all."

If it means the making of new and personal taboos, it involves a slow self-development and self-responsibility, which are not only in themselves a continual discipline, but run the risk of conflict with others engaged in the same task and with the same sincerity. For what we may still term morals, since it has now become an individual outcome, will not be entirely the same for all individuals. All our moralities, indeed, cannot fail to be modifications of a common pattern because we all belong to the same community; but the differences involve a greater degree of mutual understanding and forbearance than when uniform taboos were imposed from outside.

We come here on a conflict such as lies at the foundation of all life. On the one hand we have the disappearance of the old traditional taboos, based on external authority, with the demand that we should create a new discipline from within; on the other hand we have the insistence, which some of the most representative minds of to-day emphasise, on "the new conformity which a new social solidarity is making." How to harmonise those opposing demands? But it is in harmonising them that all life consists. In words which were meant to apply to creative art and thought, but really apply equally well to the practical art of living, an anonymous English writer has lately well said: "It would seem that for many years there can be no common emotional or intellectual background which may be taken for granted; and if in the result not a little of a man's power must be spent in creating his own scheme of values, still there is no immediate remedy, for it is in the nature of contemporary thinking that it demands an effort as individual as it must be unsparingly honest if it is to have any meaning for our generation."

So if the people of the old generation now leaving the world are often shocked to see swept away the old rigid taboos they were brought up in, they may leave it in peace. Life, after all, may not have been so hard for them, not so hard, perhaps, as for the younger generation. None the less, that younger generation, also, may continue to carry lightly its burden, on youthful shoulders, joyfully creating a new world.

Chapter 14

THE REVALUATION
OF OBSCENITY

OBSCENITY IS A PERMANENT ELEMENT OF HUMAN SOCIAL LIFE and corresponds to a deep need of the human mind, or, for all we know to the contrary, of mind generally. It is not confined to any nation or any stage of culture, low or high, savage or civilised. It definitely exists and is recognised among the peoples we often call "primitive," and it is joyfully manifested by the greatest men of genius among the higher races.[1] If we realise this fundamental permanence of obscenity we are relieved not merely from an ambiguous intellectual problem, but from a troublesome moral task, all the more annoying since, as experience has shown, it is labour in vain. Intellectual discrimination and moral tact remain necessary, but our efforts are no longer bound to be futile when we understand that it is our primary task to revalue obscenity.

Such a task has ceased to be meaningless when we remember that we have already gone far in a corresponding task: the revaluation of sex with which obscenity has so largely been associated or confused. By the "obscene" we may properly mean what is *off the scene* and not openly shown on the stage of life. That does not mean, it must be added, on the stage of the theatre, for the theatre has often shown what may not be so openly shown in life—art supplementing life—and alike in the greater dramatists and the lesser dramatists there has often been an element of what is correctly regarded as obscenity. When, indeed, we consider the recognised part which it has played on the most admired stages of the world it is astonishing that it should still be necessary to justify obscenity.

Certainly, as I have indicated, it is our new estimation of sex which necessarily involves a revaluation of obscenity. There

[1] The problems connected with the origin and meaning of obscenity were touched on by A. E. Crawley many years ago in "A Note on Obscenity," *Studies of Savages and Sex*, p. 101. He inclined to think that the root of the word "obscene" is the same as that of "obscure."

are, it is true, two kinds of obscenity: there is the naturalistic aspect of sexual processes, and there is the naturalistic aspect of excremental processes. Both are, from our normally conventional standpoint, obscene. But they are completely distinct, in spite of, from some points of view, their intimate association. This may be observed in literature where it touches on obscenity. The excrementally obscene writer is by no means necessarily the sexually obscene writer. This is notably exemplified by Swift, who delights in the excremental obscene and often goes out of his way to introduce it, but always austerely rejects even the faintest recognition of the sexually obscene. In this matter Swift represents a common tendency among the writers who are men of the Church. When they are obscene they are rarely sexual, the reason being that the taboo on the excremental obscene is only conventional and social, while that of the sexual obscene is regarded as also moral and religious. The moral and religious prohibition cannot be invoked against the excremental obscene, for we are here only concerned with custom and taste in a matter in which custom differs from age to age and taste from individual to individual.

We must not underrate the gravity of the moral and religious factors in the taboo on sexual obscenity. It is true that the moral factor, at all events, is of comparatively recent development. In old days we do not find that obsession with "immorality" with which we are ourselves so familiar. The word "immoral," said Restif de la Bretonne, writing near the end of the eighteenth century, "is a new word; but already," he added, "we hear it re-echoing on every side."[2] The nineteenth century, indeed, fell in love with the word. Was there anything to which it was not sometimes applied during that century? Previously, sexual obscenity seems to have had little relationship either to the name or the fact of immorality, and in classic antiquity—although the obscene was often regarded as a sign of ill-omen if not a cause for disgust—it would have been absurd to suggest such a connection. That is why a sixteenth-century churchman, like Rabelais, could be sexually obscene, but an eighteenth-century churchman must either, like Swift, confine himself to the excrementally obscene, or, like Sterne, be content with the prurient approach to the sexual obscene.

The religious factor in the sexual obscene is, indeed, more ancient, and we may even call it primitive. But this factor is

[2] *Monsieur Nicolas*, ed. Liseux, Vol. II, p. 102. But it was not a new word in England, where it was already used in an abusive sense as early as 1660, probably as an invention of the Puritans. Before the middle of the nineteenth century it was admitted into English legal phraseology, and it became possible to assert that "immoral contracts are void," thereby opening the way to endless discussion, since morality is in perpetual flux.

ambiguous, and in fact ambivalent, working both ways, so that obscenity is on certain occasions permitted and even prescribed by society. Here, perhaps, we draw near to the earliest social function of obscenity.

What may perhaps be regarded as a fairly typical state of things as regards this blended prohibition and injunction, under certain circumstances, of obscenity may be found in Africa, where it has been studied by Evans-Pritchard. Obscenity is here associated with ceremonial activities. Some kinds of collective obscene behaviour, in ordinary life usually taboo, are permitted or enjoined on certain occasions, all of social importance, either religious ceremonies or joint economic undertakings. The main objects, in Evans-Pritchard's opinion, are three: (1) By withdrawing a normal prohibition to emphasise the social importance of the activity in question; (2) to assist in canalising emotion into a prescribed channel at a period of human crisis; and (3) to furnish a stimulus and a reward at a time of combined and difficult labour.[8]

These uses of obscenity in comparatively primitive stages of culture furnish valuable clues to its functions generally, and may enable us to see how much we lose in civilisation by foolish and futile attempts to abolish the public expression of obscenity altogether. On the one hand, in so far as we are successful, we lose its canalising, stimulating, and relieving virtues; on the other hand, we magnify and exacerbate all its vices. We forget that we are dealing with a fundamental and inevitable human impulse, and that it is our business to preserve those aspects of it which are good and to minimise those which are evil.

As already remarked, we are, however, to-day approaching a revaluation of obscenity along the only path by which it can reasonably be reached, our new attitude towards sex. As we look on the phase from which we are emerging it would almost seem as though the whole field of sex, to its full extent, and in all its ramifications, even those of a scientifically technical character, had been regarded as obscene, and of an obscenity, unlike that found among savages, which was never socially enjoined or permitted. The subject of sex could only be approached when it was deprived of all naturalistic character by being sentimentalised, that is to say, bathed in a vague and frequently quite impenetrable mist.

Under such circumstances it was impossible to approach the question of obscenity in a rational spirit. When everything is obscene it becomes impossible to say what obscenity is.

[8] E. Evans-Pritchard, "Some Collective Expressions of Obscenity in Africa," *Jour. Anthropological Institute*, July-Dec., 1929.

Hence the endless definitions of obscenity, and their absurdity.

The absurdity was, indeed, so obvious that the official mind came to the conclusion that it was safest to punish the offence of obscenity while carefully refusing to explain wherein the offence lay. This was the attitude of Sir Archibald Bodkin, for many years the English Director of Public Prosecution and most zealous in pursuing obscenity. An International Conference was called together at Geneva, on "the suppression of the Circulation and Traffic in Obscene Publications." Sir Archibald of course appeared as the representative of Great Britain. When the delegates of the various countries concerned had all assembled, the Greek delegate tentatively suggested that it might be desirable, in order that the Conference should know what it was talking about, first to define the meaning of the word "obscene." But Bodkin rose and objected. He pointed out that there is no definition of "indecent" or "obscene" in English Statute Law. His objection strongly appealed to the officials present, and they unanimously resolved, before proceeding further, that "no definition was possible" of the matter which the Conference was called together to discuss.[4]

Nothing more clearly shows—it may be remarked in passing—the illegitimate nature of the attempt to suppress obscenity by law than the obscurantism of the legal officials who undertake it. They love darkness, and we know of whom that was first said. That love of darkness is shrewd. For, if we think of it, any attempt whatever to define "obscenity"—once we have put aside the vague emotional terms of abuse, "foul," "filthy," "lewd," "disgusting," etc.—in cool and precise terms cannot bring us to any crime against society.[5] Taken in the wide sense, we may define it as that which arouses sexual love and desire. But that is what anything in Nature may do, for some persons at some time, and that it should do so is in accordance with the whole order established by Nature, or, if we will, God. So it has been usual to define the "obscene" more narrowly as lying in a particular mode of expression, at variance with that usually employed by a particular social class at a particular

[4] B. Causton & G. Young, *Keeping It Dark*, p. 55.

[5] The sagacious refusal of the lawyers to define the term "obscenity" really involves the admission that it is not properly a legal term at all. Lord Hewart, the Lord Chief Justice, lecturing in London (March 24, 1930) on the distinction between the fields of morality and of law, well brought this out: "The moralist may say 'Blessed are the pure in heart,' but it is inconceivable that a statute should provide that 'After the passing of this Act any person who is not pure in heart shall be guilty of misdemeanour.' Nor would the matter be made any easier if the statute went on to provide that lack of purity of heart and its symptoms should be defined by a Government Department in rules and orders having the same effect as if they were contained in the Act."

period of history. But then obscenity becomes merely a defect
of pedantry, or, at the most, a failure in good taste, which
can never be a crime. It was in this sense that D. H. Lawrence's
novel, *Lady Chatterley's Lover*, was banned as "obscene"; it
was recognisably a fine and admirably written work of art, but
the author had, on two or three pages, deliberately chosen to
use sound old English words in place of the euphemisms commonly preferred in the "good society" of his age. For even
the most estimable clergyman may safely refer to the action
by which we are brought into the world by a word of Latin
source in eight or more letters without risking his chances of a
congé d'élire. But if in the course of a sermon he inadvertently
referred to the same act by a good old English word of four
letters—such as a child may chalk on the pavement without
endangering the structure of society—he is less likely to find
himself on the episcopal throne than in prison, unless by the
strenuous exertions of his friends he is sent to a lunatic asylum.[6]
So great for the official mind in this matter are the advantages
of darkness! We still live in a society which meekly permits
a man to be fined or even sent to prison for the unfashionable
use of perfectly correct synonyms.

This whole question has been made clearer by various
investigators since a new vision of the place of sex in life has
begun to prevail. Theodore Schroeder, a New York lawyer,
was a pioneer with his powerful and substantial work on *"Obscene" Literature and Constitutional Law*, privately printed
for forensic use in New York in 1911. He here dealt radically
with the whole subject in its historical, legal, and social aspects,
and his work is still valuable. Familiar alike with the sexological, the forensic, and the ethnographic experiences and researches he was able to speak with confidence and authority.
He made abundantly clear that it is an error to claim, as is
often done, that obscenity in our modern sense has ever been
an offence at common law in England or the United States.
In the Golden Age of British history, the age of Elizabeth and
of Shakespeare, when the English genius reached its highest
point in life and in poetry, as during the Victorian period in
science and social reform, there needs must have been, as always in the pre-modern world, sporadic manifestations in

[6] Even a bishop may have to protect himself against a word. I remember
being amused as a schoolboy by an incident that happened to the then
Bishop of Winchester (Samuel Wilberforce, nicknamed on account of his
extreme urbanity, "Soapy Sam"). He had preached a sermon in a country
church on behalf of the restoration fund, and the local paper reported that
he declared the church to be "nothing but a damned barn." Fortunately his
secretary was able to write to the editor that the word actually used by his
lordship was "damp."

various shapes of what we should call obscenity. But it was free and open and wholesome. There was no law against obscenity, and therefore there was no inducement to anyone to flaunt his obscenity before the world, and no encouragement to establish a pornographic press to flood the underworld of literature with its products, silly and dirty, but surrounded by the halo of the forbidden.

It was in the following century, by a side wind, that the modern conception began subtly to float into law. Before then, though it took no note of obscenity, it was the business of the law to protect the political order, and the business of the spiritual courts (a business later more or less transferred to the secular courts) to protect religion, and it must be remembered that at that time it was held, even by lawyers, that "morality is the fundamental part of religion." "Obscenity" slipped into it only in combination with charges of political disorder or of impiety. An "obscene libel"—the legal term still used—could not be brought in, as it can now, as a charge against an act or a writing that is indecent and no more. The obscenity must be associated either with violence or with impiety.

I have often protested against the common accusation that it is Puritanism which was responsible for the introduction of the movement to suppress obscenity. Puritanism was a liberating force, a force on the side of freedom. We cannot too often recall that the *Areopagitica*, the most eloquent denunciation of censorship ever put forth, was the work of the greatest of English Puritans in the world of letters. Puritanism was not responsible for any enactments against obscenity, and the Puritans were themselves prepared to be what we should call "obscene," both in word and in act.

Yet at the same time it seems possible that, if not directly, Puritanism may indirectly have been partly responsible for the legal movements against obscenity. The Puritans may have made no laws against obscenity, and may even have been tolerant of it, but when they were predominant during the English Commonwealth they brought into fashion pruderies of action and of speech which, when the Commonwealth had passed, continued to ferment in social life and to grow rather than to diminish in influence. Prudery was not Puritanism, but it may be regarded as, in part, an offshoot of Puritanism, which flourished vigorously after the vital spirit of Puritanism was itself dead or decaying, and grew able to mould social customs and sentiments altogether apart from religion. Thus it was only two years after the Commonwealth was suppressed, and when Charles II, the incarnation of the anti-puritanic spirit, had been placed on the throne amid what appeared to be general enthusiasm, that Sir Charles Sedley (with two other aristocratic young friends who afterwards also became distinguished), in a drunken freak, stripped himself naked on the balcony of the Cock Tavern in Bow Street, Covent Garden. A freak of this kind was really not so very uncommon and usually attracted little attention. But on this occasion it led to a public disturbance. Sedley addressed the crowd with a mock sermon, vaguely said to contain "blasphemy," in imitation of an itinerant quack, a favourite theme for Restoration jokes; this seems to have led to the throwing of bottles containing urine on to the crowd below, and they retorted by throwing stones. As "blasphemy" and violence entered here, it seems evident that the "obscenity" alone would have been overlooked. But even on this occasion Puritanism was not mainly responsible. Sedley was tried before Lord Chief Justice Foster, an old-fashioned and high-minded cavalier of the school of Clarendon, and it has been surmised that he was moved by anxiety for the good reputation of young Cavaliers when he inflicted on Sedley the heavy fine of 2,000 marks with seven days' imprisonment.[7] That it was violence and blasphemy which the law sought to control—not nakedness either in life or in literature—is shown by the fact that we hear of no more charges of "obscenity" till nearly half a century later. In 1708 Lord Holt rendered a decision concerning an indictment for writing an obscene book entitled *The Fifteen Plagues of a Maidenhead*. He dismissed the charge on the ground that while profanity is indictable, obscenity is only punishable in the spiritual courts.

But at this time, it seems clear, the leaven of transformed and degraded Puritanism was working in the general population. The reign of the middle class, putting upper class and lower class alike into the background, and proclaiming a Nonconformist conscience which arrogated the functions of the ancient spiritual courts, was beginning. It soon intruded into the temporal courts, and so led towards that legal enforcement of what was vaguely termed "morality" which later became a mischievous source of trouble.

I should like to add, however, with regard to the change of feeling in progress during the eighteenth century, that I do not consider it mainly, or even chiefly, a by-product of Puri-

---

[7] V. de Sola Pinto deals fully with the case in his life of *Sir Charles Sedley*, 1927, pp. 61-66. Pepys gave an account of it at the time in his *Diary*, July 1, 1663. The old Chief Justice died three months afterwards. His action in this case had been courageous, as the accused were friends and associates of the King, who might even (someone has suggested) have been of the party.

tanism becoming ingrained in the lower middle class. To some
extent, no doubt, it was that, but it was even more a result of
developing social culture, a form of snobbery, the aping of a
delicacy and refinement which was regarded as marking a
higher class in life, and therefore a thing to be struggled for,
although in reality it is not felt by those whom their inferiors
believe that they are imitating. We see exactly the same process
taking place in France in the seventeenth century (commonly
associated with the Hôtel de Rambouillet and the "*précieu-
ses*"), and proving equally triumphant. Early in the nineteenth
century the aged Northcote told Hazlitt (as he records in his
Conversations) that he remembered that when Goldsmith's
comedy first came on the stage there was a great uproar among
the populace in the gallery at some coarse expression which
subsequently had to be suppressed. Northcote added the significant remark: "The common people sought for refinement as
a *treat;* people in high life were fond of grossness and ribaldry
as a relief to their overstrained affectation of gentility." Goldsmith, nevertheless, was a man of incomparably more delicacy
and sensitiveness than the rude and vulgar mob that howled at
him. I may add, of an equally distinguished contemporary of
Northcote's, Sir Walter Scott, who carried prudery and sentiment to an extreme in his novels, that (as I was informed in
youth by a friend with Scottish literary associations) Scott
would tell coarse stories in private. For it is the populace that
tend to enforce the tone in these matters and even to mould
law.

We begin to see the encroachment of law in this field in a
case that occurred in 1727. It seems the earliest recorded case
in which a book was charged with being an "obscene libel"
and condemned on that account, simply on grounds of "morality." The book was called *Venus in the Cloister*. The de-
fendant was found guilty. His counsel made a motion for arrest
of judgment, arguing that there had never been any such prosecution before in the temporal courts, that a book of this kind
could not constitute a libel, and that morals could only be
censured in the spiritual courts. The Attorney General admitted there was no precedent, but argued that peace may be
broken without actual force, and that to destroy morality is to
destroy public order which is the peace of government. This
specious pleading was accepted by the court on the ground
that religion is part of the common law, and that "morality is
the fundamental part of religion," so that an offence against
morality is an offence against the common law. As Schroeder
points out, this decision clearly shows that obscenity, *as obscenity*, was not regarded as punishable. It was punished only

in so far as it was regarded as a form of impiety. This appears in the next case (1733) when a woman was charged with running nearly naked along the highway. There was no punishment; the action was not "unlawful."[8] All through the eighteenth century, indeed, charges of "obscenity" were only successful when combined with some other offence, usually "impiety." Schroeder remarks that, as the separation of the American colonies occurred before the end of the century, it cannot be claimed that the United States inherited from England any common law against obscenity.

During the nineteenth century, as we know, the charge of obscenity, stripped of any pretense that it made either for violence or for irreligion, boldly entered the law courts and was accepted. It stalked unchallenged—save by a few ineffective protesters—through Victorian literature and Victorian life. Many false and foolish accusations may have been made against Victorianism, but there can certainly be no doubt that it was bewitched by the fear of obscenity. Sordidness there might often be, conspicuously displayed on the surface of life, but obscenity was completely banished from that surface. Its humorists themselves, rather a feeble folk indeed, were prudish. Even its cartoonists (Rowlandson, who had more genius than

[8] I do not know to whom must be credited the dubious honour of making nakedness unlawful. But this unlawfulness was completely accepted in the Victorian period, and remains an accepted convention even to-day, although it is falling into flagrant opposition with the ideals now becoming current among educated people. I read in the London *Times* of to-day (Oct. 7, 1930) that a young man at a sun-bathing camp was brought to the police court and fined £10 for having in the course of a discussion with two young ladies in a neighbouring non-sun-bathing camp, who considered the practice was "not decent," let fall the towel around his waist and declared: "If I am not decent I will be indecent." One might have thought that this act of bad taste would be amply punished by a glance of contempt and that a young woman of to-day would possess sufficient anatomical knowledge not to be shocked by the sight of an unclothed fellow creature of her own species. But this magistrate (a Mr. Robinson) was very solemn. "Take this as a warning," said Mr. Robinson to the young man; "otherwise you will soon find yourself in prison, the proper place for people holding such views as you do. I sincerely hope you will get rid of these extraordinary views as soon as you can. You will not be allowed to continue to practise these views unless you want to be in the clutches of the law." These "extraordinary views," as Mr. Robinson considered them, are those beginning to be held by intelligent people everywhere. But, only two days before this magisterial pronouncement, an article on "Justices' Justice" appeared in the *Week-end Review*, written by a well-informed lawyer, in which the incompetence and senility of English magistrates (notable exceptions being admitted) are faithfully denounced, and it is not for me to say more, since in that same number of the *Review*, though in another connection, I read that "the record of the Robinsons is pitiful to contemplate." That, no doubt, is too extreme; nor must we forget the venerated figure of Robinson Crusoe, who has been described as the typical Englishman.

any of them, had died in 1927) were tamely conventional,
when they were not vulgar, but never obscene. The fear of
obscenity became, indeed, a haunting obsession. For really,
when you came to think of it, there was nothing that might
not be obscene. As the century grew older that became increasingly clear. For obscenity, however it might be defined—and
there was never any agreement as to how it should be defined—
usually meant at least two things. On the one side it certainly
meant nakedness; whether verbal nakedness or physical nakedness, it was the unclothing of something that in public is habit-
ually clothed. There could not be any doubt about that. But
it also meant something sexually provocative. That was evidently essential. For unless this unclothing induced sexual
activity how could it be "immoral"; why should it be prohibited?

We all know what happened under these conditions. Not
only were many scientific books inevitably "obscene"—because
science necessarily speaks without disguise—and therefore suppressed; but in the sphere of literature and art there was evidently a boundless field for the exercise of the anti-obscene
impulse. From Rabelais to Joyce a large number of the master-
pieces of literature were haled into court and condemned.
Shakespeare was obscene. Even the Bible—which a few centuries earlier had been regarded throughout Christendom as a
sacred book—was declared by the legal officials of the nineteenth century obscene, especially in American courts, and
punishment was meted out to those who published some selec-
tions from it. The naked body was also declared obscene, not
only in real life (so that there was endless debate as to how
many inches might safely be exposed), but also in pictures,
though here, I understand, a distinction was often made, and
while a back view was permissible, a front view was declared
obscene; it was the obverse of the human medal that was obscene, the reverse was indifferent.

While the origin and legal developments of the conception
of "obscenity" have been well traced by Schroeder, the two
authors of a later book *To the Pure . . .* have adequately
dealt with its subsequent growth and present position in England and the United States. These writers, Morris Ernst and
William Seagle, in fortunate collaboration, represent an active
interest in both law and literature, and their book, at once
serious and vivacious, is perhaps the most competent and attractive popular presentation of the question we at present
possess. The title, it is true, however convenient as a label, may
contain implications we do not all accept, for when St. Paul
uttered the famous dictum: "To the pure all things are pure,"

he was not discussing literature or pictures or the cinema, but a matter to which they are hardly analogous. There are many things in books and art generally which the pure may be justified in not feeling to be pure, although there can never be any agreement as to which things these are. That indeed is one of the solid and permanent arguments against a censorship of obscenity.

Fortunately it is only as a label that the authors have chosen their title for a book which is at once a competent history of the Anglo-Saxon censorship from the Victorian period until to-day, and at the same time a cogent and yet singularly temperate argument for freedom from censorship. We have too often seen the slapdash hand exercising itself in this field. The foolish and extravagant rhetoric of those who fulminate against obscenity has been matched by the random and reckless smartness, sometimes scarcely less foolish, of those who took the other side. It was fully time to approach the question in a sane and serious spirit, which is not less so for allowing the play of wit and humour.

A yet more recent book—this time of English origin—is *Keeping It Dark, or the Censor's Handbook*, by Bernard Causton and G. Gordon Young (1930). Here also the approach is sane and serious, while the whole subject is comprehensively though concisely considered. The authors advocate the complete abolition of obscenity laws as involving fewer dangers and less harm than are entailed by the present dark and subjective methods of procedure.

That, probably, is the view now tending to prevail, though we cannot say that it yet prevails. "I am firmly persuaded," says Bertrand Russell, "that there ought to be no law whatsoever on the subject of obscene publications." Every such law, he remarks, has undesirable consequences; it cannot forbid the bad without also forbidding the good, and the bad works little harm in the presence of rational sex education.[9] Still more significant is the opinion of those who have taken an active interest in the suppression of obscenity. "Many legislative acts and regulations have been passed involving prohibitions and varying degrees of censorship," it is said in an editorial note of the New York *Journal of Social Hygiene*. "All have failed to accomplish their full purpose." [10]

The test of obscenity can, obviously, only be subjective. Nothing is in itself obscene apart from the human observer. This is clearly indicated by the definition of obscenity most

[9] Bertrand Russell, *Marriage and Morals*, 1929, pp. 91, 94.
[10] *Journal of Social Hygiene*, Dec., 1930.

often brought forward—if any is brought—in law courts: "which excites or promotes sexual desires."

Such a definition reveals an unsuspected simplicity or ignorance on the part of the lawyers who formulated or accepted it. In doing so they delivered themselves unaware into their enemies' hands. There may indeed have been a time—though it must have been very remote—when the recognised stimulants of sexual desire were so crude and obvious that there could be no doubt about them. But such a time has certainly long passed away; it had passed long before the psychoanalysts arose to show, rightly or wrongly, that we live in a pan-sexual world.

The fact is that there are now few things in life or in art which may not be "lewd," "disgusting," and "lascivious" (accepted synonyms for the legal "obscene") to the feelings of some people and to the minds of others. This has long been known to those who saw and realised the facts. It is extremely common in susceptible subjects, men or women, for ordinary natural sights and incidents of constant occurrences to arouse sexual feeling ("lewd," "disgusting," and "lascivious," if you find them so). In persons sensitive to erotic fetichism, as many if not most people are in some degrees, all sorts of objects, even of the least obviously sexual character, may become thus stimulating. In recent years, moreover, the psychoanalysts, by including the exploration of the unconscious strata of the mind, find reason to believe that sexual associations may be endless. If we are to abolish the possibly obscene, we must efface the whole world.

Much the same must, of course, be said of literature and art. There is no end to the list of famous books which obscenity hunters banned or sought to ban. Some of the most famous books of the nineteenth century, now treated with reverence, were on publication prosecuted, and often successfully. There appears to be no definition of obscenity which will not condemn the Bible. Moreover, on the practical side, it is known that the young find their chief source of information concerning sex—birth, masturbation, birth control, rape, and perversions—from the Bible. This was, for instance, shown not long ago in a careful inquiry by a distinguished authority in social hygiene, Dr. Katharine Davis, among over a thousand unmarried women, all college graduates. The same women were also asked what they found most "sexually stimulating" (in the police courts it would be phrased "lewd, filthy, and disgusting"). The largest number replied: "Man." The problem thus becomes of tragic consequence, for we see that if obscenity is to be suppressed it can only be done by the extinction of one half of the human race. And as men, if asked the same question, would in an equal majority undoubtedly answer: "Woman"—why, there goes the other half. The censors of obscenity are too solemn to realise that they are perpetrating a joke, and too unintelligent to know that the joke has serious, even tragic, aspects.

It is impossible to estimate the social damage which has been done by the outworn taboos of obscenity. It is these taboos which have delayed until to-day the effort to combat venereal diseases and the discussion of the population question. The names of the evils were too "obscene" to mention, and therefore the evils themselves were allowed to flourish unchecked, or else left to specialists and officials to discuss in technical terms. In another field the difficult problems raised by psychoanalysis have been dragged from the sphere of science where they belonged, to be perverted and distorted by the fascination or the repulsion of the taboo against obscenity. Even in the sphere of history and biography, the taboo against obscenity has stood in the way of an accurate knowledge of personalities and events; while now that the taboo is losing its force there is naturally a movement to the other extreme, with a tendency to distortion in the opposite direction, and we magnify the importance of the facts that before we were not allowed to see. For it is not one of the least evils of outworn taboos that even the inevitable reaction they lead to is evil.

It seems so simple, so innocent, so entirely praiseworthy, to put down indecent literature by laws against "obscenity." We are none of us in favour of what seems to us indecent. It is impossible we should be, for the word means, if we search into it, simply what is unfit. Yet the simpler and more fundamental the conception of decency is seen to be, the more it eludes any prescription of positive law. It is determined by the nature of the individual himself, by the feelings of his social group, and very notably by fashion. Most of us are old enough to know that less than twenty years ago the whole young womanhood of to-day would have been held guilty of indecency in dress and liable to be conducted to the nearest police station. In literature fashion is even more uncertain and elusive than in life, for the good reason that it is not produced by mass action. Endless examples have been brought forward of such fluctuations of opinion regarding books condemned by law, as well as examples of books legally condemned as obscene in England and free in America, or legally condemned in America and free in England. "The obscenity of to-day," it has been said, "will be the propriety of to-morrow."

Law is made ridiculous when it is thus prostituted to the

fashions of the hour. It is made immoral when it is perverted to the supposed protection of children. It used to be women and children who were held to be in need of such protection from the danger of obscenity. It is now only children, for women have rightfully insisted that in this matter they are henceforth to be put on the level of men and not of children. The problem of the child remains. It ought to be clear that we are not entitled to protect children by laws which also extend to adults and thus tend (sometimes with too much success) to convert adults into children. It is for the parents and teachers, one cannot too often repeat, to protect the children, and to protect them, above all, by teaching them to protect themselves, which can only be done by facing evil and not by fleeing from it. Yet it is admitted (as by Ernst and Seagle) that there is "a twilight zone of disputed control between parents and government." In the realm of economics it is rightly held that the forces against the child should be restrained by laws prohibiting long hours of work and similar hardships. But to protect the child against obscenity by legislation is not only more difficult and more dangerous but less necessary. Pornography has no meaning and no attraction for the healthy child who casually comes in contact with it; the reaction is one of indifference, if not of disgust. To-day if any harm is caused it is less likely to come from pornography than from the crudely exaggerated films of vice, presented by virtuous propagandists of social hygiene, which are apt to cause a painful shock to the virginal mind, just as the tender skin of the infant is injured by the hot bath of a temperature wholesomely stimulating to the adult. There are many uncensored things in life far more injurious to the young than obscenity. "A minor's pornography law" has indeed been suggested by Ernst and Seagle, but tentatively, with much doubt, for, they add, education, through school and home, will prove the better solution. Parents and teachers must be trusted to aid the child in guiding himself safely through these risks, without injury to the freedom of adults. To-day this is being recognised, by parents and teachers alike, even if not yet always in ways that are according to knowledge.

A revaluation of obscenity is very far from meaning a justification of the things that most reasonable people find ugly and unpleasant. But it means a different attitude towards their suppression in practice. We know the results of the attitude which has prevailed in the past. We have all been the victims of it. A premium is put on things that are dirty and worthless. It is law alone which makes pornography both attractive and profitable. As Nietzsche long ago said: "One cannot do a thing a better service than to persecute it and run it to earth." In England a simple-minded Home Secretary arises and declares that he feels it to be his duty to protect the young from the awful dangers that threaten them in books, postcards, and cinemas. Needless to say, the young of to-day are not in a mood to be preserved from these dangers, which can always be reached, sooner or later, with a little trouble and money. And no doubt such things often give rise to some gloating, though, in the absence of prohibitions, they would have induced only indifference or dislike. The motive for producing them would then soon disappear. At the present time, thanks to the premium put on them, the production of obscene postcards and similar things is so large that even the number of those seized by the police soon mounts up to millions. All of us, it is probable, have once been stirred to gain access to such things simply because they were forbidden. For my own part, I remember how, long ago, in a quiet street of Seville, a furtive and shabby individual drew me aside and produced from beneath his long cloak a little book with coloured illustrations which curiosity induced me to spend several pesetas in buying. I found it pathetically crude and unpleasant, and quickly destroyed it; my curiosity was once and for all satisfied. Such things are far away from art or science, which redeem whatever they touch if it happens to need "redemption."[11]

We must not indeed lull ourselves into the belief that this question is already settled. The dead hand of the nineteenth century is still upon us, even upon those who imagine that they stand in the van of advance. We may trace it in a pamphlet on "Pornography and Obscenity," published (1929) shortly before his death by D. H. Lawrence, who had himself suffered more than once at the hands of the official censors of obscenity. Yet he falls into strange confusions and would himself "censor genuine pornography." The censorship he would establish, however, might prove more alarming than that of which he complains, and would certainly be even more difficult to work. He has a personal and peculiar definition of "pornography," under which the *Decameron* would go free as suitable alike for old and young—a statement we may possibly be willing to

[11] *The Bibliotheca Germanorum erotica et curiosa* (1912-1914) of Hayn and Gotendorf reveals the extent, progress and national difference in so-called "pornographic" literature. It appears from this scholarly bibliography that translations from the French account for a large number of items. It is possible to form curves of the rise and decline of such literature; in 1815 and in 1870 it flourished—together with, whether as result or cause, the reaction against it—more than now, since now we possess greater freedom in permitting entertaining literature. In England it has been especially the literature of flagellation and of masochism which has flourished.

agree with—but *Jane Eyre* and *Tristan* would come perilously near to condemnation, while his test of what is "pornographic" (very different from the original meaning of the word) seems to be a tendency to promote masturbation in place of normal sexual intercourse. How Lawrence could suppose that Charlotte Brontë's novel is more likely to lead to masturbation than *Lady Chatterley's Lover* (assuming that either of them is), or how he could suggest that Wagner should be suppressed, remains obscure. He realises that it is secrecy which causes the evil, and yet he would prohibit and render secret a large part of our literature and art! Nothing could be more muddle-headed.

At the same time as Lawrence's, and in the same series, appeared a pamphlet by Viscount Brentford: "Do We Need a Censor?" When Lord Brentford was Sir W. Joynson-Hicks and Home Secretary, he became conspicuous by many decisions and opinions concerning the prosecution and suppression of obscenity which caused deep and wide indignation among the friends of freedom in literature and art. So that I took up his pamphlet, expecting to find full confirmation for the attitude I had adopted in the days when he was Home Secretary."[12] But, to my surprise, the final conclusion he now reaches is entirely my own! Whether it was that his experiences had taught wisdom, or that the serene heights of the Upper Chamber had made it possible for him to see things in clearer perspective, I cannot tell. But though in the course of the pamphlet he makes some dubious statements—and still believes that so debatable a matter as morality can be brought within the sphere of law—he reaches the conclusion that this is a matter which really concerns the "heart," and that we are approaching a time when prosecutions will be out of date: "By the spread of education," he concludes (adding, like a good churchman, "the extension of religion"), "the people will themselves learn to reject all forms of unpleasant conduct, literature, art. If the people learn not merely to disregard but to detest all these forms of indecency in thought, word, and deed, the day will come when no form of censorship will be needed, when there will be no prosecutions for breaches of the law, and when acts of Parliament will be a dead letter in the Statute Book." Indeed, with the zeal of a new convert, Lord Brentford here goes far beyond what we can ever reasonably expect. There will never be a time when the whole population live up to his ideal, nor need we even desire that they should. What we may reasonably expect is that the spread of education

[12] "The Censorship of Books," *Nineteenth Century and After*, April, 1929.

—and especially education in sex—together with the wider extension of that good taste which is at present too exclusively the possession of a small though really increasing class, the evils which Lord Brentford deplores will be negligible.

What, however, Lord Brentford failed to see when he was Home Secretary, and apparently even still failed to see when elevated to the peerage, is that his ideal can never be approached through a system of repression and prohibition. "Without secrecy," Lawrence truly says, "there can be no pornography." So long as there is secrecy there will be pornography. Obscenity there will be under all systems, for it has a legitimate and natural foundation; but the vulgar, disgusting, and stupid form of obscenity called pornography—the literature and art that are substitutes for the brothel and of the same coarse texture—has its foundation not in Nature, but in an artificial secrecy. So that the net result of that system of repression which still prevails among us is—as Causton and Young well say—"to keep the world safe for pornography."

On this point I find another ally in the House of Lords, whose opinion seems sounder and more temperate, and one who speaks with greater authority, no less an ally than the present Archbishop of Canterbury. He is against censorship in the matter and against taboos. He could not conceive, he has declared (*The Times,* May 29, 1930), any form of censorship which would be tolerable. "Any kind of taboo in these matters was bound to defeat its own ends. There was only one way to prevent the circulation of bad literature, and that was to promote the circulation of good literature. That would do more than any revival of a moral censorship of the Press." When archbishops preach these sound doctrines of common sense I begin to feel that it is time for me to be silent.

For the truth is—one cannot too often repeat—that literature and art that are "obscene" in any genuinely objectionable sense, will be unlikely to appeal to normally healthy minds when not surrounded by secrecy and prohibition. *The market in pornography is artificially created.* That is the central fact of the situation. No one would read a book because the Home Secretary recommends it; there is a vast public to read a book because he condemns it. He and his subordinates are responsible, not merely for the advertisement of what may properly be termed "filthy," by conferring on it the charm of the forbidden, but, by creating the demand, they are directly responsible for the creation of the "filth" which supplies the demand. That, we must always remember, is the central fact of the situation so far as the crudest and most offensive productions are concerned. It is the point on which the whole question of obscenity and censorship ultimately turns. For wholesomely born and bred persons obscenity is no problem. Legislation is uncalled for when mischievous taboos are abolished. With children reasonably brought up—for which we need, first of all, the right parents—and progressively familiar from childhood with the central facts of life, the perverse zeal of our Home Secretaries and Public Prosecutors will no longer create a market for pornography.

It is fear—in reality a kind of fear-complex—which dominates the people who practise secrecy and enforce repression in a matter where secrecy and repression are obviously against Nature and therefore certain to produce results which are worse than futile. Fear, undoubtedly, is a valuable part of the equipment which Man has inherited from the higher apes from whom he arose. Their special mode of life, the absence of powerful weapons of defence, and the inaptitude for rapid movement render necessary an extreme degree of shyness, caution, and timidity. Man has built up many walls of protection against the inherited dangers to which he is thus liable, and within these walls, or even without them, he has sometimes shown a new courage which his humbler ape-like kin mostly failed to reveal. But the old aptitude for fear is still too deeply rooted not to be constantly in evidence, sometimes with good reason, and sometimes in epidemic panics.

Such an epidemic of panic, once prevalent in Europe, was that aroused by witchcraft. For three centuries European life suffered a strange and tragic obsession of fear over witchcraft, leading to endless horrors. A certain amount of belief in witchcraft is indeed world-wide. But even among savages it seldom becomes an overwhelming obsession. It was not so in Europe until as late as the thirteenth century, and the attitude of the Church, which is the institution chiefly in question where demonology is concerned, was one of incredulity and comparative tolerance. In the middle of that century, for instance, the ruling Pope refused to allow the Holy Office to extend its activities to the persecution of so-called witches. It was during the following century that the change occurred, and early in the fifteenth century, following a Papal Bull, tales of horror concerning the doings of witches had free course in all circles of society. In the famous *Malleus Maleficarum*,[13] published at Cologne before the end of the fifteenth century, the whole theory of witchcraft was codified and expounded, and, as it has been said, the stage was set for a tragedy which during the two

[13] This important work has been translated and edited by the Reverend Montague Summers (Rodker, 1928). Summers believes that witches have always been pursued unremittingly.

following centuries was to be enacted in more or less the same form in every Christian country. The conception was formulated in the heads of theologians and lawyers, and the victims were tortured until "confessions" were obtained corresponding to the ideas of the judges.[14] There were enlightened persons who realised, more or less clearly, how the phenomenon arose, but even in the eighteenth century and later, witchcraft was sometimes regarded as a serious matter.

As the obsession of witchcraft died down during the eighteenth century, another obsession, that of obscenity—having a curiously similar origin in perverse religious notions—arose to take its place. It seemed that the prehuman thirst for fear must have something to feed on, and when witchcraft lost its terrors the new diabolic iniquity of obscenity was found to serve as well. The witchfinders of the seventeenth century are indeed a close counterpart of the obscenity finders of to-day. The lurid halo around the witch made her a really injurious influence, just as the glamour we now cast around obscenity imparts to it an influence it could not otherwise possess. Witchcraft, like obscenity, was not always the product of the witchfinder's imagination. But so far as it was real it could not be touched by the ducking stool or the law court. It became harmless under more reasonably humane and civilised influences.

It was precisely at the time when the development of science and civilisation was leading to the proper estimate of witchcraft that the ferocity of the persecution of witches reached its height. We may say the same to-day about obscenity. The old sex taboos are dissolving. We are beginning to face openly the facts of sex with a degree of intelligence and frankness which even a quarter of a century ago was impossible. That new honesty and sincerity itself stirs up the persecutional fanaticism of the descendants of the witchfinders. Yet until the crime or "indictable misdemeanour," as we term it in English law, of obscenity goes the way of the crime of witchcraft it is idle to talk of civilisation.

The close resemblance of the later obscenity mania to the earlier witchcraft mania seems to have been first pointed out by Theodore Schroeder, in 1911, in his *"Obscene" Literature and Constitutional Law*. It has often been remarked on since. Schroeder, indeed, denied that there was any objective reality whatever either in witchcraft or obscenity. As we have seen, it is not necessary to go as far as that. There is a natural and more or less morbid element often to be found in the witch, and it is perfectly legitimate to describe obscenity as the usually

[14] Garçon & Vinchón: *The Devil: An Historical, Critical and Medical Study*. Translated from the French, London, 1929.

concealed side of natural fact. It is the development in both cases into an obsession that is unnatural and illegitimate, the tendency by which they are elaborated and formulated into sacrilegious and illegal entities to be haled before tribunals and condemned to punishment. When no such mania is working on perversely ingenious minds, the proper place of witchcraft and obscenity, even if they possess objective reality, is seen to be outside of law courts.

It is beginning to be seen to-day. The legal conception of obscenity has been carried to such dizzy heights of absurdity that it is toppling over into laughter. A new knowledge of the benefits of sunlight, with new habits of dress and new conventions of feminine modesty, has changed our vision of the human body, while the horrors of the Great War, which stands out as the chief event of the early twentieth century, brought ridicule on the pruderies in action and speech of the Victorian drawing room. The young generation of the eighteenth century, in their new philosophic enlightenment, had learnt too much to be afraid of witchcraft. The young generation of our own century, in their new sexual enlightenment, have learnt too much to be afraid of obscenity. Yet this episode in the spiritual history of our race, though shorter than that of witchcraft, has been serious enough, for it has maimed the freedom of art, and hampered the finest social and individual activities, alike in deed and speech. Nor is its day yet over. The final conquest of the human spirit over obscenity still lies before us and its decision is in our hands.

Chapter 15

THE CONTROL
OF POPULATION

THE QUESTION OF THE CONTROL OF POPULATION is usually referred to in popular language as Birth Control. The term is of recent origin. It was devised in New York by Mrs. Margaret Sanger and a few friends in discussion. There was already, indeed, the term "Neo-Malthusianism," invented in England, together with the movement it indicated, in the middle of the last century. But it was felt that that term assumed a particular economic theory which might not necessarily be accepted, or even understood, by many who would still be convinced and even ardent advocates of the movement on its practical side. At first, however, the new term was little used, even by those who had devised it; they were content with other terms, like "Family Limitation," which is less satisfactory because it is narrower, "control" not necessarily involving "limitation" at all, and yet being of the essence of the process because it makes clear that children have ceased to be the result of mere chance but that their coming has been desired and deliberately willed. So that when I first came upon the term "Birth Control," which was before it became general, I at once seized upon it as the best term and have often used it since. It is true, there are some precise people who find that it is not absolutely accurate; but it is a term that cannot fail to be understood, and the more accurate alternatives have not commended themselves.

The name is recent. But what it stands for is ancient. "Birth control," indeed, and its substitutes—especially the latter—have been in active operation ever since birth began to take place on the earth, and even earlier, from the commencement of animal life, even of plant life, and it is estimated that only about five per cent. of the blossoms on our fruit trees mature. That is why it is possible to look at this question as one having an evolutionary meaning.

An old friend of mine, a physician who was also something of a philosopher and keenly interested in the problems of life, once had occasion at his dentist's to take nitrous oxide gas.

It not infrequently happens that in this state we are brought before fundamental problems of the world, and my friend found himself in the presence of the Almighty. He took advantage of the occasion to seek the solution of the mystery of life. What is it for, all this toil and trouble that fill the earth? And the awful reply came in one word: *Reproduction*. We may accept the statement as the statement of the biological "end"—so far as we may use such a word—of all life on earth.

So vast indeed may be said to be Nature's desire for reproduction—speaking in our human way—that in the multiplication of offspring an enormous margin has always been allowed for accidents. A great many more creatures are produced than could possibly subsist if they reached maturity. All but a few do, in fact, fail to become mature. That is fortunate; for it has been roughly estimated that a single infusorian, if allowed to its full capacity, would soon produce a mass of protoplasm larger than the volume of the sun, and another minute organism produce in a year a sphere which would extend beyond the limits of the known universe. A single oyster, if all its progeny survived, would speedily accumulate, it is estimated, a heap of shells eight times the size of the world, while, as a cod may yield seven million eggs and a ling twenty-eight millions, it would need a very short time indeed for a single pair to render the whole ocean a solid mass of fish. The omnipresent English sparrow, it is said, if none died but from old age, would in a few years cover the earth, one to every square inch. Even a single pair of elephants, the slowest animals to breed, would in much less than a thousand years produce ninety millions of elephants. It might be supposed that Man is an exception to this rule. But it is not so. Civilized Man, in some regions, as in the United States in the past, has been known to double his numbers in twenty-five years, and Darwin estimated fifty years ago that at this altogether possible rate of human increase, the population of the United States alone would in a few centuries cover the whole surface of the globe so thickly that four men would have to stand on each square yard. There is indeed one important difference, when we compare Man with other animals in this respect, that while they generally do not increase or diminish at all on the whole (except by human interference, designed or undesigned), any excess or deficiency in one season being soon smoothed out, and the general balance of life thus preserved, Man retains no such equable level, but in a few places tends to die out altogether and in most places tends to overcome the obstacles to increase, though he never anywhere even approximately reaches the rate of increase possible were all obstacles removed.

These are elementary biological considerations. It is necessary, however, to hold them clearly in mind, because they are the foundation on which any human policy of living must be built up. It is necessary, that is to say, in establishing any ordered system of life, that we should remember that life was built up at the first under conditions which presupposed the absence of intelligence, and that there was consequently the need of an enormous margin, to allow for the certain destruction at an early age of the great majority of living beings. As life has evolved towards the higher mammals, living things are better equipped to contend with the destructive agencies of the world, and therefore the offspring of the higher mammals are not nearly so numerous as of the fishes and other lower vertebrates. Yet even the most civilised human races inherit the aptitude to produce an enormous surplus. Whenever, therefore, Man takes up the task of ordering life on a rational and human basis he has to meet the problem of deciding what is to be done about this surplus.

All human societies have been perpetually concerned with this problem from the outset, to a large extent unconsciously, to an ever increasing degree consciously. Malthus, at the end of the eighteenth century, in his famous *Essay on the Principle of Population,* by a systematic survey of the various races of the world, made clear how the natural tendency to excess of population was among every human race naturally checked in a great variety of ways, *preventive,* by the exercise of a restraint on procreation, and *positive,* by the destruction of the excess due to unrestrained procreation. These positive checks, he considered, were extremely various and included every cause, whether arising from vice or misery, which in any degree contributes to shorten the natural duration of life. Under this head he enumerated all unwholesome occupations, severe labour and exposure to the seasons, extreme poverty, bad nursing of children, great towns, excesses of all kinds, the entire train of common diseases and epidemics, wars, plagues, famines. The whole of the obstacles to increase of population, preventive and positive, he regarded as resolvable into moral restraint, vice, and misery. The wide survey which Malthus made of this process among all the peoples of the earth up to then observed is quite independent, it must be remembered, of the particular theory of the ratio of human increase compared with the ratio of the increase of the means of human subsistence, with which his name is associated and which has often been violently attacked, no doubt with more or less reason. The facts remained, whatever might be thought of the details of the theory put forward to explain them.

Half a century later Charles Darwin appeared, inspired by the ideas of Malthus, but working in the totally different field of biological evolution. In his *Descent of Man* Darwin briefly discussed and enumerated the influences preventing the indefinite growth of population. The primary or fundamental check he held to be the difficulty of gaining subsistence and of living in comfort, this primary check acting among civilised nations chiefly by restraining marriage. He added, as very important among the poor, a high death-rate of infants and a generally greater mortality from disease at all ages. The effects of epidemics and wars, he pointed out, were soon counterbalanced, under favourable conditions more than counterbalanced, while emigration he realised to be only a slight and temporary check. He considered that prudential restraints, by delaying marriage and in other ways, are common among savages, and that the offspring of savages are subject to many risks and dangers. He observed that Malthus failed to lay enough stress on infanticide, which is probably the most important of all checks to population. Following Hume, Malthus believed indeed that the permission to practise infanticide was not a check at all but an actual encouragement to population. Malthus also passed over abortion.

During the period that has followed Darwin's work in this field the activity of ethnological observers all over the world has accumulated a vast amount of facts concerning the attitude of different races to the question of population and their actual practice with respect to offspring. The results are summed up in a work, *The Population Problem*, by Professor A. M. Carr-Saunders, which is likely long to remain a landmark in the study of a problem of the first consequence for human happiness and civilisational advance. Carr-Saunders made clear that among all savage peoples one or more methods of limiting population are adopted, and that by these methods, of limiting automatically and often consciously, the population is preserved at an almost or quite stationary level. As this holds good of peoples living a nomadic life as hunters or fishers, like primitive men, it seems probable that such controlling influences came into action early in man's career, certainly in the later Paleolithic period, and probably before then.

The methods by which population is consciously or automatically controlled, and increase limited, are numerous. They fall into two groups, the first acting before conception, by decreasing fertility, and the second after conception, and indeed throughout life, by increasing elimination. Most of these two groups of methods are found among peoples even in very early stages of culture.

The methods of the first group, which naturally tend to become ever more prominent as civilisation and the foresight which accompanies it develop, are least important in the earliest stages. Nor are they always to any high degree effective. Thus pre-pubertal intercourse, which has been included among such influences, seems of doubtful efficacy; it might even be held to act in the opposite direction by ensuring pregnancy at the earliest possible moment, though it may not be favourable to a high quality of offspring. Prolonged lactation is a more effective method, and is not unknown to the lower social classes in civilisation. The women of some savage races continue to suckle their children sometimes for very long periods. Thus the women of the extinct Tasmanians, who were an extremely primitive people, prolonged lactation for from two to four years, the Australian women about the same time, and sometimes even until the child is five or six years old. In quite another part of the world, in North America, the practice is similar. Among some Californian tribes, Schoolcraft (as quoted by Carr-Saunders) found that the child was sometimes not weaned until five years of age. Further north the same practice prevails, sometimes for a still longer period; and in Greenland Nansen even heard of children of ten or more continuing to take the breast. Similar reports come from all parts of the world, not only as regards hunting and fishing peoples, but also agricultural tribes; thus in Africa the suckling period is estimated to last nearer three than two years. During lactation, as is well known, pregnancy is unlikely to occur. That is further ensured, in many parts of the world, by the prohibition of intercourse during lactation.

This is probably the most important of the taboos which constitute a special group of methods for controlling birth. They were especially studied, first by Robertson Smith and later by Frazer and Crawley, who have shown how for primitive peoples matters of sex are felt to be dangerous, only to be approached with many precautions, and frequently to be altogether avoided.

There are a number of occasions in life when, for peoples living in many parts of the world, intimate intercourse between the sexes is held to be full of risk, spiritual or material. Some of these taboos were only operative under circumstances (such as war and hunting expeditions) when intercourse was not likely to take place. Yet they were so numerous and sometimes so prolonged (the entire population of Egypt, according to Diodorus, had to abstain from intercourse for seventy-two days after the death of a king) that they could not have been without effect. What we now consider the most important method of limiting population, and specifically term "birth control," the method of permitting intercourse but preventing conception, is, and so far as we can tell always has been, rare among primitive peoples of any type.[1] It is not surprising when we remember that there is reason for believing that many primitive peoples have not known what precisely caused the production of children and have attributed it to various fantastic causes. Even when we know or suspect its existence, it is often practised in ways so ineffective, and even of purely magical character, that its influence can scarcely have been great. We must not, however, suppose that it was entirely unknown as altogether without effect. The story of Onan in the book of Genesis shows that the practice was recognised in the ancient traditions of the Hebrews. It is worth noting, also, that that story cannot be taken to indicate that the practice was reprobated; it was the motive of Onan that constituted his sin: he objected to obey the divine ordinance to raise seed to his brother's widow, on the selfishly individualistic ground that the resulting child would not be counted as his own; therefore, we are told, the Lord slew him, but we are not told that the Lord had any abstract abhorrence of his method of birth control.

When we survey the general working of these methods of the first group—the methods of limiting fertility—we are bound to conclude that, though an undoubtedly real influence, they are hardly adequate to account for the very low birth-rate which we everywhere find among the lowest, and therefore probably the most primitive, human races. Nearly everywhere, all over the world, the savage family seldom consists of more than three or four children, counting all births. A family of five children is usually a large family.

When, indeed, we consider broadly the question of the sexual impulse among primitive and savage races we seem to be brought to a conclusion which I set forth some years ago in an Appendix to the third volume of my *Studies in the Psychology of Sex*. It used to be thought that savages were more licentious and more sexually inclined than civilised peoples. But the more we know of them the more we are compelled to conclude that that is often the reverse of the truth.[2] Savage peoples must for

[1] Malinowski, among the Trobriand Islanders of New Guinea whom he studied so elaborately, found that, though youthful pre-marital intercourse is common and recognised, pregnancy is rare. This remains a puzzling phenomenon.

[2] We must of course admit wide variations. Thus while among the Trobrianders Malinowski found youthful sexual indulgence generally accepted, in another part of New Guinea Margaret Mead (*Growing Up in New Guinea*) found sex minimised, even in early life, by shame, puritanism, and the fear of spirits.

the most part lead a hard and strenuous life, with little about it to arouse the softer emotions. It would frequently seem to be only under special circumstances and on the occasion of some periodic festival orgy that sexual activities are strongly aroused. They remain latent in a much greater degree, and for much more prolonged periods, than is normal among the civilised, even though among the civilised there are usually more restraints on their more easily aroused desires. The small procreative activity of savages and primitive peoples would thus be due not so much to strong measures for controlling and restraining conception—though these often play a large part—as to the presence of a temperament which is without the need for strong measures of control and restraint. Nature herself limits procreation by limiting the impulse to procreate.

This is rendered the more probable when we recall that—as has been pointed out by Walter Heape, the pioneer of the modern study of sexual physiology, as well as by others—we see precisely the same difference between wild and domestic animals. Wild animals, in their natural and strenuous conditions of life, are comparable to savages, and domestic animals, in their easier and more artificial life, to the civilised. And we find that there is just the same corresponding sexual difference. Not only is the sexual impulse aroused much more easily in the domesticated, but breeding tends to occur more frequently than in the natural wild condition, and reproductivity is increased. Thus (as Beebe has shown in his splendid monograph on the Pheasant Family) the Red Junglefowl of southeastern Asia, which is the aristocratic ancestor of our Domestic Fowl, resembles his rather degenerate descendant in many respects, but in his sexual habits he is notably different. He is monogamous, not polygamous, and in place of the servile submission of the modern hen and the easy callous dominance of the modern cock, she is independent and hard to win, and he must spend much time in a long, arduous, and skilful courtship in order to gain her favours. That is the common and almost universal difference between wildness and domesticity in animals, as between savagery and civilisation among human beings. Thus the conclusion is confirmed that while restraints on the sexual impulse are easier to impose and carry out in savagery than in civilisation, that is because the impulse itself is less imperative and for long periods in a natural latency.

So much for the ways in which among primitive and savage peoples births are controlled by prevention. We may turn to the other group of ways in which, births not having been prevented, the only control must be by subsequent elimination. The chief of these methods are infanticide, hardship, ignorance, and lack of proper food leading to high infantile mortality, wars and feuds, disease, the killing of the sick and infirm. It is the first of these that is the most important, and also the most interesting because deliberate and apparently unnatural. As we have seen, Malthus failed to realise its importance, which was emphasised by Darwin, and even exaggerated by McLennan. How important it is among savage peoples is clearly brought out by Westermarck in the careful and learned summary of facts concerning its wide prevalence and great extent in his *Origin and Development of the Moral Ideas.* It is frequently not merely permitted, but enjoined by law or custom, even against the parents' wishes. Sometimes not more than two children are allowed to a family; in some regions nearly every woman has destroyed four or five of her children. But everywhere this can only be carried out shortly after birth; later, it would be murder and as such punishable. Moreover—as indeed we might expect—it is usual for the children selected to live to be treated with even an excess of tenderness and indulgence, to a much greater extent than is common among the poorer classes in civilisation, among whom large families, even when not felt to be an infliction, are beyond the strength of the mother to tend. It is found that in small islands, as in the Pacific, the stress on infanticide is very stringent: without it, the population would soon outrun the means of subsistence, for their territories are strictly limited by intertribal arrangement and so will only support a limited population. But it is also curious to observe that the real reason for limiting the growth of the population is seldom understood by the peoples who practise it, and they commonly assign all sorts of reasons, or merely "custom," for the economic reason which renders infanticide, in the absence of any sound method of birth control, really imperative. The other methods for the restraint on population by elimination are mostly independent of human will, like disease and hardship, or at all events not primarily directed to this end, like wars and feuds. They do not seem to be so important as infanticide. We might expect disease to be full of danger for primitive and savage peoples; but it is not so. Carr-Saunders has well brought together the facts and arguments indicating that disease is rare among such peoples, of many of whom it can be said, as of the Tasmanians, that "before connexion with the whites the aborigines were a healthy as well as a happy people." Diseases, on a broad survey, seem to be mostly of comparatively modern origin—some of them indeed probably of very recent development—and due partly to the artificial conditions of civilised existence and partly to the excessive aggregation involved by civilised life, conditions which only begin to be overcome by hygienic and medical skill in the most advanced stages of civilisation. It is hardship and deficient food, common to savage life, rather than diseases, which cause infantile mortality at this stage.

When we turn to peoples in a higher stage, the stage of barbarism leading on to civilisation, which comes within the view of history, the picture is modified. There are the same methods of decreasing fertility and of increasing elimination—one or more of which is found in powerful operation among every people on the surface of the earth—but their relative importance is changed and their forms sometimes modified. Infanticide became still more common, among those that were the leaders in civilisation almost universal. Egypt, China, Japan, Arabia, Palestine, Greece, Rome, northern Europe—in all these cradles of high civilisation infanticide has flourished; nearly always the infants of obviously inferior quality have been destroyed, but the practice was seldom strictly confined by that consideration. Moreover, infanticide tended to be supplemented, and gradually in part or altogether replaced, by the attenuated form of abortion. This was indeed found among many of the primitive and savage peoples, but with the growth of refinement it became more common, and it has now largely replaced infanticide altogether. As physicians well know, women to-day of all social classes feel no horror of abortion, though they would not dream of contemplating infanticide, and seem often to find it hard to realise that by the man-made laws of most countries abortion is counted a crime.

Another check to fertility which begins to acquire a new prominence among the historical races is celibacy, alike in its religious and secular forms, or delay in marriage. Among the primitive and savage races, as we know, though taboos on intercourse were frequent and sometimes prolonged, everyone who was not hopelessly imbecile married, usually at the earliest possible age, and the tendency to a single life, which increases with civilisation, cannot but powerfully aid the checks on fertility. At the same time we find, though still so rare as to be negligible until recent years, a slightly increased attention to the methods of what we now specifically term "birth control."

All these checks on procreation are then increased. But the increase was necessary, for the energy of procreation itself had increased. Among the historical races families have always been larger than among the primitive and savage peoples. The more settled life of Neolithic times, out of which the great historical races arose, the organisation in closely knit communities and ordered towns, the consequent accumulation of wealth, made life easier, and the earlier restraint of hard conditions on life which had itself prevented large families was removed. So that even the increased checks on fertility were not enough to restore the balance, and an increased severity of the methods of elimination was also needed. A new importance attaches among historical races to disease. Carr-Saunders believed that it was, precisely, amid the aggregated centres of population developed during the Neolithic period that many of our modern parasitic diseases arose. So that the same influence which caused the increase in population also caused an important check to population. Wars, too, began to acquire a new effectiveness as a method of eliminating the superfluous human populations, especially when the Iron Age introduced more adequate methods of human slaughter than had hitherto prevailed, a process which has gone on with an accelerated skill and rapidity to our own day, so that it is now estimated that before long, unless some new methods of control are established, it will be possible by pressing a button to destroy the whole population of large areas. The mortality of wars in the past, however, has been due more to the pestilences and famines following them than to actual slaughter in battle, and, as we know during the last Great War, the deaths due to influenza in various parts of the world were far greater than those due to the war.

These are the general tendencies which have been at work during the ten thousand years or so of the historical period; such have been the influences increasing fertility, and such have been the influences counteracting that fertility. On the whole they have been fairly successful in maintaining, not without much friction and misery, an even balance. It has been roughly estimated that up to the year 1800 the natural increase from the beginning, perhaps during millions of years, had only attained a world population of 850 millions. But since then a cataclysmal change has taken place which, in one way or another, has affected nearly the whole of the earth's population. This change has been of a threefold nature. There has, firstly, been the immense stimulus furnished by the industrial revolution beginning near the end of the eighteenth century and associated with the steam engine and the subsequent outburst of mechanical inventiveness; therewith the whole of life—production, consumption, procreation—was speeded up. Secondly, following on this and to some extent its natural outcome, there came the development of the medical, sanitary, and hygienic sciences and arts which not only countered the new risks to health and life of urban overpopulation caused by the industrial revolution, but went further, increasing the health and longevity of the whole population everywhere, and vastly diminishing the mortality and the prevalence of some of the most devastating epidemic diseases all over the world. Thirdly, and acting in the same direction, the slow development of humanitarian feeling, the feeling of Christianity in particular and civilisation in general, has largely suppressed many of the methods by which fertility had always been diminished and most of the chief methods by which the population is directly and deliberately reduced. Thus three new forces of world-wide influence, yet unknown in the world before, all began to exert pressure in the same direction at the same moment, early in the nineteenth century.

These three great movements are still working among us, still developing, even taking on new forms, and leading to new social impulses never dreamt of by those pioneers who first worked to initiate them.

I do not propose to discuss in detail these new forms, and it would indeed be premature, for it is not profitable to deal with situations which are independent of our determining influence until they actually arrive, all the less perhaps since, until they have arrived, they are apt to arouse a ferocious antagonism in many excellent people. Any remarks I may here put forward are, therefore, uttered *sotto voce*, as it were, in a kind of self-communing which no one need overhear.

In the first place, one cannot but note that the stimulus of the eighteenth-century industrial revolution is entering a new and totally different phase. The revolt of the workers in the early nineteenth century in the belief that the machine would destroy the worker with the machine-destroying riots in the north of England, was on the short view mistaken. The immediate effect of machinery was to create a real and effective working class. "Labour" in the modern sense was born, and soon gained power, and therewith came trades unions, socialism, communism, and the rest. But in the long run that dread of the workers lest machinery should extinguish them is likely to prove to some extent justified. Man has harnessed Nature to the car of labour, all the natural forces are being utilised or transferred to replace human work.[8]

The workers are reduced to a minimum, while, on the other

---

[8] As I write I come on an excellent statement of this process by Professor Leopold Ziegler (*Forum Philosophicum*, Vol. I, No. 1, 1930): "There is no flowing water, no seam of coal, no metallic stratum or oil field, perhaps soon no ray of the sun nor lightning flash, nay, no atom, no elemental quantum of matter which will not yield up its chained energies to the insatiable hunger for more power. Man is being freed from manual labour and nature allowed to create and work. Here stands, the centre of all admiration, the power-plant automatically set and kept in motion, from whose clear and well-lighted halls the occupants have almost completely disappeared, while generators, dynamos and turbines run by themselves. If the modern strategist is proud of the 'empty field of battle,' the engineer, the real man of the hour, is no less proud of the empty field of work."

hand, the production of commodities, which the unemployed workers cannot afford to buy, is accelerated to a maximum.[4] This phase, which we are now entering, is sometimes termed that of "rationalisation." But at the present moment the process, however rational, means that the world contains far more workers than it can employ and far more goods than it can consume. So that we view an unexampled world-wide condition of unemployment and industrial stagnation, which, while it will not in its present state prove permanent, represents a temporary exacerbation of what must be a permanent tendency until we have stabilised industry and prices, and that can only happen when we have stabilised population. One result will be an internecine struggle (such as at the moment exists in Australia) between Labour and the industrial system which Labour was created to carry on, a struggle in which one party can only strangle the other and therewith itself. Industry, which once loomed so conspicuously on the stage of the world, is retiring into the background as a comparatively unimportant though still essential part of life. The workers will shrink into a comparatively insignificant, though still valuable, section of the community, and will be transformed in mental and physical characteristics, for in many spheres, with the new mechanical delicacy now secured, a child can perform to-day what it needed a navvy to perform yesterday. That indeed is recognised as an essential part of the process now going on, for as industrial progress becomes more specialised, skill becomes less so, and labour is tending to become to a large extent merely automatic machine-tending. The proletariat—at the very moment when its triumph is being proclaimed—is approaching extinction, and as it draws nearer to the goal its mental abilities dwindle.[5]

But though the labouring class shrinks, it remains alive—even more alive under our present comfortable conditions of life than ever before—merely becoming the "unemployed."

[4] Thus in the United States, even if we go a few years back, it was found in 1927 that with 5 per cent. fewer employees American factories were turning out 7 per cent. more product. No end can be seen to this process, for the possibilities of technological improvement are practically unlimited.

[5] These lines were scarcely written when a statement absolutely in harmony with them appeared from the pen of a distinguished economist, J. M. Keynes ("Economic Possibilities for Our Grandchildren," Nation, London, Oct. 18, 1930). "The economic problem," he here declares, "may be solved, or be at least within sight of solution, within a hundred years." But this can only happen, he points out, provided we control population, avoid wars and dissention, and give to science the control of those matters which concern science. Meanwhile, he continues, let us encourage, and experiment with, "the arts of life." This has been my own view of the problem for over forty years (as in the introduction to The New Spirit, 1890).

While human skill is, on the one hand, working to make human beings comparatively unnecessary, it is, on the other hand, working with equal zeal to keep human beings alive and even to multiply their number. With that fantastic absurdity which puts him apart from all other animals, Man undoes with one hand what he does with the other; he creates life with tremendous energy, even as though he were thereby fulfilling a divine mission; and at the same time he devotes an equally tremendous energy to the task of making life almost impossible. Thus in England at the present moment forty million pounds a year (quite apart from an equal sum devoted to ordinary Poor Law relief, as it used to be termed) are spent on keeping alive the vast unwanted army of workers no longer needed, and all the resources of science, medical, hygienic, and sanitary, are employed to prevent or cure disease and increase still further the ever-increasing longevity of the population and the ever-diminishing chances of death.[6] At the same time the governments of the nations are blind to the devastating effects of the vast flood of human life which they recklessly let loose on the world, not only doing nothing to stay it, but on the contrary seeking to tie the hands of those who would educate the nation in the vital task of controlling procreation. This has brought about what has been called a "systematised lunacy." It was fabled of old that the world was destroyed by a flood; it is by a flood that the world is threatened to-day, but not of water, and not by Jehovah, but by Man himself.

Ziegler believes that, by transferring its handwork from human workers to mechanical automata, society is making of the displaced working class its own mortal enemy, and perhaps preparing the downfall of our civilisation. The cloud castle of prosperity is fading to nothingness, as an unintended secondary result of the inevitable rationalisation of commercial life. At the same time the vast industrial army of unemployed and unemployables, bred in intensive culture as parasites, prey upon the marrow of the nations, and being hopelessly demoralised by the compulsory idleness which soon becomes second nature, will become, Ziegler believes, the vengeful soldiers of any upheaval.

But, I have asked myself before and would ask again, why need this now unprofitable army be maintained? If the old industrial system, which involved a vast proletariat army of often ill-used units, is now over and done with, why should we not recognise facts, rejoice in them, and prepare the way for a new and better order? No doubt there must be a pain-

---

[6] Thus, as regards infant mortality, the average in London at the middle of the last century was 157 per 1,000; in 1927 it was only 59.

ful stage of transition. But to allow the continued procreation of an army of workless parasites which may at any moment turn and rend those who feed them is a kind of lunacy which scarcely deserves even to be called systematised.[7]

Our period of rationalisation, which cannot be carried on indefinitely, needs to be followed, as Ziegler himself states, by "a period of deliberate irrationalisation"; that is to say, a deeper and wider grasp of the elements of reality in life. There will always be workers, and work is always good, while a workless class—whether the masters of old Rome or the unemployed parasites of to-day—is an evil and destructive element in society. But the possibilities of work are infinite.

The extinction of the industrial proletariat of the past does not, it must be added, mean that workers will be abolished. On the contrary, it may more truly mean that there will be no class but that of workers, with the important distinction that none of them will constitute a proletariat, and that even the machine-tenders, who must always be a considerable body, will be left free by their simple activities to develop themselves in some wider field. Work, it must be remembered, is natural; all animals tend to work; idleness and parasitism only occur among creatures whose ordinary or previous channels of work have for some reason or other been closed to them, and without work they degenerate. There is, therefore, no disrespect to work or the workers if we state that the machine-workers of the coming industrial age are tending to be extinguished, for that merely means that, ceasing to constitute what is called a proletariat, they will reappear as a higher working class with greater possibilities of absorbing all other classes.[8]

I am not called upon to say what the chief forms of work will be that lie before that coming class. If I were, I should say that they can only be what in the widest sense may be called art. For the possibilities of art, and the variety of mediums in which it may be exercised, are practically endless.

[7] By Act of Parliament (Mental Treatment Act, 1930) there are legally no longer any "lunatics" in England; but it is a good old English word, and I propose to continue to use it, when it seems to me required, any reader who objects being requested to substitute mentally for the term "lunatic" the term "fitting inmate for a mental hospital."

[8] When this was written I had not read the admirable essay on "Revolutions" in Aldous Huxley's *Do What You Will* (1929), in which the disappearance of the Proletariat is discussed and explained. But I consider that Aldous Huxley views the outlook too pessimistically. Even in the worst ages of the world there have been delightful redeeming points, and even the same age has often been glorified or damned according to the standpoint of the spectator. For even in the worst age it is open to us to find ways of following our own daimon, and if men therefore seek to kill us, well, as Charles Kingsley would have stammered, "L-l-l-let 'em!"

It must needs be so, since art, rightly understood, enters into all human activities and all the satisfactions of human needs. I speak of art without mentioning science, by no means to belittle science, but because even science, when it is not debased, is itself an art. All the great representatives of science have been great artists, and while life is not possible without the everlasting thirst of science, it is also true that science is not wholesome unless it is kept true to the whole of life, which is essentially art. And if there is any one art which comes before us as of fundamental importance and immediately urgent, it is surely architecture. To take only the city with which some of us are most familiar, the destruction, the replanning, and the rebuilding of the greater part of London are tasks that cannot be too soon undertaken, for the comfort of its inhabitants and the joy of future generations.

The third movement, that of humanitarianism, which acquired such enormous momentum during the nineteenth century, is, above all, the modern movement which now needs to be guided into the channels it must in any case sooner or later inevitably find. With its earlier forms we need not quarrel; we can recognise them as beneficial and even necessary. The task of making sanitation, wholesome hygiene, the extinction so far as possible of devastating epidemics, the cure and prevention of disease, the preservation of life, and the extension of longevity into national aims, has been a social discipline of inestimable value. Even its cost in time and labour and money has constituted a precious part of that discipline, and the fact that it has been faced and accepted is a promise that the same courage will be found to face and accept the new forms of humanitarianism which now lie before us.

The discipline was needed. When we look back at the social history of even a century ago, as recorded in the newspapers of that age, we see prevailing a degree of callous brutality if not of absolute cruelty, in an atmosphere of indifference and sometimes of complacency, which to-day seems to us appalling. The voice of humanity was, indeed, from time to time vigorously raised, but it with difficulty effected any practical change, and humanitarian social feeling had no existence even as a phrase.

Humanitarianism has now become a part of our civilisation. It has been indeed so intensified, so driven into special channels, and these have been so fossilised, that it needs to be revived and reinvigorated and enlarged. There is such a thing as a morbid humanitarianism, and beneficent as was its first movement a century ago, it now needs fresh blood and the energy for new movement. Consider, for instance, the present so-called humanitarian attitude towards capital punishment. When a man was hanged for burglary and even lesser offences, that question was rightly regarded as urgent. To-day the abolition of capital punishment may still be desirable, but to regard it as urgent, to make of it a cause for energetic propaganda, to show so much anxiety to preserve for the torture of lifelong imprisonment the lives of feeble and anti-social specimens of humanity while yet tolerating the destruction of hundreds of thousands of the best lives in war—that is an attitude which would be ludicrous if it were not pathetic.

The humanitarianism that will soon be called for, if it is not already demanded to-day, is at once both broader and more discriminating. The excessive horror of pain is out of place when we realise that pain is an essential part of all growing life, and that it is only unessential and unprofitable pain that we should seek to prevent. The destruction of life, similarly, has been a part of all life from the beginning. It was rooted in Nature long before Man appeared, and Man cannot with impunity escape it, though he may exercise control over it. That control is most wisely exercised by ensuring, so far as possible, that the finest specimens of our race are not destroyed. To foster wars, in order to kill our "heroes," as we regard them, while taking so much care to safeguard the lives of our "criminals" is not the course of wisdom.[9] We cannot expect, and we cannot desire, that the vast army of persons who become maimed or diseased through no fault of their own should be killed off. Future ages may well look back with horror at the days when everything in life was planned except death, and men and women were meekly content to let their exit from the world be ordered by the chances of disease. We can at least ensure that those who find life an intolerable burden should have social support in the courageous resolve to throw off that burden and accept what is termed euthanasia. Moreover, we can adopt beneficent meas-

[9] It may be that the future, instead of trying to safeguard the lives of criminals, will cultivate a more enlightened conception of criminality. If, as is now held, the criminal is essentially the anti-social person, the murderer or the burglar is not the only anti-social person, or even perhaps the worst. The person in authority who impedes the accomplishment of any great beneficial movement, bringing health to body or to mind, whether of the individual or of the community (some, no doubt, will think of those who impede the spread of birth control or censor the manifestations of art), is, in accordance with the great principle long ago magnificently asserted by Milton, worse than any ordinary criminal and may some day be considered more worthy to be hanged. A crude and narrow view of criminality is the inevitable consequence of superficial life values and so long as our public retail a crude and narrow intelligence we shall have all—or more than all —the criminals we deserve.

ures to diminish at the outset the number of those who are, or will probably prove, maimed or helpless.

It is here, indeed, that we still have an opportunity of manifesting that heroism which so many think we shall lose when war and the militaristic attitude are things of the past. It is, of course, a foolish thought. There is just as much room for heroism in peace as in war, and it is just as often being manifested, though for the most part in unobtrusive ways that are not announced in newspaper placards. But the militarists may be cheered to think that even when war is totally abolished, there is still a place in morality for killing, and an infinitely more humane place than that occupied by murder in war, that is to say by killing the unfit, not by killing the fit. Only so can we be true to the instincts that have created Man.

It is the aim of eugenics to eliminate, so far as possible, the unfit stocks, which by their constitutional defects lower the level of human achievement and increase the difficulties of social life. But in the state of our knowledge to-day, and probably for some time to come, this is extremely difficult. So complicated is heredity, so various the order followed by the inherited genes in constituting the new individual, that the more cautious Mendelian investigators sometimes think it may take thousands of years before we can make much progress, through methods of deliberate selection, in raising the level of the race.

But there is a simple method of working towards the purification of the race which has perhaps prevailed from the beginning and been held in honour in the highest civilisation, including those of Greece and Rome, from which we ourselves so largely descend.[10] It is one of the unfortunate results of Christianity among us to-day—amid other results more fortunate—that we were led to reject infanticide, and that we still feel compelled to our own pain and trouble, to the injury of the race, and to the misery of the victims of our supposed "humanitarianism," to keep alive even the most hopelessly maimed and defective of new-born infants. We know in the back of our minds that we only do it out of a quaint superstition. So timid a race have we grown, so meekly crushed by the dead hands of a tradition that for us has ceased to have any meaning, that our "humanitarianism" is now a ghastly spectre! We suffer the fate we deserve.

[10] While a general right of life and death over the newborn infant was recognized in Greece and Rome, it was usually only as regards defective and monstrous offspring that the duty of destruction was enjoined. (See e.g. Westermarck, *Origin and Development of the Moral Ideas*, Vol. 1, pp. 408-411.) This limitation seems altogether reasonable and desirable.

It used to be said that the Great War had cut us off from the past and led us into a new world. It is not probable that many still cherish this delusion. There seems to be no animal so thick-skinned as Man. A sharper prick than that of the Great War—sharp as that seemed at the time—is needed to pierce his tough hide, to arouse into action those sensitive impulses of which, now and again, we catch a glimpse that quickly passes out of sight. I have faith that some day, in whatever poignant shape, the truth will come to Man that life is an art, and that in art there is no place either for violence or for sentimentality.

Yet a sane attitude towards life may be nearer than perhaps we know. When once we have put war out of the world —as sooner or later we are bound to do in a world that is growing so small and so closely knit together—and all the wanton and cruel and mischievous methods of destruction associated with war, we shall be able to face life more reasonably. Pain and death are a part of life. To reject them is to reject life itself. But we have to learn how to apply them and to put them in their right place. There is no longer any room for war in the world, but there will always be room for heroism, and with the highly sensitive and sympathetic dispositions that civilisation may in time generate, the choice of pain and death, for others and even for oneself, cannot fail to call out the heroic spirit. The old humanitarianism, with its morbid terror of pain and death, effected much that was good. But its day is nearly past. The abolition of war, when that comes, will finally abolish it. We are reaching the day of the New Humanitarianism.

These statements, I repeat, though intercalated here, are not put forward for discussion. They merely express the vision of the things that await humanity along the road we are now following. Nothing is gained by discussion. The most vital revolutions spring up from within; they are born in the heart and not in the tongue. They come, and are there before we know it.

How enormously effective these three great forces have been we witness to-day, although so novel is the situation that few have yet grasped its terrible significance. The population of the world, which during millions of years had grown so slowly, suddenly, in the mere flash of time which a century is in the earth's growth, doubled its numbers, and at the present moment is increasing more rapidly than ever in history before. Knibbs, a statistician in this field of the highest competence, estimates this increase as nearly twenty millions every year, so that every two years the world has to provide fresh food for the equivalent of a new France. Professor East, content to be more cautious, estimates the increase as fifteen millions per annum, and making a careful survey of the possibilities of the earth's surface and of the development of agriculture, he believes that the maximum population the earth can support is a little over five thousand millions. Here, he says, is "the heart of the matter." At the present rate of increase the time when there will be no more room left on the earth is not so far distant but that some of our grandchildren will live to see it.

Now it is certain that the present rate of increase will not be maintained. The growing difficulty of obtaining food must cause an ever larger number to perish long before every swamp has been drained and every desert and mountain top rendered available for agriculture. But, if we assume that Man will continue to make but feeble efforts to control his own fate, while the final catastrophe will thus be delayed, it will not be averted. All life, when left to itself, follows the same laws, and it is quite possible to devise a small closed universe with lower organisms and to observe the result. Dr. Raymond Pearl, of the Johns Hopkins University, has done this with a small family of fruit flies of the genus *Drosophila*. He took a pint milk bottle and furnished it with a soil of banana pulp and agar-agar sown with yeast, roughly corresponding to the closed-in universe of the earth on which we live, but of more convenient size. As the Adam and Eve of this universe a couple of flies were introduced with a normal progeny, and the bottle was stoppered with cotton wool, which admitted nothing but air, and kept in a uniform temperature. Every three days a census was taken. Life went on as in the larger universe, and it was found, moreover, that the rate of increase followed just the same course as that of Man through the ages. At first very slow, the rate gradually increased, reaching the maximum—probably the point at which Man is now arriving—and then began to decrease in rapidity, though numbers still increased, finally reaching a point at which the density of the population resulted in complete saturation.[11] There are disturbing influences in our larger universe not found in this smaller one, but the general drift of events is evidently the same. The rate of increase will be slackened. But it lies with us to decide whether this shall happen destructively, with accompanying misery and degeneration, or constructively, in accordance with increasing knowledge. The "unclean spirits" which now possess Man may rightly be termed Legion. We know what happened to those Gadarene swine who were possessed by the spirit of Legion. But it is still

[11] Raymond Pearl, *The Biology of Population Growth*, 1926.

not too late for mankind to check the swift career down that
steep place into the sea where the two thousand swine were
choked. The goal of human life on earth, to return to Pearl's
conclusion, is now visibly in sight, and the great question before us is: What kind of people are they to be who will inherit
the earth? Today it is still in our power to determine the answer to that question.

Here, at the threshold of eugenics, we must conclude our
brief survey of the course of "birth control" and its substitutes
in the past. Those methods of the past are no longer practicable; they are too crude, or too ascetic, or too cruel; that
is why they have decayed. The method which comes before
us to-day as a reasonable practical instrument, whatever its
defects, for limiting the family and eugenically moulding the
future race is the method of contraception, henceforth the
most obvious though not the only form of "birth control." It is
practically a new method, and as yet it has no measurable
influence in restraining the ever increasing flood of human
fertility. The pessimists may shake their heads, but it is too
early to despair of the future of humanity and meekly become the humble adherents of the Gadarene swine. Some day,
let us be sure, the world will recognise all that it owes to those
noble pioneers who, at the risk of obloquy, had the vision to
see the fate that threatens Man and the courage to face it
with hope.

Chapter 16

EUGENICS AND THE FUTURE

THUS WE ARE BROUGHT TO EUGENICS, a study in which all races of living things have from the first been unconsciously concerned, though it is only in the higher forms of human civilisation that it becomes a conscious concern. The word "eugenics" has, it is true, together with the supposed aims of its partisans, often been the object of cheap witticisms. Ground for amusement has, in fact, not seldom been afforded alike by cranks and by well-meant cranky legislation. It is just as foolish to suppose that a new race can be created by legislation as that a new morality can be established. Professor East remarks that the word "eugenics" has been so bandied about by the self-complacent and the waggish that he hesitates to use it at all. But there is no occasion to allow weak brains to rule in this matter; the word is a good sound word, and it was the word finally chosen by Galton, to whom we owe the modern foundation of this supremely important study. The figure of Galton, indeed, grows greater as the years pass. He was not only a highly original and versatile man of science— a supreme representative, one may indeed say, of the scientific spirit—but charmingly human, with a humorous common sense which preserved him from the fads which have been associated in some eyes with "eugenics." All his general pronouncements on the matter, as apart from scientific studies, are gathered together in one small volume written in simple language; and to read this is to realise how far the chief exponent of eugenics was from those silly notions which have filled the minds of the opponents of eugenics.[1]

The details of the methods by which the human race may

[1] Sir Francis Galton, *Essays in Eugenics*, 1909. *The Life, Letters and Labours of Francis Galton*, completed by Karl Pearson in four large volumes (1914-1930), now renders possible a comprehensive study of his work.

be purified and invigorated Galton always left free and open;
he knew that at the present stage of investigation they cannot
be determined. He would rather have eugenics to be a kind
of religion than a subject for legislation, doubtless realising
that Parliamentary statutes are only sound in so far as they
approximate to common law and merely assert that which
the community is already spontaneously doing. It is education
that, above all, we need, education in existing knowledge and
a determination to aid the further growth of knowledge,
together with training in personal and social responsibility.
The English Society for the Promotion of Eugenics, founded
under the inspiration of Galton, was originally called the
Eugenics Education Society. Hasty or injudicious legislation
has sometimes impeded real eugenic progress, which must
work mainly through the free and deliberate choice of the
individual. It is true that the most urgent eugenic task appears
to be, not the promotion of what we imagine to be good
stocks, but the elimination of those which, certainly or probably, are injurious to society or to themselves, and that the
members of these stocks must sometimes in the last resort be
induced by social pressure, and even perhaps by legislation, to
undergo sterilisation. But it is beginning to be recognised that,
in our social state, the really serious factor is to be found in
the class of the population above that comparatively small
stratum unquestionably unfit for society. A decrease among
the grossly defective class may be accompanied by an even
greater increase among the less defective class just above them.
This is the opinion of Professor East as regards the United
States, and Major Leonard Darwin—son of the great Darwin
and long the distinguished president of the Eugenics Society—
believes that such a process is now probably taking place in
England, with a threat of national decay, for "the whole tone of
a nation is permanently affected by the moral and intellectual
contagion which is due to the presence in its ranks of persons
of inferior type," even though they are not of the lowest type.
No compulsory sterilisation can be enforced here; it is a problem which must be met indirectly.

This, we have to recognise, is one of the problems of
eugenics which stretches beyond eugenics. For these are people
who pass muster in the crowd, and they are so numerous that
they have a controlling voice in the policy of a nation. These
are the people who, whether they belong to the labouring class
or the capitalist class, can take in times of industrial prosperity,
but cannot let go in times of industrial depression, with no intelligence to see that they are thereby cutting their own throats;
these are the people who think a country can sell goods to

other countries without buying from them; these are the people who in time of crisis snatch at the easiest and quickest and cheapest policy, without the foresight to know that they will repent of it at leisure; these are the people who are perpetually passing laws for the reform of other people, which produce results the exact opposite of what they were intended to effect; these are the people who daily make their more far-sighted fellow citizens realise that, even if democracy is to-day the only tolerable form of government, a democracy of fools can but lead to ruin. Our eugenical prescriptions are helpless here. We cannot expect a democracy to eliminate—either by violent or by mild methods—the kind of people whom it often elects as its chosen representatives. It is probably education, in the largest sense of the word, that alone helps here, the education that lies in the ever wider expansion of the vision of that world which the few slowly create, together with the increase of the sense of social responsibility which must in the end bind together all the peoples of the earth.[2] We must never imagine that eugenics alone can cure the ills of humanity.

Equally, however, it is not education alone. The danger to-day is, not that eugenics will be overvalued, but that education will. We find abroad in our democratic world an immense faith in a crude conception of education, witnessed, for instance, by the anxiety of Labour governments to prolong the school age, a step which may or may not be beneficial, and is probably not beneficial if applied indiscriminately to children whose capacities are limited and who might be better enabled to develop if removed from the confusing atmosphere of the schoolroom to the larger field of the world. Instruction, the piling in of facts, is not education, and cannot safely be pursued with children of limited capacity; it is merely the overloading of weak stomachs, a process leading to various unpleasant results, none of them beneficial. Education, as the word implies, is the leading out of aptitudes latent in the individual to be educated, of which one of the chief is intelligence. But supposing the aptitudes are not there? We have to learn either to cut off the education at the point where it ceases to be beneficial and probably becomes mischievous, or to cut off the stocks who fail to show in sufficient measure that prime quality of intelligence which, with the stable nervous system on which it normally rests, is essential to a whole-

[2] As J. A. Hobson has well pointed out (*New Statesman*, 18 April, 1931), the world itself is now becoming "the true and final economic system," and while political states retain regulative functions, international government must override national sovereignty in matters affecting the wider human interests.

some life in our difficult and dangerous world. So that, even when we follow the path of education, we are brought up to eugenics.

The chief instrument by which eugenics must work, as we view it to-day, a more essential and reliable instrument than the only less important one of birth control, is sterilisation. In former days sterilisation meant castration, and while it was carried out extensively in that form, not only in the East for the production of eunuchs, but even in the West, where it was approved by great moral theologians of the Catholic Church as a remedy for sexual offences, or (with Papal approval) adopted merely to preserve the singing voices of boys, it has now been superseded.[8] Castration, it is recognised, is harmful by depriving the organism of the internal secretions necessary for full development, which was indeed precisely why it was adopted for the Papal choirs. The methods of sterilisation now employed have no evil effect whatever on the organism. They merely prevent the sperm cell or the ovum from reaching their normal exit, and so inhibit procreation, while leaving sexual desire and sexual potency intact for either man or woman. The operation itself is so slight that, on the man at all events, it can be carried out without interference with his daily work. That is why sterilisation has become the safest and surest method of contraception when procreation is undesirable. So simple it is indeed that the fear has been expressed (as by Dean Inge) that it "might become popular among men who for selfish reasons did not wish to have children." That possibility, however, it should be added, is by no means to be regretted. People who do not wish to have children are the last people who ought to have children; they could only make undesirable parents, and it is in the

[8] Minor ecclesiastics and even the present Pope Pius XI (in his Encyclical *Casti Connubii*) have fulminated against sterilisation. But the Church attaches immense weight to tradition (I recall how, as a boy, a friend once told me he had heard an eloquent sermon from Cardinal Wiseman, and the impressive refrain throughout was: "The Church never changes!"), and it must be remembered that the great moral theologians have found no objection to castration. The greatest of all, Thomas Aquinas, approved of it. Liguori, also, and other prominent moral theologians, had no word of criticism for the castration of the soprano choir in the Pope's private chapel, which went on for centuries, until, indeed, it was considered that soprano voices were not needed. Dr. Joseph Mayer, a Roman Catholic priest, has studied the question of the Church's attitude to castration exhaustively in a work which has received the imprimatur of his ecclesiastical superiors (*Gesetzliche Unfruchtbarmachung Geisteskranker*, 1927). He came to the conclusion that the Church approves of sterilization in suitable cases. Indeed, the practice in the Papal Chapel alone shows that the traditions of the Church admit sterilisation, even castration, for a useful end.

social interest that they should be shut out from parenthood. This is beginning to be seen.

Yet there are many prejudices and misunderstandings still lingering on from the past. The castration of old days left behind it traditions of punishment, ignominy, and obloquy, at the least of a kind of shameful dishonour, and such notions, it is likely, still largely prevail among the populace and became attached to the new sterilisation. Even scientific men, ill-informed concerning recent advances of knowledge in this field, have thrown doubts on the desirability of sterilisation. Especially have they questioned the eugenic benefit of sterilising defectives. Such arguments, when they are not directed against extravagant claims for sterilisation, usually rest on fallacies, and it would be out of place to discuss them here.[4] There can be no reasonable doubt that it makes for some benefit to the race, and is certainly for the benefit of the children who remain unborn and the parents who are spared the pains and trouble of begetting them, that parents who are mentally abnormal or defective should not beget or conceive children.

It is true, and well recognised, that a large number of defective children are the offspring of parents who are not under restraint and approximate to the normal; so that they cannot be brought under legal control for purposes of sterilisation. But these parents usually belong to neurotic groups, and it is possible to recognise them and to bring social influences to bear on them. Cases constantly occur in which to parents of this kind child after child is born in rapid succession, all more or less defective, one way or another, or even in the same way, as in a family of eight, all epileptics. After the first child in such a family (if not before), sterilisation might automatically take place, either voluntarily or by social pressure; yet, as Norman Himes and others have pointed out, how seldom is this done!

A question of frequent debate is how far sterilisation should be voluntary and how far regulated by legislation. My own prejudices in this matter have always been strongly on the voluntary side. Some surgeons appear to have a nervous terror that if they sterilise they may be doing an illegal act, even if they do so at the wish of the patient, and some legal opinions seem to support it, though it is difficult to see who could dis-

---

[4] All aspects of the question are discussed in the *Eugenics Review*, the organ of the English Eugenics Society, and sometimes in the New York *Journal of Social Hygiene*, as well as in *Eugenics*, the organ of the American Eugenics Society. I may add that Dr. E. G. Conklin has dealt with the special and rather radical objections of Raymond Pearl to eugenics in Cowdray's *Human Biology and Race Welfare*, 1930, Chap. XXIV.

pute a voluntary sterilisation, and on what grounds.[5] A law to regulate sterilisation, standing by itself, would look like class legislation and be in consequence resented by those who ought to feel, not that a punishment is being inflicted on them, but that a privilege is being brought within their reach. That result is best achieved by the free and open practice of voluntary sterilisation among all classes of the community.

At the same time, provided that such voluntary sterilisation is openly encouraged and practised, I am now willing to admit that legal facilities may be desirable to bring this method within reach, not only of the poor, who otherwise would not have the means or the opportunity to secure it, but of the insane and feeble-minded under control, who can legally only give their consent through their nearest relatives, but for whom, alike in their own interests and those of their possible offspring, procreation is undesirable. It is quite possible for such parents to have tolerably normal children, but, with our increased sense of social responsibility, we begin to realise that in so serious a matter no risks must here be run.

In the United States a number of laws have been passed in many states for ordinary compulsory sterilisation.[6] These laws were often badly made as well as premature, frequently repealed or declared unconstitutional, and sometimes never carried out; they have even at times had the effect of preventing the operation from being any longer performed, thus, as it were, sterilising sterilisation. It is in California that a sterilisation law, not indeed entirely admirable, has been most effective, having been applied to many thousands of subjects and worked in a reasonable way.[7]

The sterilisation of the insane or defective in California, being in the ordinary course carried out by agreement with the husband or wife or nearest relations when the patients are not legally competent to give their consent, it is interesting to know what on liberation they ultimately think about

[5] The opponents of sterilisation have even fallen back for support on the ancient principle of common law concerning *mayhem*, or main, a word so old that its origin is unknown, though it was an important principle in a primitive community where everyone needed his own strong arm. "The loss of those members which may be useful to a man in fighting alone amounts to *Mayhem* by the common law," Blackstone stated. Moreover, to constitute an indictment of *mayhem* there must, it is said, be "lying in wait," which covers the whole question of consent, while minor wounds, such as sterilisation is, were, it seems, not held to amount to *mayhem*. It is fantastic to invoke that ancient principle in this connection.

[6] The position of the laws in the various states was fully set out up to date in 1922 by Laughlin in his *Eugenical Sterilization in the United States*.

[7] Dr. Paul Popenoe has dealt in detail with the results in numerous articles in the *Journal of Social Hygiene* (1927-1928) and elsewhere.

it. Those who oppose sterilisation seem to be under the impression that sterilised persons would regret an operation done on them in a legally irresponsible state. In Californian mental hospitals, indeed, sterilisation is not performed if strong objections are offered to it, though, by a wise precaution, the inmates of mental homes are not allowed out, even for a short period, without sterilisation. Yet, in spite of the operation being, at all events by law, compulsory, there is no reason to believe that the sterilised persons often resent it. A special inquiry at a later date among persons who had formerly been inmates of such homes elicited the fact that only a small proportion, whether of males or females, regretted it or were displeased, while none showed any indignant resentment. This is the more notable as, among such patients—abnormal, morbid, and sometimes liable to strong and fantastic prejudices—such resentment might well be expected.[8]

The insistence on sterilisation is needed because of late the subject has become a battlefield for the opposing opinions of those who assert and those who deny its eugenic value and general advantages. The belief in its value is growing, but there are always those who, on the other hand, bring forward arguments which are sometimes sound, though we may believe that they are far from carrying all the weight that their advocates would attribute to them. Thus it is said that the compulsory sterilisation of certifiable defectives alone would have but little effect in diminishing the number of defectives in the next generation. This may well be, but those who bring forward this argument do not seem to be aware that, none the less, the majority of defectives come of parents who are totally unfit to procreate, subjects of mental instability, subjects whose germ cells are in some way faulty, and who are the carriers of defects more serious than their own. These people constitute a considerable proportion of the community, and are often worthy members of it. But they are unfit to procreate, and, in so far as they do so, they are anti-social members of the society to which they belong. It has been estimated that the sterilisation of even one-tenth of the population would produce an appreciably beneficial eugenic effect on the whole nation.[9] To make such a statement should also be to state by

[8] Paul Popenoe, "Eugenic Sterilization in California," *Journal of Social Hygiene*, May, 1928.

[9] This is the estimate that has repeatedly been put forward by, for instance, the *British Medical Journal* (e.g., July 5, 1930, p. 27), though it is not sufficiently emphasised that such sterilisation must be in the main voluntary and that legislation here would, even if possible, prove futile and mischievous.

implication that there is here little room for legislation. It is by the increase in the knowledge of heredity, by the spread of education among the masses of the population, and—perhaps above all—by the growth of the sense of social responsibility, that alone real progress is possible.

The study of eugenics, regarded as a biological science, will, we may expect, throw light on our path through difficulties which cannot be confined to a single nation. It is probable that the United States of America will play a conspicuous part. Just as Germany has taken a leading part in the study of sex on its psychological side, and the Institute of Sexual Science in Berlin is the first of its kind to be established in the world, so the seed of that special branch of the study of sex on its biological side which we call eugenics may be said to have been planted in America. It was Noyes, an American whose name is not likely to be forgotten, who threw out the first modern suggestion of "Stirpiculture" in practical shape. Half a century later it was in the United States at Cold Spring Harbour, and in close association with the station for Experimental Evolution, that was erected the Eugenics Record Office, the first building to be devoted solely to the study of human evolution or race biology, under the direction of Dr. Charles B. Davenport producing so much fruitful work.

Social movements embodying the impulses of racial regeneration must necessarily be altogether apart from purely scientific studies in biology, though they cannot fail to derive inspiration and guidance from them. Sexual choice, sexual mating, to some extent even the production of offspring, remain personal matters. They belong to a sphere in which the individual is supreme. In this field, as we know, a change is taking place which, though not originated, has been accelerated by the Great War, and may be observed alike in Europe and in America. What is needful is that this movement should follow lines that make, not for deterioration, but for real social and racial progress.

We see that the real question of population has become the question of eugenics: how can we now replace the aim of quantity by that of quality? When we grasp that problem in all its branches we see that it is most intimately bound up with our personal lives. And when we recognise how the problem presents itself to-day we shall realise that, from the wider human standpoint, it is also the most vital problem of society.

II

"What remains to a legitimate eugenics movement," it has been asked, "when the race problem is dropped from its programme?" It is a reasonable question. At a time when the eugenics programme of many eager would-be eugenists contains so many items that had better be dropped, one may well ask what remains.

As I am one of those who, like Dr. R. H. Lowie, who asks that question, believe that much remains, I should like finally to state the grounds and the nature of my eugenic faith. And in the first place, as Dr. Lowie states, it is important to clear away the rubbish that merely encumbers the ground on which a sound eugenic faith has to be built up.

The race problem, with which some have sought to obscure the eugenic problem, may indeed be eliminated at the outset. It is another question, and a question only profitable for the historian to consider. Even apart from the important fact that there is probably not a single person of really pure race to be found anywhere, the eugenist, as such, is not concerned to decide which is the best race, nor even to assume that any race is better, taken all round, than any other race. There is something to be said for every race, and the more to be said the better we learn to know it. The preference for one race above another is little but the outcome of prejudice, often due to the fact that one believes, rightly or wrongly, that one possesses oneself a strain of that preferred racial blood. The eugenist is not called upon to prefer one race above all others and to work for the extinction of the others.[10] If we come to that, it is quite likely that, on a referendum being called, the darker races of our earth, who happen to be in a large majority, might vote for the extinction of the white race, and, moreover, find many excellent reasons for that decision. Ultimately, we are bound to conclude, pigmentation is a question of exposure to the sun's rays, whether ingrained in race by natural selection or acquired by heredity; it is a problem, not for the eugenist but for the biological anthropologist. The eugenist, whether the dark-skinned eugenist or the white-skinned, is not called upon to make any decision in the matter. He is simply called upon to improve the stock of the race within which he belongs. So far as Europe is concerned, and the lands which have been peopled by migrations from Europe, there are, as we know, three main races, though it might be possible to reduce them ultimately still further: the Mediterranean race of dark long-heads; the Nordic, or, as it might be better to call it, the Baltic race, of fair long-heads; and, as a wedge driven in between these two from the East, the Alpine race, round-heads of medium pigmentation. Each of these races finds its parti-

[10] Elie Faure has suggestively discussed the virtues of white, yellow, and black races in his *Trois Gouttes de Sang*, 1929.

sans, especially among those persons who believe that they themselves belong to it. The Mediterraneans may claim that they were the pioneers in human civilisation and progress, the larger part of classic antiquity, and the still more ancient cultures on which that antiquity was founded, being to their credit; the Alpines boast their proficiency in the arts of peace and point to the fact that the man of genius tends to approximate to their type, whether or not of their race; the Nordics claim to be the most adventurous, the most individualistic, and sometimes the most warlike. It is the Nordics who have perhaps been loudest in proclaiming their own virtues, above all in Germany, where, however, they do not predominate, but also to some extent in France and in England and in America.[11] It may perhaps be permitted to a largely Nordic person, ancestrally rooted in a mainly Nordic region, to attempt to take a reasonable and impartial view.

There are some persons, to-day, who deplore the approaching extinction of the Nordic race, for they believe, on the most dubious grounds, that it is perishing. But without the least wish to deny the great achievement of the Nordic peoples in the world, it may well be that the Nordics possess many qualities which have sometimes proved mischievous. It has, for instance, been possible to maintain that it was mainly the lust of conquest, the ferocious procreative instinct, the immoderate greed for wealth, the cunning intrigues, of largely Nordic peoples, not on one side only but on both sides, which led up to the Great War, as well as to many European troubles of earlier times. If there is any likelihood of the Nordic race leaving the earth, it is to be feared than many will be overheard to murmur: "Thank God."[12]

These, however, are not problems which directly concern the eugenist as such. It is really sufficient for him to know that, excellent or pernicious as Nordic blood may be, we scarcely find it unmixed, but nearly always blended with Alpine or Mediterranean stocks or both, and that when we do find it comparatively pure, we find peoples who are of less account.

[11] The rather careless statements into which even a moderate champion of the Nordic race may sometimes fall are illustrated by Professor McDougall in his Lowell Lectures: *Is America Safe for Democracy?*

[12] Professor Nicefero, the distinguished Italian sociologist, in his learned work, *I Germani,* has dealt faithfully with the extravagant claims of Nordic champions. In the reaction against such claims, however, we must not undervalue the great Nordic qualities of individualism, essential to all high culture, and too easily submerged at a time like the present when collectivist movements, alike in Russia and America, are so pronounced. See a thoughtful and well-balanced discussion by Dr. Lars Ringbom, *The Renewal of Culture* (1929), written from the standpoint of Finland, where the opposing ideals are both racially represented.

The same, indeed, may be said also of the Alpines and the Mediterraneans. Wherever any of these three races are comparatively pure, whether in Sardinia, or in the isolated mountainous districts of the Central European Highlands, or in remote Northern regions, we are in the presence of peoples who have been left behind in the race. It is the hybrids who have come to the front, not only as individuals but also as nations. Germany, France, Great Britain, the Scandinavian countries, Russia and Holland, that is to say, the chief lands in which there is a large Nordic element, also possess a large Alpine or Mediterranean element, if not both. This is notably so as regards France and England. In both those countries all these races are blended, and that, without doubt, is a large part of the secret of their powers of achievement in the world. It is open to the narrow-minded partisan to assert that one race alone in the blend is the superior element. This has been amusingly illustrated in England during recent years. Before the Great War it was commonly believed that this superior element was the Nordic. But the war caused many people to think that terrible vices might be inherent in the Nordic race, and so-called anthropologists came forward to assert that the English nation was largely of Mediterranean race. They were quite right. If Spain and Italy had joined in the war on the opposing side, these same people would have come forward to declare that, after all, the English nation was largely of Alpine race. They would still be quite right. Eugenics, properly understood, has nothing whatever to do with these squabbles. It accepts the race of a human stock, or its blend of races; it desires that the stock shall produce the finest results of which it may be capable.

We must not only dismiss from eugenics the endeavour to foster one particular race of mankind under the impression that it is superior to all other races, we must also refrain from trying to cultivate, within the race, only one particular type of individual man as our exclusive ideal. It has taken some time to understand this point. Even Galton, the founder of modern eugenics, so moderate and reasonable in most of his demands, was inclined at first to think that we should actively seek to promote the production of the best stocks. There are two possible divisions of eugenics: positive eugenics, directed to the improvement of good stocks, and negative eugenics, directed to the repression of bad stocks. In 1901 Galton thought that to increase the productivity of the best stocks is far more important than to repress the productivity of the worst. But seven years later he declared that this latter task of repressing the worst stocks is "unquestionably the more pressing subject."

It is evident that he was on the way to the conclusion that it is negative eugenics with which alone we can be, directly, that is to say actively, concerned. It must not, however, be supposed that Galton had an unduly limited conception of what the "worth" of good stocks meant. One has heard it stated by ignorant persons that he advocated an ideal of civic worth which would shut out from life all who were not stodgy, narrow, commercially minded, and probably hypocritical Philistines. It was not so. Galton himself remarked that "society would be very dull if every man resembled Marcus Aurelius or Adam Bede,[18] and he even asserted that in ascertaining the desirable hereditary qualities "we must leave morality as far as possible out of the discussion," for otherwise we entangle ourselves in hopeless difficulties, since goodness or badness of character is not absolute but merely relative to the current form of civilisation. Health, energy, ability, courteous disposition were the desirable qualities on which Galton insisted, since "all creatures would agree that it was better to be healthy than sick, vigorous than weak, well-fitted than ill-fitted for their part in life." He summed up the three eugenically desirable qualities as physique, ability, and character, and he put character last, though in real importance it stands first of all, because of the difficulty in rating character justly.

In putting aside positive eugenics, to which so much importance was once attached, I was careful to say that it is the *direct* furtherance of good stocks that we are called upon to avoid. Even by devoting ourselves directly to negative eugenics we are thereby really effecting much for positive eugenics, more indeed than we could possibly hope to achieve by more direct efforts. This in two ways, the one material, the other what I should like to call spiritual. (1) The material way is that, by accumulating among us, as for a century we have been actively doing, all those who are in any category of unfitness, enabling them to be procreated, guarding them on every side from disease and death, protecting them and supporting them in expensive institutions, we are placing an ever greater burden on the fit, who, the more fit they are, the larger the burden they are thus called upon to bear, so that if they exercise foresight—and foresight is one of the chief qualities which constitute fitness—they are compelled to consider how far they can themselves play a procreative part in the world. The

[18] Bateson, similarly, in his characteristically pungent way (Herbert Spencer Lecture on "Biological Fact and the Structure of Society"), remarked that, "if we picture to ourselves the kind of persons who would infallibly be chosen as examples of 'civic worth' the prospect is not very attractive. We need not for the present fear any scarcity of that class, and I think we may be content to postpone schemes for their multiplication."

result is that, as compared with the less fit, they are ever taking a relatively smaller part in the reproduction of the race. By working towards the elimination of the unfit we are indirectly lifting a great weight off the fit and conferring upon them far more power that we could hope to impart by direct action. (2) The evils on the spiritual plane which are inflicted on the fit by the growing predominance of the unfit are even more serious, especially in that democratic phase of society where it is quantity rather than quality of votes which is the decisive factor. It is to the short-sightedness, the callousness, the selfishness, the greediness, the hysteria of the unfit majority in any age that the evils of the human world, its criminal wars, its sometimes yet more criminal peaces, and all its manifold disorders, are to a considerable extent due, and in these evils it is the fit, and sometimes the fit first of all and above all, who are called upon to suffer. Nor is it only in the major evils of the world, in its minor evils also the unfit are forever exerting a limiting and lowering pressure on the fit. Their illegitimate activities are constantly making impossible the legitimate activities of the fit. All the immense web of taboo I have already discussed—the bylaws and regulations, formulated or not, which society is weaving and binding round itself— is merely meant to restrain the unfit, although in so doing it also restrains the reasonable activities of the fit. It is easy to give examples: I read in the newspaper, for example, that the Countess of Derby, finding the chestnuts in her park so plentiful this season, resolved to share the harvest with her neighbors and threw open the park to the public with permission to gather the nuts. But she speedily had cause to repent: so much damage was done to the plantations and fences that the Countess was compelled to close the park and invoke the services of the police. The unfit were unable to see that their selfish and mischievous activities were curtailing even their own privileges, and the fit were compelled to suffer for offences they had not committed. It is a process which, in one field or another, is going on unceasingly.

There is yet another item to be eliminated from every sane programme of eugenics, and that is the mania for an ill-judged or premature appeal to legislation. It is common, indeed, but sometimes mischievous, and usually futile. We do not know enough to legislate on eugenic schemes, and even if we knew more, we cannot legislate ahead of public opinion, because our laws will be evaded, while if public opinion is educated up to the level of the laws, those laws will be superfluous. All this has been well illustrated in the United States. But I pass by this point, since it may be unnecessary for any reader who has followed me so far, and turn to yet another form of activity which, immensely important as it is even in its influence on eugenics, we must refrain from including under eugenics, and that is the amelioration of the environment. There are two ways in which we can work socially for the good of mankind: by acting on heredity and by acting on environment: they have been ingeniously termed eugenics and euthenics. Others term the two ways that of Nature and that of Nurture, though this terminology is not very sound, for the main object of Nature, teleologically speaking, is Nurture, and there is nothing in Nurture which is not ultimately Nature. There can, indeed, at the roots be no conflict between eugenics and euthenics. Each form of social activity is equally necessary; both are indispensable. To dispute whether one is more important than the other is to carry absurdity to its extreme limits. It is a discussion just about as profitable as a discussion on the problem whether our legs are more useful than our arms. It remains true that the task of the eugenist is distinct from that of the euthenist. Each must walk along his own lines and in his own field. The more faithfully each keeps within his own sphere, the more completely will be revealed the beautiful harmony between them, and the more powerfully will each be found to aid the other.

You eliminate racial competition from eugenics, one may be told, you eliminate positive eugenics, you eliminate compulsory eugenics by law, you eliminate action on the environment—why, what is there left? There is very much left, so much that it might well fill all our lives and still take centuries to accomplish.

Galton, to whom I once more appeal—for modern eugenics owes far more to him than its name—was accustomed to declare that it is the task of eugenics to act upon Public Opinion. That itself is a never-ending task, for opinion, to be effective, has to become so deeply rooted as to be entwined with the instincts and so to be a guide to action. It might be supposed, indeed, that the paths of eugenics are pleasant, for as the eugenically fit people are the attractive people and the unfit the unattractive, to bid youths and maidens fall in love only with the fit seems a piece of advice that is not hard to follow, provided there is sufficient insight to discriminate between genuine attractiveness and its merely meretricious and superficial counterfeits. But, as we know, it is less easy than it seems, for, in civilisation, there are many qualities other than eugenic attractiveness which prove seductive, some of them qualities which also prove fatal to the mate who is seduced by them. Evidently Public Opinion has still much progress to make.[14]

Moreover, there is at times a more intrinsic difficulty in the fact that there are at least three qualities—physique, ability, character—that go to make up "fitness." Ability and character, for instance, may sometimes prove attractive when there is no physique to speak of, and when this happens various problems arise. Is this attraction a justifiable instinct? Should it lead to marriage? If so, should it also lead to children? And if not, what measures ought to be adopted?

It is evident that the growth of Public Opinion, however sound and instinctively operative a conscience it might in time implant in the heart, is not enough. To deal with the difficult problems that arise, intelligence and knowledge are required, and these cannot be secured in a day. A greater degree of intelligence is, indeed, itself one of the gifts which we hope some day to secure through eugenics, and knowledge can only be slowly built up. On one point, certainly, knowledge—and practice in accordance with knowledge—has been accumulated and widely disseminated during the past century, especially the last half century, and that is in regard to birth control. It is worth mentioning that point again, because, although eugenics can by no means be reduced to birth control, it is yet vitally true that without birth control there can under modern conditions be no eugenics. Eugenics without birth control is simply a castle in the air, a beautiful vision in the clouds, no doubt, but not to be brought to earth. Birth control—in the wide sense which includes sterilisation and some day perhaps even more radical measures—is the chief instrument vouchsafed to civilised men wherewith from the infinite possibilities of brutal procreation to carve the great race of the future.

It is knowledge, as well as goodwill, that is needed to learn how to use that instrument wisely. The field that opens before

[14] At the same time it must always be remembered that even here the individual, in every state of society including those we count primitive, instinctively acts in accordance with laws and follows unwritten taboos which limit his choice. There are thoughtless libertarians who do not seem aware of this elementary fact. In some parts of the world there are so many prohibitions that the marriage class open to a man to choose from may be very small. (See, for instance, Mrs. Brenda Seligman, "The Formation of Marriage Classes," *Journal of the Anthropological Institute,* July-December, 1927.) Among ourselves marriage in the same social class is the rule, and there are difficulties, with frequently unfortunate results, in marriage outside the same class. We even have a tendency to marry within the same caste, and I note among my own ancestors in the seventeenth and eighteenth centuries that the parsons tended to marry the daughters of parsons or the widows of parsons. There is nothing unnatural or difficult in the formation of eugenic marriage classes.

us is large. And a more fruitful field than that of biological genetics could not well be found. Not all may be equipped to explore it. But every man, if he will take the small trouble needed to acquire the necessary data, will find in his own family and ancestry a fascinating study full alike of interest and profit. Every honest investigation, however narrow, helps to build up the great watch tower from whose heights the paths of a new race can be traced in the future. We cannot all learn to be wise, but we can all learn to know and to will in accordance with knowledge. With so noble a task before us it matters little that there are still some among us content to wreck folly and destruction. Their time may be short. The path is slowly growing clearer. The future is to those who have the insight to see it, the skill and the energy to work towards it.

No community of Man, it is true, has ever known before-hand the fate of its civilisation. It has left future ages to dis-inter and attempt to reconstruct the dead civilisations of the past, and we are always discovering more. We cannot doubt that there are advantages in not knowing that fate. There would not be any advantage whatever in fixing our attention on the annihilation which is Man's final end. Exuberance and effort and hope are of the essence of life. It is the dead amongst us, and not the living, who shake their heads over eugenics.

Let us remember, moreover, that we have already ascended from the ape, the wisest of animals, and that it is our privilege to press on consciously towards those highest things he so daringly pioneered, meanwhile casting aside, if we can, some of the acquired foolishness of which he would never have been guilty.

INDEX

SIGNET and MENTOR Books
on Psychology

SIGNET Guides
to Better Health

☐ **THE NEW AMERICAN MEDICAL DICTIONARY AND HEALTH MANUAL (revised) by Robert Rothenberg, M.D.** Over 7500 definitions of medical terms, disorders, and diseases, with more than 300 illustrations, make this the most complete and easy-to-understand book of its kind. Also includes a comprehensive first-aid section and guides to better health. (#Q3451—95¢)

☐ **LIFE BEFORE BIRTH by Ashley Montagu.** Vital information for the mother-to-be to increase her chances of bearing a normal, healthy baby. Introduction by Dr. Alan F. Guttmacher. (#T2690—75¢)

☐ **PREGNANCY AND BIRTH by Alan F. Guttmacher, M.D.** A handbook for expectant parents by the Director of Gynecology and Obstetrics, Mount Sinai Hospital, New York. (#T3446—75¢)

☐ **YOUR BODY AND YOUR MIND by Frank G. Slaughter, M.D.** The famous doctor-novelist shows how emotions influence health, and how anger, fear or worry can cause serious physical illness. (#P2302—60¢)

☐ **MEDICARE AND YOU by William Adler and Sayre Ross.** A step-by-step guide for senior citizens and their families, this is the first comprehensive explanation of Medicare, covering every aspect of the program from the method of enrollment to the collection of insurance. (#P3049—60¢)

☐ **HEALTH IN THE LATER YEARS by Robert E. Rothenberg, M.D.** A comprehensive guide to medical problems for men and women over forty. Includes a special handbook of information about the new Medicare program and the 1965 Social Security Amendments. (#Y2900—$1.25)

THE NEW AMERICAN LIBRARY, INC., P.O. Box 1478, Church Street Station, New York, New York 10008

Please send me the SIGNET BOOKS I have checked above. I am enclosing $ _____(check or money order—no currency or C.O.D.'s). Please include the list price plus 10¢ a copy to cover mailing costs. (New York City residents add 5% Sales Tax. Other New York State residents add 2% plus any local sales or use taxes.)

Name_____

Address_____

City_____State_____Zip Code_____

Allow 2 to 3 weeks for delivery

SIGNET Reference Books

☐ **PULL YOURSELF TOGETHER or HOW TO LOOK MAR-VELOUS ON NEXT TO NOTHING by Barbara Johns Waterston.** An easy-to-follow guide for self-improvement, providing valuable pointers on clothes, skin, hair, make-up, diet, exercise and on money. (#P3343—60¢)

☐ **THE NEW AMERICAN WEBSTER HANDY COLLEGE DIC-TIONARY edited by Albert and Loy Morehead.** An easy-to-use dictionary, with more than 100,000 clear defini-tions of useful words; illustrated. (#P2174—60¢)

☐ **THE NEW AMERICAN ROGET'S THESAURUS in Dic-tionary form.** Synonyms, antonyms in an alphabetical listing. Easy to use. A must for every library. (#P2175—60¢)

☐ **THE HANDY BOOK OF GARDENING by Albert E. Wilkin-son and Victor A. Tiedjens.** A complete, fully illustrated handbook on growing flowers, vegetables, fruits and house plants; using insecticides; caring for lawns; and landscaping. (#T3422—75¢)

☐ **THE I NEVER COOKED BEFORE COOKBOOK by Jo Cou-dert.** A basic guide in plain English on how to prepare simple, delicious foods with ease . . . and the certainty of success. No experience necessary. (#T2797—75¢)